# LEGALISM

# Legalism

*Law, Morals, and Political Trials*

## by JUDITH N. SHKLAR

HARVARD UNIVERSITY PRESS

CAMBRIDGE, MASSACHUSETTS
LONDON, ENGLAND

*To  G. S.*

# PREFACE, 1986

I wrote this book over twenty years ago in a state of considerable innocence. Because it had not been my intention to attack the integrity or the social functions of the American bench or bar, I was surprised to find that I had offended almost all the lawyers who read it. With a few notable exceptions, they felt that I had criticized their profession unfairly. Ethnographers have long lamented the distance between their point of view and that of the natives. I came to appreciate what they mean, for while I knew that I was an outsider looking at a highly cohesive group, I did not realize then how different the view from within was from mine. There does not seem to be an obvious way to bridge the gap between self-perception and observation, and I have no remedy for that obstacle to mutual understanding. I can, however, try retrospectively to restate my main points and general meaning in such a way that the degree of misunderstanding may at least be reduced.

The chief culprit has been, I think, the always ambiguous word "ideology." The sociological vocabulary cannot do without it, but nothing one can say will remove its sting. I used "legalism," moreover, in two different senses, and thus may have created unnecessary confusion. One is as an ideology internal to the legal profession as a social whole. Most historically enduring groups with a recognizable identity and set of functions have belief systems that inform their practices and act as guideposts for their members. They are educated to respond to them and to maintain them. A belief system is their map within their group and conditions their responses to others. Above all, in this case, it gives them their sense of what it means to be a lawyer. The military and the medical profession also have their respective internal ideologies, which differ from each other and from the ethos of lawyers as well. These group belief systems exist despite enormous individual and group differences within each profession. The majority of lawyers in the United States are solo practitioners, and in many ways the rather small group that makes up the big law factories in large cities is unlike them. Academic lawyers also have their own peculiarities. Nevertheless, the shared characteristics are striking, and there is nothing aberrant in speaking of legalism as the operative ideology of lawyers. I may of course have got this or that detail wrong, but I think there is no hostility in describing it as I did, as the extremity of rule-oriented thinking.

The second sense in which I spoke of ideology should have been labeled more clearly as political. Here legalism is projected into the greater political environment of multiple and competing ideologies. And in this political context it assumes a different character. In this sense legalism is not at all restricted to lawyers, although the court of law remains of necessity the most legalistic of all public agencies. The values of impartial judgment, according to rules, are the courts' overt reason for existence. If we place them at one extreme of an ideological continuum it becomes evident, however, that courts do not have a monopoly on legalistic values. Tribunality is inherent in functioning legislative assemblies, bureaucracies, mediators of all kinds, and extends even down to parents as they try to be fair in distributing rewards and penalties. At this end of the continuum obviously other values count for more; for instance, the health and education of a child call for qualities far more primary than fairness. Historically, moreover, the legalistic frame of mind has had to compete with a considerable number of ethical and political alternatives. At one extreme might be placed the pure antinomians, of whom there are far more than the legalists care to admit. Inner-light Christianity, Plato's primacy of rational psychic order, Marxism in its revolutionary and utopian phases (in which the community distributes according to need and receives what it requires according to the abilities of its members), the military values of discipline and courage, the devotion to friendship and charity as our foremost needs and goals, all these are pretty remote from the values pursued by matured legal systems and the ideology of those who run them. At the other end of the spectrum one should look for the Old Testament, for Aristotle and syllogistic logic, and for all natural law theorists, to name only the most obvious of those who think in terms of rights and duties fairly distributed. Legalism, in short, has a wider range of adherents and a greater variety of antagonists in the world of ideologists than most legal theorists are willing to recognize.

It cannot be said that the upholders of legalism recognize it as part of a continuum. Overtly they see legal institutions and legal thinking as highly discrete practices, clearly marked off within society and deriving much of their validity from their immunity to influence from, and participation in, the normal course of political activity. The tendency to dismiss both the political provenance and the impact of judicial decisions especially, and of legal practices generally, remains very common in legal theory. This is what I meant by saying that legalism tends to treat law as just "there," and that legal formalism has always been the most articulate defense of this stance.

I nevertheless know quite well that compared to English legal thinking American legal theorists have not ignored the political functions of the law. How could they, with so many jurisdictions, with state and federal judicial review, and with the American habit of shopping for favorable laws, first in local legislatures, then in Congress, and finally in the courts? Yet the quest for the holy grail of perfect, nonpolitical, aloof neutral law and legal decisions persists and remains a test for acceptability. It is also still often said that a politically oriented legal system spells the end of judicial legitimacy. In fact, although it is philosophically deeply annoying, human institutions survive because most of us can live comfortably with wholly contradictory beliefs. Most thoughtful citizens know that the courts act decisively in creating rules that promote political ends—to name only civil rights—of which they may approve. They also insist that the impartiality of judges and of the process as a whole requires a dispassionate, literal pursuit of rules carved in spiritual marble. Changes in these rules are to be made by legislative agencies, but never by the judiciary. All criticism and praise of judicial performances is couched in phrases drawn from this belief, which may seem ridiculous but is not at all socially or psychologically indefensible. Indeed, if we value flexibility and accept a degree of contradiction, this paradox may even seem highly functional and appropriate.

These reflections are scarcely original or damaging to the legalistic outlook. What seemed to disturb many readers was my placing of legalism within the contentious environment of rival ideologies, and my discussion of that confrontation in the vocabulary of political theory, which is neither abstract nor specialized. In this respect, political theory has differed all along from the style of moral philosophy to which much contemporary legal theory has resorted. That there is a natural affinity between these two highly structured modes of social theorizing is undeniable, but I am not persuaded that it is altogether wholesome, for it only confirms legalism in its disposition to think of itself as an extrapolitical, isolable mode of thought. It must again be said that thanks to its inevitable, historic court-centeredness, American jurisprudence has always had at least one alternative style of exposition to the extreme deductive, ahistorical abstractness that has in recent years marked legal theory in the Anglo-American academic world.

My view of legalism is overtly liberal, but it is not the liberalism of the "rule of law" ideal promoted by Friedrich von Hayek and his followers, because it does not suggest that the only function of a legal system is to provide a secure framework for the spontaneous order of the free market. I would still not add anything to what I originally said about that subject. The restrictive definition of liberalism as this sort of "rule of law" is not, however, limited to traditional conservatives. It has now been adopted also by their avowed radical, egalitarian, and communal critics. Like Hayek, the advocates of "critical legal studies" believe that the welfare state has destroyed the liberal order which aspired to a neutrality it could maintain only by doing or pretending to do very little. This ex-liberal state is now a mere open battlefield for pressure groups with no claim to legitimacy. The "rule of law," the radicals contend, cannot survive as a framework for contemporary pluralism nor act any longer as a mask for a hierarchical system of domination. The law itself exists to reinforce and to hide the realities of this essentially criminal political order, acting as its prime agent. The law of contract is often used to illustrate these assertions, with the object of unmasking the real ideology of formalism and with it the pretensions of the liberal state. It goes without saying that at the end of the road there will be a communitarian, unatomized, united society which is said to be imminent even as the liberal order is collapsing under the burden of contending interests, which have become more manifest in the active welfare regime. Here is recognition with a vengeance of the political role of the law. It obviously is not the same message as the one I tried to convey, which was that within the record of our century the collapse of liberalism has in no case come to anything but an extremity of horror. There is no warrant for expecting any other outcome.

Because it is so derivative in its view of the "rule of law," and because of its obvious affinity to traditional ideologies of agreement that used to go under the name of natural law, the radical political criticism of liberal legalism is not intellectually very innovative. For that one might have to wait for the work of Lon Fuller's successors. His own vision of an inner morality of the law, even when it was broadened to include meeting the expectation of the citizenry at large, was flawed. Its standards could be met by any rigid bureaucratic regime as long as its repressions were not random and the expectations of its unfortunate citizens were small. If these expectations, however, include first and foremost a recognition of equal rights, as Ronald Dworkin claims they must, then the morality of the law is opened up. It enters the real world of politics and its controversies. The self-understanding of legalistic thinkers, however, has always turned around the proper relation of law to morality, rather than to politics, and that inclination has again served to maintain equal rights as *moral* rules already "there" in some sense. Since moral rules prevail in society, it is possible for judges to form moral decisions in hard cases. That claim is not entirely plausible, even though it is a highly traditional legalistic view. It assumes that when *moral* rules are applied in court, the judge can escape the normal political conflicts of a pluralistic society. In fact, I argue, the contest would be political from the outset and, as in all ideological politics, the organization and directior of political power and the mobilization of opinion are part of the substance of the process. Such conflicts may or may not be a contribution to the legal politics of the United States, but they cannot be pictured as a simple integration of morality into the law by acts of pure practical reason.

The emphasis on hard cases in the latest effort to relate law and morality has its intellectual advantages. Legalism, like all political ideologies, reveals itself most at the margins of normality, such as unprecedented Supreme Court decisions and the international trials of major war criminals at the end of the Second World War. A considerable part of *Legalism* is devoted to these trials and most of its arguments were meant to lead up to them. The real point of the book lies there. I think that subsequent events have not proved me wrong. There have been many wars since then and endless crimes against humanity, but there has been no repetition of the trials that followed the Second World War. That does not mean that they were politically useless. They have had a very strong impact not only upon Germans, but upon political thinking and action in Europe and America. That remains their ample justification. Nor was the revival and reinforcement of the principles of a decent legal system and of the ethos of legality in vain. Indeed, it may well be that confronted by a choice among principles in the hardest of hard cases, a judge might well ask what political outcome would do most to maintain the integrity of the judicial system in the political order of his time and place. Such a question might well entail an intellectual escape from legalism, but it would also save its values for political society as a whole.

It is a real pleasure to thank all those who have helped me with this book. I am grateful to the John Simon Guggenheim Memorial Foundation for awarding me a fellowship to study modern legal theory in the year 1960. I hope that my friends who encouraged me to write this book and who read, criticized, and corrected it will not find it embarrassing to see my thanks to them in print. Stanley Hoffmann, Isaak Kramnick, Robert McCloskey, Martin Shapiro, and Paul Sigmund all have so great a claim upon my gratitude that I cannot ignore it here, nor forbear to express my affection for all of them. I should also like to thank Paul Shupack for helping me with the proofs.

# CONTENTS

# LEGALISM

# INTRODUCTION

## *Law and Ideology*

What is legalism? It is the ethical attitude that holds moral
conduct to be a matter of rule following, and moral relationships to consist of duties and rights determined by rules. Like
all moral attitudes that are both strongly felt and widely shared
it expresses itself not only in personal behavior but also in
philosophical thought, in political ideologies, and in social
institutions. As an historical phenomenon, it is, moreover, not
something that can be understood simply by defining it. Such
a morality must be seen in its various concrete manifestations,
in its diverse applications, and in the many degrees of intensity
with which men in different places and conditions have abided
by it. It is, in short, a complex of human qualities, not a
quantity to be measured and labeled.

Legalism, so understood, is thus often an inarticulate, but
nonetheless consistently followed, individual code of conduct.
It is also a very common social ethos, though by no means the
only one, in Western countries. To a great extent it has provided the standards of organization and the operative ideals
for a vast number of social groups, from governmental institutions to private clubs. Its most nearly complete expression is
in the great legal systems of the European world. Lastly, it
has also served as the political ideology of those who cherish

these systems of law and, above all, those who are directly involved in their maintenance—the legal profession, both bench
and bar. The court of law and the trial according to law are the
social paradigms, the perfection, the very epitome, of legalistic
morality. They are, however, far from being its only expressions. Indeed, they are inconceivable without the convictions,
mores, and ideologies that must permeate any society which
wishes to maintain them. Yet the spirit of legalism is not now,
and never has been, the only morality among men even in
generally legalistic societies. The full implications of this moral
and political diversity, though its existence is commonly
acknowledged and often regretted, has rarely been thoroughly
investigated. This is by no means surprising, since almost all
those who have devoted themselves to the study of legalistic
morality and institutions have been their zealous partisans and
promoters, anxious to secure their moral empire.

Even though it is no sign of disaffection for legalism to
treat it as but one morality among others, such a view has not
been congenial to any of the traditional theories of law. These
have been devised almost exclusively by lawyers and philosophers who agree in nothing but in taking the prevalence of
legalism and of law for granted, as something to be simply
defined and analyzed. The consequences for legal theory have
not been altogether fortunate. The urge to draw a clear line
between law and non-law has led to the constructing of ever
more refined and rigid systems of formal definitions. This
procedure has served to isolate law completely from the social
context within which it exists. Law is endowed with its own
discrete, integral history, its own "science," and its own values,
which are all treated as a single "block" sealed off from general
social history, from general social theory, from politics, and
from morality. The habits of mind appropriate, within narrow
limits, to the procedures of law courts in the most stable legal
systems have been expanded to provide legal theory and

ideology with an entire system of thought and values. This procedure has served its own ends very well: it aims at preserving law from irrelevant considerations, but it has ended by fencing legal thinking off from all contact with the rest of historical thought and experience.

As an alternative to this unsatisfactory situation, it is suggested here that one ought not to think of law as a discrete entity that is "there," but rather to regard it as part of a social continuum. At one end of the scale of legalistic values and institutions stand its most highly articulate and refined expressions, the courts of law and the rules they follow; at the other end is the personal morality of all those men and women who think of goodness as obedience to the rules that properly define their duties and rights. Within this scale there is a vast area of social beliefs and institutions, both more and less rigid and explicit, which in varying degrees depend upon the legalistic ethos. This would provide an approach suitable to law as an historical phenomenon, and would replace the sterile game of defining law, morals, and politics in order to separate them as concepts both "pure" and empty, divorced from each other and from their common historical past and contemporary setting.

The object here, then, is not only to understand legalism, but also to suggest other ways of thinking about law. Accordingly the first part of this book is devoted to an argument with both analytical positivism and natural law theory and, especially, their respective ways of distinguishing law from morality. The second part, equally critical in tone, deals with legalism as a political ideology which comes into conflict with other policies, particularly in the course of political trials, both international and domestic. Throughout there is an effort to explain and judge legalism as an ideological manifestation. Now the very word "ideology" is apt to create misunderstandings as soon as it is uttered. Unhappily there is no nice, safe substitute available. Since nothing is to be gained, moreover, by arguments about the real meaning of this unfortunate word, one can do no more than offer a simple statement about its significance in various contexts. Thus it is important to explain, firstly, the meaning of the term "ideology" as it is used here; secondly, the author's own ideological commitments; and lastly, the purposes that this critical analysis of the ideological preferences of others is meant to serve.

The term "ideology" is not intended tó mean anything very complicated. It refers simply to political preferences, some very simple and direct, others more comprehensive. There have, of course, been ideologies that have claimed to be far more, to provide an explanation of the entire past, a program for the present, and a blueprint for the future. These might well be called grand or total ideologies in contrast to the more modest formulas that are the subject of this book. In no case is there any effort to use the word "ideology" as one of simple opprobrium. On the contrary, it may well be doubted whether political theory, of which legal theory is a part, can be written without some sort of ideological impetus. Nor is there any reason to feel that the expression of personal preferences is an undesirable flaw. It must seem so only to those who equate objectivity with remoteness from their own experiences and especially from those they share with their contemporaries. However, if one thinks of ideology as merely a matter of emotional reactions, both negative and positive, to direct social experiences and to the views of others, it is clear that ideology is as inevitable as it is necessary in giving any thinking person a sense of direction. To be sure, ideological responses are often difficult to recognize in oneself, as they insensibly come to condition one's interests, one's methods of study, one's conceptual devices, and even one's vocabulary. However, if we did not think of ideology as a gross form of irrationality, we would be less anxious to repress it and our self-awareness would be correspondingly greater. Political theory might well benefit from it, for one of its tasks is to articulate and examine the half-expressed political views that the various groups in any given society at any time come to hold. Ideology, thus conceived, is eminently a matter of attitudes common to groups of people. It is the sort of preference that arises in the course of common social experiences. In the present case, legalism as a political ideology finds its strongest adherents in a professional group, the lawyers. It is also probable that the notion of objectivity as, above all, a matter of de-ideologizing social theory is an ideological reaction among academic intellectuals, appalled by the fanaticism engendered by the grand ideologies. One can hardly blame them. For an historian it is enough to observe that such political preferences are held by a number of people, with some degree of consistency and continuity, to know that ideology is prevalent. No more is needed.

By now it must be fairly evident that this book is not to be a contribution to the literature of de-ideologizing. It is not an exercise in the art of impersonally recording the views of other writers. It is therefore necessary to state the ideological contribution that the author is about to make to the debate. It is, at its simplest, a defense of social diversity, inspired by that barebones liberalism which, having abandoned the theory of progress and every specific scheme of economics, is committed only to the belief that tolerance is a primary virtue and that a diversity of opinions and habits is not only to be endured but to be cherished and encouraged. The assumption throughout is that social diversity *is* the prevailing condition of modern nation-states and that it *ought* to be promoted. Pluralism is thus treated as a social actuality that no contemporary political theory can ignore without losing its relevance, and also as something that any liberal should rejoice in and seek to promote, because it is in diversity alone that freedom can be realized. A free society is not one in which people are merely allowed to make effective social choices among a variety of alternatives, but one in which they are encouraged to do so. The range and the number of choices available and the mutual tolerance among those who choose conflicting paths are what determine the degree of freedom that the members of any modern society can be said to enjoy. If one must be a hero, a saint, or at least enormously courageous and self-confident in order to pursue a manner of life or to express views other than those agreeable to the powers that be, both governmental and social, one cannot be said to live in a free society. These views are at least as old as John Stuart Mill, and hardly novel. No one today can claim, nor did Mill assume a hundred years ago, that everyone frantically yearns for personal liberty or regards tolerance as a virtue or finds the self-control it demands easy. It cannot even be said, as he did, that freedom is needed for "progress." What is evident, however, is that diversity and the burdens of freedom must be endured and encouraged to avoid the kinds of misery that organized repression now brings. This is a type of liberalism quite common among members of permanent social minority groups, and it surely reflects both the apprehensions and the positive experiences which their situation creates.

Obviously no one who writes in defense of an ideology is in any position to complain about others who do the same thing. That is certainly not the aim here. Not the mere presence of ideology but the reasons for and consequences of pretended immunity to ideology will be considered at length and, perhaps, with an undue lack of charity. There are three quite distinct ideological aspects of contemporary legal thinking to be taken into account. First of all, there is the manner in which ideology has conditioned the entire structure of thought among Austin's heirs, the analytical positivists. Secondly, there is a critical evaluation of the ideology implicitly and explicitly attached to theories of natural law. Lastly, legalism in general, especially in its pervasive influence upon all legal thinking, must be established in its place as one ideology competing with other political preferences.

In the case of analytical positivism it undeniably is a criticism to show that political preferences have contrived to inspire and condition its whole development and inner character, often with unfortunate results—because this theory regards its ideological neutrality as the very core of its position. Imperviousness to ideology is regarded as the foremost condition of legal "science"; indeed, the latter is defined by its immunity to ideological contamination. Moreover, the image of law that analytical positivism has devised consists of sets of rules carefully divorced from ideology. Its whole theory of the separation of law from morals is designed to achieve this end. This is also what leads it to an excessive formalism. For only thus can the neutrality of law as a concept and of legal science as an intellectual discipline be maintained. However, it will be shown that these efforts are themselves conditioned by ideology and that the failure to recognize this has made analytical positivism a far less persuasive theory than it might otherwise have been. This is not meant to be one of those jobs of debunking that try to expose the "real," and presumably unworthy, hidden tendencies of ideas with which one disagrees. Since the ideological inspiration of analytical positivism is liberalism and a skeptical view of ethics, it is obviously quite congenial to its present unmasker. It is not the aims of ideology, but the results of treating political preferences as the logical necessities of any valid theory of law, that are highly questionable.

To charge natural law with being an ideology would, on the other hand, be ridiculous. Natural law theorists not only recognize that they are presenting a set of moral preferences, however flexible, but insist that this must be part of any legal theory. Here it is not the presence but the specific content and character of ideology which, from a liberal point of view, is disheartening. The argument to be developed is that natural law theories set a premium on moral agreement and social cohesion and that these ends are not compatible in practice with freedom in a diversified society nor agreeable ideologically to those who wish to promote diversity and tolerance.

Lastly, there is legalism itself. To say that it is an ideology is to criticize only those of its traditional adherents who, in their determination to preserve law from politics, fail to recognize that they too have made a choice among political values. In itself this would hardly be a new accusation, nor a very important one. What does matter is again the intellectual consequences of this denial, and the attendant belief that law is not only separate from political life but that it is a mode of social action superior to mere politics. This is what will later be discussed as "the policy of justice," for legalism as an ideology does express itself in policies, in institutional structures, and in intellectual attitudes. As a social ethos which gives rise to the political climate in which judicial and other legal institutions flourish, legalism is beyond reproach. It is the rigidity of legalistic categories of thought, especially in appraising the relationships of law to the political environment within which it functions, that is so deleterious. This is the source of the artificiality of almost all legal theories and is what prevents its exponents from recognizing both the strengths and weaknesses of law and legal procedures in a complex social world.

Legalism as an ideology is the common element in all the various and conflicting modes of legal thinking that are to be discussed here. It is what gives legal thinking its distinctive flavor on a vast variety of social occasions, in all kinds of discourse, and among men who may differ in every other ideological respect. Legalism is, above all, the operative outlook of the legal profession, both bench and bar. Moreover, most legal theory, whether it be analytical positivism or natural law thinking, depends on categories of thought derived from this shared professional outlook. The tendency to think of law as "there" as a discrete entity, discernibly different from morals and politics, has its deepest roots in the legal profession's views of its own functions, and forms the very basis of most of our judicial institutions and procedures. That lawyers have particularly pronounced intellectual habits peculiar to them has often been noticed, especially by historians and other students of society whose views differ sharply from those of the legal profession. As one English lawyer has put it, "A lawyer is *bound* by certain habits of belief . . . by which lawyers, however dissimilar otherwise, are more closely linked than they are separated. . . A man who has had legal training is never quite the same again . . . is never able to look at institutions or administrative practices or even social or political policies, free from his legal habits or beliefs. It is not easy for a lawyer to become a political scientist. It is very difficult for him to become a sociologist or a historian. . . He is interested in relationships, in rights in something and against somebody, in relation to others. . . This is what is meant by the legalistic approach. . . [A lawyer] will fight to the death to defend legal rights against persuasive arguments based on expediency or the public interest or the social good. . . He distrusts them. . . He believes, as part of his mental habits, that they are dangerous and too easily used as cloaks for arbitrary action." [1]

These remarkable observations come from an academic lawyer, forced perhaps by the demands of scholarly objectivity and daily contacts with non-lawyerly teachers to look at his profession from the outside. Another academic lawyer has noted in a similar vein that "it is possible for the commercial lawyer and the economist, for the family lawyer and the sociologist to regard one area of social activity from standpoints so far apart that contact becomes infrequent and indeed almost fortuitous." [2] A practicing lawyer might not rest with noting the difference between himself and others; he would insist that his was simply the right and true view. That is the meaning of legalism as an ideology.

The dislike of vague generalities, the preference for case-by-case treatment of all social issues, the structuring of all possible human relations into the form of claims and counter-claims under established rules, and the belief that the rules are "there"—these combine to make up legalism as a social outlook. When it becomes self-conscious, when it challenges other views, it is a full-blown ideology. Since lawyers are engaged in their daily lives with political or social conflicts of some kind, they are bound to run up against perspectives radically different from their own. As law serves ideally to promote the security of established expectations, so legalism with its concentration on specific cases and rules is, essentially, conservative. It is not, however, a matter of "masking" a specific class and economic interest. Not only do lawyerly interests often differ from those of other conservative social groups, businessmen's, for example, but legalism is no mask for anything. It is an openly, intrinsically, and quite specifically conservative view, because law is itself a conservatizing ideal and institution. In its epitome, the judicial ethos, it becomes clear that this is the conservatism of consensus. It relies on what appears already to have been established and accepted. When constitutional and social changes have become inevitable and settled, the judiciary adapts itself to the new order. The "switch in time" from 1937 onward, after all, involved the whole federal bench eventually, not just one Supreme Court justice. For the judiciary to remain uncontroversial is the mark of neutral impartiality. Adjustment is therefore its natural policy, whenever possible.

The limits to such adaptation are to be found not in judicial attitudes but in society itself, when no consensus prevails to allow the judiciary to appear neutral. When a consensus does emerge, as it rarely does, adjustment is easier. The ease with which the English judiciary not only accommodated itself to socialist legislation, but even bent backward to facilitate its enforcement, shows how the belief in statute law as "there" can help an immensely conservative set of lawyers to adapt itself to political *force majeur*.[3] Yet in 1911 Winston Churchill had said in Parliament that it was impossible for trade union-ists to expect fairness or understanding of the nature of social conflicts from the judiciary. Even before turning to Marxism, Harold Laski assumed that no amount of personal impartial-ity could save the English judiciary from its upper-class out-look.[4] That English barristers have not as a group been drawn to the cause of socialism remains true. It is not likely that the judiciary is now composed of ardent Labour sympathizers. Far from it. However, men live up to the expectations that their own ideology imposes upon them and to the demands of public office. Faced with the consensus that supported the reforming legislation of the first years after the war, the judiciary demonstrated its neutrality by adapting to the new order as it had supported the old.

Aloofness from politics and impartiality depend upon avoid-ance of conflict with other, more powerful political agents. The politics of judicial legislation is exposed as such only when there is conflict. As long as there is no opposition to them, decisions seem to be not choices but accepted necessities. There is no reason to suspect the "legal caste" of using the "thereness" of law as a cover in order to exercise political power irresponsibly.[5] Ideology is rarely so rational or so purposefully designed a Machiavellian scheme. Neither natural law nor positivism is "there" to hide anything. They are not contrived to protect the judiciary or the bar. They are ideas that correspond, each in its way, to the professional experiences and necessities of bench and bar, and that help to maintain their identity, their social place, and their sense of purpose. However, both natural law theories and analytical positivism allow judges to believe that there always is a rule somewhere for them to follow. The consensus of society or of its wise men, a statute (however broadly interpreted), a precedent (however twisted in meaning), all are somehow present to serve as rationalizations to which a judge must resort if his decisions are to meet the demands that a legalistic conscience and his office make upon him.

If many lawyers, in America especially, do recognize that the courts do legislate and make basic social choices, this is less true and even less accepted in other countries. Even in the United States, moreover, the public at large and important sections of the bar do not perceive their functions thus. The courts are expected to interpret the law, not to alter it. Professional ideology and public expectations, in fact, do mold the conduct of the judiciary and its perception of its role. To seek rules, or at least a public consensus that can serve in place of a rule, must be the judge's constant preoccupation, and it affects his choices in ways that are unknown to less constrained political agents. To avoid the appearance of arbitrariness is a deep inner necessity for him. The trouble is that the possibility of aloofness does not depend on the judge's behavior alone, but also on the public responses to it. In England, given the acceptance of Parliamentary sovereignty, the judiciary is not exposed to controversy as extensive as that in America. Here both the nature of the issues placed before the courts and the greater scope of choice available put the judiciary inevitably into the very midst of the great political battles of the nation. Elective state judiciaries, moreover, are bound to remain subject to public scrutiny, which the English judiciary is spared.

In any case, no basic social decision, whether made by court or legislature, can ever meet with unanimous approval in a heterogeneous society. Without consensus the appearance of neutrality evaporates. Every offended party characteristically responds to a decision by accusing the judges of "legislating." It is not the law, which is clearly far from self-evident, but the judge, who is at fault, and an erring judge is a legislating judge, since the losing party begins its case by presenting its version of the true law. The result is that, as denunciations of "lawmaking" multiply, the legalistic ethos is reinforced and the likelihood of judges satisfying it becomes increasingly rare. As long as substantial interests and expectations are disappointed by judicial decisions, there can be no realization of legalistic hopes for a neutral judicial process. Law exists to satisfy legally argued expectations, and the loser is sure to feel that the judge, not the law, has arbitrarily deprived him of "his own." The easiest resort, under such circumstances, is for judges to escape into formalism when they can. For American judges this is frequently not possible. In England it is. As for analytical legal theory, it is more than anything an effort to enhance the formalism that is already a built-in feature of legal discourse. Modern legal theory would be incomprehensible if it were forgotten that its creators are themselves lawyers and that professional habits of mind exercise a real influence upon them as they strive to extract the formal essence of law from the confusion of its historical reality.

Another instance of professional attitudes may be seen in the way in which such a citadel of conservative lawyerdom as the American Bar Association addresses itself to social issues. Matters are taken up one by one, in isolation from the social context and without discussion of the basic issue. Precisely because the A.B.A. regards itself as the official spokesman of the bar it must present its views in a formal manner that gives the appearance of being supra-political and almost without concrete content. It is the independence of the judiciary, the separation of powers, the preservation of fundamental rights, or just fairness, the policy of justice—never the specific social interests or purposes of policies—that is discussed. This formalism makes for adaptability in the long run, but it also represents a rooted conservatism. When it comes to changes that affect the judicial establishment directly, moreover, conservatism becomes immobility. An A.B.A.-sponsored survey of the American legal profession concluded that when it came to reforming procedure, for instance, lawyers were unreasonably obstinate.[6] Observers of the English bar have reached the same conclusion. The English barrister tends to regard the common law as an inheritance to be preserved and technically perfected without being in any way altered. The changes that the bar wants, if any, are not those that the public is interested in.[7] It is, moreover, doubtful that change of any kind is to its liking. "The lawyers could no doubt reform their education and training, reform the practice and processes of the law, even reform the law itself, if they felt like it. But probably they will not feel like it."[8] On the contrary, the more the bar concentrates on formal perfection of established rules and procedures, the more removed it may become from the social ends that law serves. The judiciary, happily, is forced by the institutional demands of its office to keep moving.

The antiquity of legalism as an ideology is, in fact, one of the wonders of history. It is itself the expression of the continuity of the legal profession and its basic tasks. Whereas science has rendered the practice of modern medicine quite unlike the pre-nineteenth-century profession of the same name, the heirs of Coke resemble him closely in vocabulary, outlook, and concerns. De Tocqueville's description of the legalistic ethos is as accurate today as it was when it was written. Order and formality being the marks of the legal mind, he wrote, it is natural for lawyers to support the established social order. As long as they are not deprived of the authority which they regard as their due they will rally to the regime in power. The radical village lawyer of the French Revolution was an aberration that the aristocracy foolishly brought upon itself. In the normal course of events conservatism is inseparable from legalism. "If they prize freedom much, they generally value legality still more: they are less afraid of tyranny, than of arbitrary power." [9] One might add that, if they fear tyranny, it is because it tends to be arbitrary, not because it is repressive. The fear of the arbitrary, however, is what gives legalism its political use. That is why it is not a conservatism without content. To the extent that change means uncertainty, the hatred of the arbitrary is inevitably conservative, but it is a conservatism that has a specific direction which distinguishes it from other conservatisms, especially on those occasions when the independence and professional standing of the bench and bar are directly involved; for they, and they alone, stand to protect "justice" against the arbitrariness and "expedience" of politics.

Almost a hundred years after de Tocqueville wrote, Max Weber could still present a picture of the ideology of the legal profession that was virtually unaltered. Lawyers remained as wedded to formal justice as ever and so to all the interests that relied on permanence and predictability in social procedures. Weber felt that this was even more true of the bureaucratized Continental lawyers than of those in common-law countries. And one can readily see how bureaucratic formalism would reinforce legalistic conservatism to a degree unknown in the Anglo-American legal systems where the free legal profession is less insulated from the shifts and turns of everyday politics. The liberalizing effect of involuntary politicization on the American higher bench, doomed to interpret and adapt its constitution, is evident enough. It is historical phenomena such as these, moreover, that make it so necessary to think of legalism as a matter of degree, rather than as either "there" or "not there," as lawyers think of law. Weber certainly thought of it dynamically, and he was far from complacent in his views

of the intensification and rigidity of the legalism that he saw
about him. If, as he argued, it was worse on the Continent
than in England, his general remarks still are far from inapplicable to Anglo-American lawyerdom.

What he and de Tocqueville saw was that a legal caste,
once it had established the "rule of law" securely against
threats from absolutist arbitrariness, was bound to prefer order
to liberty. What de Tocqueville called aristocratic habits of
thought, Weber believed (rightly) to be more a matter of
"internal professional ideology." The importance of the inner
dynamic of legal reasoning and the professional preferences
of lawyers tend to separate them from other social groups.
Capitalist entrepreneurs have their own interest in stability
and calculability, but the excessive formalities of lawyers' law
are uncongenial to them. The conflict between jurists and psychiatrists is another example of tension engendered by incompatible professional views. As Weber was quick to note,
these are not class struggles but acute differences between
groups which belong to the same economic stratum in society.
Looking at German lawyerdom mainly, he thought that its
self-absorption, the extreme formalism of the legalistic spirit,
would make it inevitably hostile not only to all radical social
reform but to democracy in general.[10] Since democracy was
a radical ideal in Imperial Germany, he was quite right. However, as de Tocqueville noted, democracy is not necessarily
incompatible with legalism. Law in America, then as now,
is a profession open to talent, the poor boy's classical road to
middle-class eminence. One might add that political democracy in America has been so conservative, in general, as to give
the legalistic consciousness relatively little cause for complaint.
Only occasionally, in the fear of radical state legislation and
the Progressive movement for popular recall of the judiciary
in the decades before the First World War, have legalism and
democratic ideology clashed directly. Nevertheless, the main

thrust of legalistic ideology is toward orderliness, and formalism can readily reinforce an inherent preference for authority. The ease with which German lawyers accepted "Adolf Légalité's" pretensions to legitimacy, the support they gave Nazism until its radical anti-legalistic tendencies revealed themselves (and even after), more than justify de Tocqueville's and Weber's suspicions. It cannot be repeated often enough that procedurally "correct" repression is perfectly compatible with legalism. That is the cost of conservative adaptability.

If traditionalism tends to favor liberal constitutionalism in America and England, as it did not in Germany, other aspects of legalism transcend the historic differences which Weber stressed so much and which certainly are very important. The differences in the respective attitudes of American lawyers, psychiatrists, and businessmen are still much as he described them. If the American corporation lawyer, the "house lawyer," comes to identify himself completely with the "organization" for which he works, there are lawyers who are wary of the informality of businessmen. There are, moreover, plenty of businessmen who find "lawyer's law," and expenses, unwelcome—and not only crude robber barons like Ryan and Whitney at that.[11] The resort to arbitration under chamber of commerce auspices, from which lawyers were at first explicitly excluded, represented a significant preference for direct negotiations over formalism and, worse, litigation.[12] On another level, businessmen do not want regulatory governmental agencies to become too courtlike, but prefer to maintain direct access to them in order to bargain with officials. The official program of the A.B.A., on the other hand, calls for judicialization. In this the lawyers, true to their ideology and habits, express their traditional distaste for the politics of negotiation, expediency, and arbitrariness. It is the popular acceptance of this legalism in America that surely contributes its share to the general cynicism toward politics as inevitably "dirty." The belief that negotiations aiming at peaceful settlements represent defeats for justice, for the politics of legalism, has led the official American bar to take at least one stand that separates it noticeably from most other conservative groups. From the first it has lent its support to international law, and especially to the International Court of Justice, on the ground that adjudication alone can prevent war and establish the reign of justice. Here, as in domestic politics, disputes between states are treated in isolation, apart from world politics in general. Here, too, the adjudicative process is held up as the model for government, the substitute for politics. So devoted a business lawyer as Joseph Choate headed the American delegation to the Second Hague Conference, and the "World Peace Through World Law" movement has today the ardent support of the A.B.A.[13] This in itself would suffice to demonstrate the existence of a professional ideology among lawyers.

It also shows that lawyers are not indifferent to their public responsibilities, as has often been charged, but that they conceive of these in terms of their professional experiences and ideology. These give legalistic politics its identifying marks. It would be foolish to underestimate their prevalence or the depth of their roots in tradition, in the very structure of judicial institutions, and in the professional life of bench and bar. That is why one may well doubt the efficacy of the many schemes devised to reorient the thinking of lawyers by altering legal education in America. These proposals come mostly from academic lawyers who, like their medical-school counterparts, have a rather different view of their profession than do their client-oriented former students. Many academic lawyers would like to see a public-spirited political elite replace the private-law practicing lawyers whom they now teach. It is, to be sure, true that many lawyers do participate in politics. These men especially, but the profession as a whole, too, cannot, it is said, be prepared for their public duties by the case method or other traditional ways of teaching lawyers. Men as far apart in their political preferences as the late Justice Vanderbilt and Professor Hurst agree that special training for public service must replace the old curriculum.[14]

That changes in the curriculum are the answer to all public deficiencies is, of course, in keeping with the great American tradition of painless reform. Everything from the study of Chaucer to the pursuit of "social science" has been proposed to this end. What has not been shown, however, is that changes in the content of courses alter the social behavior and attitudes of students once they enter upon their professional life. Given the very real demands for his services in our society, there is no reason why the young lawyer should not follow Lord Coke and make *meum* and *tuum* his favorite words, rather than the vocabulary of social science. Nor is there any reason to suppose that tinkering with the curriculum will, in the absence of significant social changes, alter traditional attitudes that are as firmly grounded as is legalism, not only among American lawyers but in popular opinion as well. The policy of justice, which despises arbitration, negotiations, bargaining, as mere "politics" arbitrary and expedient, will continue to appeal to lawyers. Adjudication of private *lites inter partes* will remain the model for public rectitude, the best way to solve all social conflicts, and "the law" will remain "there." Moreover, a great deal of analytical legal theory will continue to thrive on conceptions that have their roots in this nexus of beliefs. However formal the arguments and abstract the concepts, analytical jurisprudence reflects the same ideological climate as the legal profession as a whole, in spite of that minority of the legal profession in some American law schools which has long protested against formalism in jurisprudence, no less than against the ideological legalism of the bench and bar.

If one is to treat legal thinking in ideological terms, one must also look at its relationships to other ideologies. Indeed, the complex relations between liberalism and legalism form one of the major themes of the present study. Some of the most obvious bearings of legalism upon both liberalism and conserv- atism are, of course, well known. "Freedom under law," "a government of law, not of men"—the limitation of private and public power through the vigorous application of general rules—is inseparable from liberalism. The conservative has no less reason to cherish that security of expectations, guaranteed by the impartial application of rules, which insures the en- forcement of established rights and values. Vested interests are rights, too, depending upon enforceable rules. Such views are too well known to require much examination. They are indeed still prevalent. There are, however, other ideologies fundamentally hostile to legalism. Of these, Fascism and Nazism are the most obvious in their glorification of spon- taneous violence as a fit replacement for the morality of rules. These are not, indeed, the only manifestations of that nihilism which simply wants revolution as a form of authentic self- expression, quite apart from any future ends that it might serve. There are also those extreme forms of anarchism and communalism that reject any ethics of rights and duties in favor of a common life based on mutual service, fellowship, and self-abnegation. These are but a few of the ideological competitors of legalism. They are also all integral parts of the moral history of the West. This is an important considera- tion, because it is as part of the current preoccupation with *"the* political tradition of the West" that law has now become a major item of ideological discourse. This development, and also that highly traditionalist liberalism which has made "the rule of law" the core of its program, would in themselves justify a study of law as an ideological manifestation. They must, at the very least, be mentioned in order to place legalism in the general ideological picture of the present age.

The conspicuous concentration on *"the* West" today is

clearly a response to the Cold War and to the political organization of ex-colonial, non-European societies which now challenge the European world. These events have made us all culturally self-conscious. The result is a search for an identity, for a positive and uniquely Western tradition. The core of that tradition, for those who have discovered it, is essentially legalism, the rule of law. It is not an entirely new notion. The contrast between European legal government and Oriental or "Turkish" despotism is as old as European political theory. There have occasionally been advocates of enlightened despotism who used the Eastern potentate as a model of rational government. However, the main object of these comparisons has been to fortify the rule of law by warning Europeans of the dangers and miseries that await all those who abandon it in favor of Eastern absolutism. Today the confrontation of East and West is not quite so simple, but its ideological core has hardly altered.

The most elaborate, erudite, and influential of modern efforts to expose the contrast between "the Occident" and the rest of the world has been that of Max Weber. It is clear that his object was not to analyze the non-European world, but to discover, by comparing it to Europe, the unique cultural traits of the West. The question he asked was not what are they like, but why are they different from us, and therefore what makes us what we are? To him it seemed that it was a matter of "rationality," by which he meant exactly what has here been called legalism. The predisposition to discover, construct, and follow rules was, in his view, the distinguishing mark of European culture. This alone accounted for those phenomena which appear "only in the Occident": Roman law, the legal profession, judicial institutions, capitalist economics, rational social ethics, and Puritanism in religion. In glaring contrast to these stand the patrimonial and kadi justice of China and Islam and the inner-worldly ethic of the Orient.[15]

The issue here is not whether this provides an adequate account of Asian history. The question is whether it is valid to extract a quintessence of "the West" by subtracting from its history all that it shares in various degrees with the rest of mankind. The result inevitably gives Europeans an unwarranted appearance of consistency and uniformity. The aim of this exercise, moreover, is not difficult to guess: as always it is a matter of defending the "essential" West against other ideological forces, revolutionary, national, and violent. The difficulty is that these too are Western.

Because the threat to "the West" is external at present and so more obviously non-Western in character, the ideological defense of the Western tradition has become increasingly rigid. It is no longer just a matter of emphasizing that legalism has been far stronger in the West than elsewhere, which is certainly true. The ideology of "the West" now goes well beyond that, insisting as it does upon a single Western political tradition. It always comes down to a political tradition of freedom under law or the rule of law. The difficulty with this self-congratulatory view of the Western past is that it flies in the face of the most obvious facts of history. There is no *one* Western tradition. It is a tradition of traditions. Moreover, political freedom has been the exception, a rarity, in Europe's past, remote and recent. It is indeed the very diversity of traditions and conditions that makes European history so turbulent and various. To say that *a* political tradition, "freedom under law," ties all that together into a neat pattern is an ideological abuse of the past. It falsifies the past, and renders the present incomprehensible. What it expresses is the nostalgia of a liberalism that has ceased to look to the future and which seeks to maintain itself not as a hope but as an ancient possession, to be valued more for its familiarity and age than for its intrinsic merits.

Conservative liberalism also inspires that ideology of the

rule of law which has Professor Hayek as its most persuasive and consistent advocate.[16] This indeed is grand ideology, with its own theory of history, of psychology, of epistemology, of economics, and of politics. History is seen as a battle between the healthy instincts of society and the destructive power urges of the state. The battle is fought essentially in terms of intellectual conceptions, especially in terms of economic theories, for it is economic policy that is fundamental. Once the free market is tampered with, even by such a policy as professional licensing, the swift decline of society into absolutism and destruction is inevitable. The chief agents of this destructive urge in the modern world are the intellectuals who want to plan society, not grasping that this requires unobtainable total knowledge of society as a whole. Since their plans must fail, they end by becoming tyrants. The answer to these false political aspirations is the rule of law. The rule of law is the miracle of liberalism, government without coercion. By coercion, Professor Hayek does not mean any exercise of power, but only what occurs when one man issues a direct command to others to perform a specific action to serve his own ends. The chief source of such coercion is government, for it is seen, essentially, as a military agency. Coercion can, however, be eliminated if men are governed entirely by general rules which are applied impersonally and equally to all. These rules must, moreover, be accepted by those to whom they apply directly, as well as by others. Such general rules, indeed, have the character of a natural necessity and, as such, people adjust to them spontaneously. It is, of course, not obvious that men do accept natural necessity. The very existence of technology argues against such a notion. It is even more difficult to imagine what laws other than traffic rules can possibly have the character that is ascribed to genuine law here. Certainly no other examples are offered.

It is not clear at all that the contrast between direct commands and general rules can be maintained. There are direct commands which are general: "Fasten your seat-belts," for example. There are general rules that are highly coercive: "No one may travel abroad," for instance. The difference is clearly not one of form at all, but of the ends served by both laws and commands. The purpose of this division is, in fact, to show that administrative action is not lawlike in character. Only general legislation providing for the barest needs of peace and order in society may truly be honored by the name of law. All else is not natural but coercive. Law, to be law, may merely articulate those standards that are already immanent in society, else it becomes destructive impositions. Although freedom is clearly the end of such a vision, it is also a deeply conservative one, for the natural is the prevalent. That is why law ought to have nothing to do with politics, with that dangerous realm of purposive social action. It exists, rather, to limit politics. To be sure, rules of law do exist to ensure the security of expectations, but here security and freedom, tradition and legality are totally identified. As such, this too, like the ideology of "the West," is a liberalism that clings to legalism because of its conservative implications.

These prevailing ideologies of law would suffice to justify a study of legal thought in ideological terms. There is, however, another consideration. There has been a great tendency toward formalism in philosophy in general, and in political theory especially, in recent years. Mostly it is a matter of reducing political thought to exercises in definition. Of course, playing with words has always been the favorite intramural sport of academicians, and bickering over definitions is far from being a new occupation for philosophers. Nevertheless, not even in the later middle ages were the learned more concerned with language, words, and definitions than they are today. This is so evident that one can hardly avoid wondering how and why it has come about. To anyone interested in contemporary social and intellectual history this general verbalism must be a subject of considerable interest in itself. Moreover, since this is now a feature of all forms of social theory, it might be profitable to look at some of the ideological pressures which have stimulated the passion for definitions and the disputes about them in at least one corner of our intellectual world. Legal theory offers the most promising starting point for such an inquiry, because it has traditionally been the battleground of wars of definition. Perhaps an examination of some legal ideas might serve to illuminate a few of the more fundamental issues of political theory.

There is nothing inherently odd or silly about the passion for clarity and precision which inspires classifications and definitions. What is curious is that there should be such endless disputes about the "true" meaning of words and phrases. Since these arguments tend to center on words which refer to subjects about which few of us are neutral, such as "law," "religion," "ideology," or "justice," it is of considerable practical importance to know exactly what friend and foe mean in using these explosive words. One might also assume that here the issues are basically ideological; they are semantic only in appearance. This can be seen in the effects created by that very fear of "bias" which is so widely shared among American social scientists and which tends to encourage exercises in definition and "methodology" as a means of "coming clean" about one's "values." For, however honest these efforts may be, they seem to be futile. Somehow the definitions and categories remain only covert or open expressions of ideological preferences and as such inevitably become subjects of bitter dispute. Nor, on the other hand, is there any reason to believe that the elucidation of "common usage" as a means of evading "right" definitions can succeed in bringing even limited agreement. To say that to insist upon "true" meanings is a species of verbal self-righteousness misses the point. We protest because words arouse incompatible emotions in us. Until the unlikely event of our ceasing to be different from one another, even a complete analysis of how words in fact behave in our language will not diminish the tensions created by our responses to them. It is not the words but the feelings behind them that cause men to fight.

In fact, however paradoxical it may seem, the urge to define and the various forms of linguistic analysis which oppose such rigidity and finality in the use of words seem to have a common origin. Both arise from a general anxiety about our ability to communicate with each other at all, which is the legacy of the great ideological struggles of the recent past and the verbal warfare and distortions they induced. It is just because the Western world is no longer torn by the life-and-death political passions that raged in it before the Second World War that we have become both aware of the damage done to us by the systematic abuse of language and eager to de-ideologize and de-emotionalize our discourse. However, there is no cause for rejoicing yet. If both the desire for one clear set of definitions and the readiness to admit that "anything goes," as well as the various intermediate positions, show that the great ideological disputes are past and that in different ways we are prepared to settle for limited agreements, there is no evidence that we are succeeding. There is no end to the persuasive use of definitions and classifications and no end to arguments about them. All that has happened is that the issues have shrunk. There are no more great militant ideologies, but this has not produced any agreement. On the contrary, we are now deprived of the cloaks which clothed our temperamental and private differences in the garments of great causes. Now we stand psychologically quite naked before one another, our intellectual dispositions and social preferences openly displayed as expressions of habits and experiences rooted in our very characters, and, as such, probably quite beyond reconciliation. This applies most of all to those who by instinct are believers and those who by nature are skeptics. And it is between these two, the man who is drawn to faith and order and the man who doubts and debates, that most contemporary social, as well as purely philosophic, antagonisms arise. The entire debate about "facts" and "values," about "cognitive" and "non-cognitive" ethics and their political offshoots, is rooted in this conflict. For the questions are not, as the old ideological battles were, matters of concrete substance. The disagreements are not about what we should do, how we should act in specific situations, but about how we should feel and think about morals and politics, above all about how certain we should be, with what degree of conviction and self-assurance we should insist upon our preferences.

It must then seem that the end of the "age of ideology" has left only pettiness and triviality behind it. So the veterans of the 1930's tell us daily, and this too is the complaint of the various "commitment at any price" enthusiasts. For them the end of the great ideologies is the end of all genuine thought. In fact, however, two things are left: ideology in the simple sense of personal and group political preference, and those perennial questions of political philosophy that have concerned the reflective part of mankind since well before the French Revolution—since classical antiquity, in fact. What has gone is grand ideology, those inspiring "isms" that still shake the non-European world. These great social faiths were total world views, explaining the past, predicting the future, serving both as programs of collective action and as the primary ends of individual lives. However, political thinking did not begin with them, nor need it disappear now. While it is a vain tribute to academic vanity and pretended aloofness to say that political philosophy can be divorced from all preferences and all ideology, we are not doomed to a choice between grand ideology and intellectual extinction. We need not even stay modestly within the limits of linguistic clarification. On the contrary, the most obvious task of political theory has always been the elucidation of common experience, the expression of what is inarticulately known to groups of people at any time. It is the re-examination of inherited ideas, their adaptation, and even their utter rejection. It is not a work of discovery, but one of illumination through discussion. We all carry with us a mixed bag of *idées reçus,* and in order to travel with it through an everchanging world we must shift it around occasionally—drop something here and add something there. Above all, we share a variety of common encounters and reactions, and to give these a coherent form, a clear voice, is the task of political theory.

# PART I

# Law and Morals

### DEFINITIONS AND IDEOLOGIES

Philosophical controversies are rarely resolved, but some do fade away. There are a few, however, which have an extraordinary capacity for survival. Of these the argument between natural lawyers and legal positivists is a notable example. Modern legal theory amounts to little but a repetition of the assertions and counterassertions of these ancient opponents, neither one of whom really expects to convince the other. On the surface their differences appear to be a matter of irreconcilable definitions of the word "law." In fact, however, their durable antagonism involves not just words but fundamental social ideologies. The natural lawyer has generally been quite ready to recognize this. Indeed, the moral and political implications of legal positivism have been the main objects of his attack. The positivist's case, however, rests to a large extent upon denying any political commitment on his own part. This is not surprising, since the necessity of separating law, politics, and morals entirely from one another is, ostensibly, his main concern. While this enterprise is pictured as a disinterested pursuit of intellectual clarity as an end in itself, it has from the first been a counter-ideology, a theory whose life depends upon a negative assertion.

If the core of natural law theory is the proposition that law
and morals intersect, positivism lives to deny that proposition.
This does not mean that natural lawyers are not interested
in distinguishing law from morals. On the contrary, both
positivists and natural lawyers agree not only that the aim of
legal theory is the definition of law, but that the way to define
law is to discover those specific characteristics which set it
apart from other social rules, especially those of morality. If
this common preoccupation has provided the chief bones of
contention, it has also come to make the two contestants seem
increasingly similar. Long-standing enmity is, after all, an
intimate human relationship, and old enemies often resemble
each other more closely than they suppose. In the present case,
as a result of concentrating on each other, the subject of debate
between natural lawyers and positivists has been limited to
those issues, and those alone, which bear on their dispute. The
scope and relevance of legal theory has been unnecessarily
restricted by both debaters because they talk only at each other.
This bond of similarity has been enhanced by the fact that
both reflect the concerns of the age in which their quarrel
began, the period of the early modern state. The political
vocabulary of both, filled with terms such as "sovereignty,"
"the state," "the public," "the society," is that of a rather
remote political age. It not only shows a common tendency
to think in terms of static, tangible social entities—a legacy
from the past—but it also reflects an ideological preoccupation.
As long as natural lawyers and positivists remain mesmerized
by each other, neither will feel inclined to question the contemporary relevance of their own positions, or even of their
whole quarrel. This must, therefore, be the task of an outsider. For the student of modern political ideologies the
argument between positivists and natural lawyers is of interest
as an ideological manifestation. To the student of political
theory the issues that it raises and ignores are inherently

important because law and ideas about law are now, as ever, vital aspects of political experience. From these perspectives a series of critical questions presents itself which the "insiders" of legal theory are not apt to see. Why does legal theory in general, and positivism especially, concern itself so much with formal definitions? What do most legal theorists mean by morals and politics when they define the relationship between law and morals and between law and politics? Why do they treat these relationships as they do? What alternatives may be offered?

To an outsider—an historian of ideas, for instance—both natural lawyers and legal positivists seem at first to be primarily interested in definitions. Indeed, most legal theory looks like a heap of definitions piled one upon another. This is particularly true of that part of legal theory which concerns itself with analytical jurisprudence. This is solely a science of definitions. The major part of any work entitled "jurisprudence" consists of demonstrations of the "real" meaning of such terms as right, duty, tort, crime, and contract. In England there has always been a considerable body of opinion that would prefer to limit legal theory entirely to this task. The great question "What is law in general?" is to be shelved in a philosophy designed specifically for lawyers only. Some have gone so far as to reject any "general jurisprudence" altogether. This has been done by denying that there were concepts common to all legal systems and that any one set of definitions could apply to more than any one system.[1] In effect, the same conclusion is reached by those who feel that the sole task of legal theory is to clarify the meaning of the language of lawyers in a given municipal legal system in order to establish all the ways in which terms actually are used.[2] This, it is claimed, will be of immense use to lawyers and will untie all sorts of legal knots. In fact, lawyers remain monumentally indifferent to these labors, have never found any use for courses in jurisprudence (apart from their possible prestige value), and do not regard their professional difficulties as linguistic at all. The claim of linguistic analysis to serve practical ends and to resolve legal conflicts is far from being justified, very probably because verbal confusion only masks conflicts of interest which no amount of analyzing can remove. Even apart from its failure to redeem the legal profession, it is unsatisfactory as jurisprudence, for it offers only more or less generalized accounts of technical terms. It does not deny that such questions as what is a legal system or what is law are interesting, but it brackets them, or simply passes on the responsibility for definition to the political theorist or sociologist. As such, moreover, the analysis of the language of briefs, statutes, and decisions is in itself of no more concern to the student of history or politics than the philosophy to be drawn from a plumber's manual. It is not even relevant to the judge who might be interested in a theory that helped him decide what to do. And this has, in fact, been at times admitted by the champions of a lawyer's jurisprudence.[3]

There is another level at which definition becomes a vital issue, and one which *is* of general relevance. It is *the* question of legal theory. What is law? Can it be defined? Is there one way of using the word correctly, or are there at least a limited number of ways? Should one, in view of the great variety of definitions that has been offered, give up altogether? After all, the wretched word has been used in so many incompatible ways and in such totally disparate areas of discourse that it has become quite hopeless to try to pin it down. Why not let every man choose the definition that happens to suit his mood, his purpose, and his moral and political preferences and, as long as he is clear and consistent, let him have his way? To insist on one universally valid definition of so general a term, and then to squeeze a select number of phenomena into this classification, only reveals "an essentialist" or "realist" bias in philosophy. It is an expression of the belief that words always refer to identifiable entities and that general categories correspond to essences which define individual phenomena and designate their place and purpose in a universal order.[4] In fact, it is quite wrong to hold either philosophical realism or Platonic idealism responsible for this urge to define. The freezing of concepts, the reification of abstractions, is too common for that. Even those who claim that their definitions of law are only pragmatic, of limited usefulness and applicability, often end by treating them as if they referred to a block of matter. Judicial activity is treated as capable of global definition and law as a quantity, even by those quite innocent of philosophic essentialism.[5] It is this excess of conceptualism rather than any given philosophic commitment which has made definition seem purposeless and false.

Another approach, if one does not wish simply to shrug one's shoulders in the face of inevitably "persuasive" definitions, is to allow only an extreme formalism. Such a formalism would admit a possible schema for definitions, or even Kelsen's "pure theory" which purports to offer a skeleton by means of which the essential characteristics of any conceivable historical manifestation of the legal may be identified. By this means it is hoped to achieve the true purpose of definitions: to bring order into one's thoughts without the ideological bias or the historical and cultural myopia that afflicts all more concrete and specific efforts. However, there is less neutrality here than one might suppose. The possibility of treating law as a conceptual pattern entirely distinct from all political, moral, and social values and institutions is simply taken for granted. That law is something "there"—a discrete entity, however abstract—is assumed to be self-evident.

The idea of treating law as a self-contained system of norms that is "there," identifiable without any reference to the content, aim, and development of the rules that compose it, is the

very essence of formalism, for formalism does not just involve
treating law mechanically as a matter of logical deductions
from given premises. It consists rather of treating law as an
isolated block of concepts that have no relevant characteristics or functions apart from their possible validity or in-
validity within a hypothetical system. But what aim is served
by this "homeless ghost"?[6] Why do both the wide formalism
that seeks a single universal pattern for all law and the narrow
formalism that limits itself to analyzing the language used
by lawyers in a municipal legal system insist on validation as
the sole task worthy of legal theory? Is it really a self-evident
procedure? To be sure, the question of what is valid *is* the one
the practicing lawyer must ask in the course of his activities.
There is, however, no reason to assume that it is the only
intellectually worthwhile question to be asked about law.
There is no particular reason why it is to be the only true form
of legal thinking, or why formal definitions alone should
prevail. On the contrary, the notion of the legal as something
that begins at the outer door of the place of legislative activity
and ends with a judicial decision is a highly artificial one. It
is something that the legalistic ethos always demands, but it is
not even partially realized under many historical circumstances. It corresponds to only one historical condition and to
only one ideology. Yet these are the self-imposed boundaries
of formalism. This narrowness is in itself unassailable as long
as it does not pretend to exclusiveness or to the title of the one
true method in legal theory.

This deliberate isolation of the legal system—the treatment of law as a neutral social entity—is itself a refined
political ideology, the expression of a preference. As a description of law it does some considerable violence to political
actualities. While it is clear that arbitrariness is the cardinal
sin from which law must be kept at all costs, it does not follow
that it is necessary to separate law in *theory* from all contact

with the society of which it is an integral part, or even to
ignore the very circumstances which make that neutrality of
law a partial possibility. To do so is to allow the ideal purposes
of law to govern all one's thinking about law in general. It
means thinking of law only as it ought to be—as legalism
wants it to be, not as it actually is. For even if social theory is
not a purely descriptive enterprise, it is difficult to think what
relevance it can have if it becomes totally divorced from all
the contingencies of historical actuality. Formalism in legal
theory here reflects only the legal profession's own assessment
of its functions, the ethos of both bench and bar in what
Austin called "matured legal systems," or, as we might say
more generally, in those states where an independent judiciary
is a valued institution. Here a legal system can be treated as
something "there," an entity to be analyzed only by looking
at it in purely formal terms, even if it does not have the static
timelessness really required for such an enterprise.[7] The
"thereness" of legal systems as historical institutions is, however, far from self-evident. Nothing in human history is self-
evident. Formalism creates this "thereness" because its promoters think that a legal system *ought* to be "there" in order
to function properly. To be "there" it must be self-regulating,
immune from the unpredictable pressures of politicians and
moralists, manned by a judiciary that at least tries to maintain
justice's celebrated blindness. That is why it is seen as a series
of impersonal rules which fit together neatly.

Formalism, on the level of history, is thus also an effort to
say "is" about a legal system where "ought to be" would be
more appropriate. It is necessary to emphasize this because
analytical positivism is driven to formalism precisely because
it makes so much of its own "purity" and freedom from
morals and political ideology. Both the creators of the theory
of "legal science," especially Kelsen and his followers, and the
vision of law that it offers are again and again said to be dis-

tinguished by a perfect remoteness from "external" influences. Yet the theory is incomprehensible unless it is seen as a counter-ideology, as an attack on a different kind of confusion of "is" and "ought"—that which is characteristic of every kind of "higher law" theory. Indeed, it is all but impossible to understand the definitional obsessions of analytical positivism, especially of "pure theory" and of all legal formalism, if one does not recall its ancient enemies, the various theories of natural law. The total refusal to engage in general definitions in order to rivet one's attention on the language of the law itself, no less than the conceptual analysis of highly general jurisprudence, is primarily conceived as an alternative to natural law.

If the verbalism of analytical jurisprudence is covertly ideological, that of moralistic jurisprudence is at least openly so. Perhaps that is its main, indeed its only, merit. It insists that any proper definition of law must include some reference to the higher values law should serve. A law that is not conducive to certain desirable ends, in short, ought not to be honored with the sacred name of law. Definitions ought to be framed so as to avoid such a possibility. Classification and evaluation are here openly joined. If, however, one asks why it should matter so much whether one says, "This is a bad law," having defined law in some way that does not touch upon its merits, or "This is not law because it fails to meet my standard of goodness," one can see at once that it is not a question of linguistic practice at all. The desire to say this "is" non-law arises partly from the known propagandistic punch of "persuasive" definitions. The feeling that what one does not approve of "is" not, either because it has been or soon will be destroyed, is a real necessity for many people who have a "cause." Here the logical difficulty of deriving an "is" from an "ought," or vice versa, is of no importance compared to the sense of security to be gained from the feeling that a true law, a rule that is genuinely valuable, "exists" as a natural, universal necessity. One is not only to be right, one is also to "be"—to have a grammatical and ontological status above those who are wrong. Otherwise how is one to have that certain feeling of being perfectly right and triumphant, while one's opponents languish in error and defeat?

The difference between people who would fall into despair if their moral convictions were not anchored to a universally valid order and those who find a state of doubt not only endurable but positively enjoyable is one of incompatible intellectual-psychological types. This is a difference far deeper than the urge to proselytize by means of confusing "is" and "ought." The tradition of philosophical realism or essentialism also has roots deeper than propaganda. Indeed, the propagandistic aspect of persuasive definitions itself expresses the desire to overcome doubt and diversity.[8] Behind the urge to convince lies a belief that we ought to agree, because agreement is in itself valuable. The realist sees a harmonious universe to which we must adjust morally because this ultimately is God's design for His creation. To overcome moral and political doubt and diversity is for him not an expression of intolerance but the fulfillment of an impersonally imposed obligation which is entirely lawlike. A serviceable definition of law must include only law that conforms to this higher law, because otherwise it would be untrue to his own fundamental moral experience. To those who do not share that experience, however, it is nothing but his private law. Impersonality, objectivity, for those who accept doubt and diversity in morals means necessarily repressing such individual moral inclination.

Thus, the "isness" of such positivist and formal definition of law as "a hierarchy of sanctioned rules," "sanctioned norms," or "the command of a sovereign," and even "what the courts have done and will do" is historically frail. However, they all do spring from a determined desire to avoid an obvious inclusion of personal values in the acts of defining and classifying. Therein lies positivism's intellectual appeal and its practical weakness. Impersonal judgment and the striving for objectivity are intellectual virtues of the highest order. But they are the virtues of observers, of technicians, and of strategists, not of those who must make social choices for themselves and for others in situations where it is far from clear what ends can and should be pursued, however much the participants may long for clear rulebooks to guide them. The appeal of natural law lies just here. However inadequately, it does satisfy a widely felt need. It has always addressed itself not so much to lawyers as to judges and politicians. Not only has it been built into our judicial institutions, but it has always been directed at those who must act and decide. That is why its intellectual partiality, so often exposed, has not destroyed the practical appeal of its system of definitions. Positivist formalism is the intellectual expression of the skeptic's wish to de-ideologize political discourse and political life in general. This is as true of legal theory as of other types of formal political theory. The natural lawyer appeals to a very different sort of moral need, the need for certainty and for shared standards of moral judgment, which does not decline in a morally diverse society but may even grow stronger. This tends to exacerbate conflict, of course, but formalism offers no answer to that particular practical circumstance. Therein lies its real weakness, not in its purported "falseness." Since it is doubtful that any social theory can rise to the degree of detachment which the "pure theory" of Kelsen claims (erroneously) to have achieved, the price which this formalism has paid in terms of excessive abstractness and remoteness from law as a social phenomenon seems particularly exorbitant.

In view of these considerations it becomes clear that the quarrel over "what is law" is not a matter of proper linguistic usage. Even when one remembers the professionally induced preoccupation with words, definitions, and classifications that afflicts lawyers, one cannot believe that this dispute between legal theorists is a purely verbal affair. The quest for impartiality, for that "perfect" judicial poise, cannot give to even the most formal "science of law" the neutrality it seeks. Indeed, the very quest for an intellectual purity analogous to the ideal of judicial autonomy reflects a moral and political partiality. That the natural lawyer is not just looking for a simple definition is openly admitted in any case. All this becomes perfectly clear when one looks at that standard subject of all legal theories, the classification of law and morals, for this evidently is the heart of the dispute.

THE DIFFERENTIAL CHARACTERISTICS:

SIN, IMMORALITY, AND CRIME

One of the main efforts of the various traditional schools of legal theory has been to define law by separating it from other bodies of social rules, especially from morals and customs. For purposes of clarity it seemed most important that a list of differential characteristics be established so that any rule could at once be identified as either moral or legal. The "tendency to confound Law and Morals is one of the most prolific sources of jargon, darkness and perplexity," wrote Austin.[9] No legal theorists, whether positivist or natural lawyers, would disagree with him. Why should it be so? There is no particular reason to believe that lawyers and their clients, for instance, are deeply confused by an inability to keep law and morals apart. It is not a difficulty that afflicts us in our daily lives ordinarily. Moreover, just what sort of confusion is to be dreaded? It is here that the classifiers begin to disagree. Is it purely intellectual confusion that is dangerous? Or does the danger lie in the possibility that people will err in their social conduct if they cannot tell moral from legal rules? This is certainly the view of natural law. It is also the view of Hobbes,

Austin, and Kelsen. Now natural lawyers may be liberal or authoritarian, and they may fear that an inability to tell law from morals would lead either to excessive or inadequate degrees of civil obedience on the part of private citizens and to either overgovernment or undergovernment on the part of rulers. Among positivists, fear of religiously and ideologically inspired anarchy was great, and as long as the state was held to be a neutral peacemaker it was important to preserve "law" from disorders inspired, presumably, by morality. The tenor of positivism in England and America has, however, for many years been liberal, and it is to preserve morality from law that positivists now classify the two with all possible linguistic rigor. It is perfectly clear that the fears of confusion are inspired by a concern for neither law nor morality, primarily, but for the proper spheres of private and public life. This, to be sure, is one of the great issues of politics, but it is not really a question of logical classification.

That classification as an intellectual sport is not the real issue becomes even more evident when one considers the way in which morals are treated. For purposes of classification alone the term "morals," whatever its relations to law, would have to cover every conceivable moral theory and every known form of moral belief. Since many of these are mutually incompatible, it is not possible to single out the essential characteristics of morality without, in fact, limiting oneself to only one type of morality. That is, moreover, just what has happened. In the case of natural lawyers this is not surprising or obscure, since the moralization of law is the ultimate end of classifying the two. It is assumed that there is *a* morality and that this intersects law whenever the citizen, lawyer, judge, or legislator asks himself whether he should accept a given rule as binding upon himself or others. The "pure" formalist might appear to escape from choosing one set of morals by saying that morality is all that is not law, and bracketing it as irrelevant to legal "science." Even this, however, involves a view of morality which at least assumes that law and morals *are* distinguishable, a point which some moralists might deny.

This does not imply any sort of deliberate subterfuge on the part of any legal theorist. Ideology is not conscious distortion. It is, rather, a series of personal responses to social experiences which come to color, quite insensibly often, all our categories of thought. The liberalism of Kelsen or Hart, for example, is perfectly open and avowed, as is that of many of their admirers. It is that very liberalism and the standards of intellectual objectivity that it demands, however, which make it apparently difficult for those thinkers to recognize the extent to which their preferences mold their conceptions about law and morals. In fact, it is clear enough to an historian that it is not fortuitous that Kelsen's "pure" theory has its origins in the Vienna in which psychoanalysis and logical positivism also had their home. All these concentrated attacks on traditional myths and irrationalities of every sort arose in the midst of a veritable caldron of religious, social, and ideological conflict. All are negative responses to the fanaticized consciousness and the distortions which it engenders. In such a situation it may well be that intellectual integrity and freedom may need protection more against the currents of grand ideology and absolutist morals than against the powers of a faltering state. Here liberalism is bound to identify itself with the ideal of a strong but neutral state that stands above and aloof from the wars of ideology and thus morality.

The pure science of law is a vision of the law of such a state. Intellectually it expresses the belief that science is defined by its non-ideological character, its formal purity. The task of law in practice is to preserve order against ideology; that of theory, to structure a notion of law free from all that is subjective, contingent, or ideological. The price of historical irrelevance does not seem too high in that case. As for Professor Hart, what liberal denies that his attacks upon those who want to improve the moral conduct of their fellow citizens by applying governmental pressures are as necessary and valid as were those of John Stuart Mill?[10] There is nothing one can object to in these efforts to protect the private life of every individual against the absolutism of those moralists who would employ the force of government to impose their preferences upon others. It does not, however, follow that, because this is desirable, it is also logically necessary or conceptually possible to separate law and morals. No one argues that this separation has ever been maintained in practice, either in the past or in the present. Indeed, the age of totalitarianism is one in which this separation is rejected more than ever by a greater number of governments. The simple point is that the separation of law and morals is not self-evidently necessary, even on that most empty, formal, and "pure" plane where history is purposely forgotten. The entire formulation is not a matter of logical classification, of conceptual clarity, of "science," or of analytical coherence. It is an expression of the liberal desire to preserve individual autonomy, and to preserve the diversity of morals which is in constant danger of ideological and governmental interference. To this end, however, an open discussion of the political issues can contribute much more than positivist and formalist dogmatism can.

Actually, there is no compelling reason for choosing one system of morals, one criterion of evaluation, in order to discuss the relations between the moral and the legal. On the contrary, while the insistence upon a single set of values is capable of yielding a neat scheme, it is a scheme neither complete nor in any correspondence with historical experience. Whether one wishes to moralize politics by demonstrating the superiority of moral values over legal ones in order to rouse rebellion in defense of the "higher law," or, more likely, in order to prop up an established political order by covering it with moral blessing, the higher law schematization of differential characteristics has no concern with and no use for social realities. Its purpose is to establish the "necessary" relationship between true morals and good politics. The positivist denial of such a relationship is, moreover, just as useless historically and just as indifferent to actual practice. It only widens the separation of law and morals in order to prevent political oppression by the adherents of some one system of religious and moral values. Historically it is, of course, quite true that the secular state and the religiously neutral legal system have been the cornerstones of individual moral freedom, just as the contemporary ideological state has been its scourge. It is, however, one thing to favor the ideal of a *Rechtsstaat* above all ideological and religious pressures, and quite another to insist upon the conceptual necessity of treating law and morals as totally distinct entities.

The first outcome of these mistaken strivings is a series of elaborate lists identifying both the essential attributes and the proper relations between law and morals as distinct entities.[11] Almost all these accounts begin with the assertion that law is concerned with external action, while morality is directed at inner states of mind. Law demands mere conformity of behavior, while morality by definition demands that action be motivated by the voice of conscience. This is said to be logically necessary, either on ontological or on psychological grounds. Either this is what the essence of value in law and morals is, or these are two different human responses. In the former case there is a difference of standards of evaluation, as well as of aim. In the second case, different attitudes are said to be involved. The merely legal is seen as something one does because of external pressure, the moral as something that springs from the depth of one's personality. Usually this outer-and-inner dichotomy is followed by the consideration that morals derive their validity from a *summum bonum* while law is relative, both historically and ethically. Law, in short, is social, objective, and coercive; morals are individual, subjective, and voluntary. The first deals with men in the gross, in generalities; the latter seeks the personal and particular. The law, lastly, is more modest in its demands, insisting only on abstention from what is forbidden, while morality demands the willing fulfillment of positive duties. In law an agent may act for us; to be moral, we must carry out our responsibilities ourselves. Either because it is in its "essence" limited, or as a matter of psychological fact, law cannot make us good Samaritans. It can enforce a sort of minimum social morality, a standardized general code. The unique situation, demanding a direct, individual choice, is beyond its scope. In any case, much of law is morally indifferent, while the truly moral act cannot be legally enforced even if the content of individual moral and legal rules is the same, because the sources of their respective validity, or at least the attitudes involved in each case, are by definition different.

Even those positivists who are most anxious to avoid committing themselves to a too specific notion of morality concede that there is at least a difference in the kind of pressure that is brought to bear upon people. Moral pressure takes the form of an appeal to a person's own standards. It is a call to what is commonly spoken of as conscience. Moreover, morality is voluntary, and so "I could not help it" is an excuse in morals but not necessarily in law. The pressure exerted by law is ultimately coercive, and in any case refers to a rule outside the individual's private system of values. In addition, it has been suggested, again by a convinced positivist, that morality is more important to the individual ultimately than law. What "important" means is not very clear, but the implication is that it refers to behavior and ideas that should not be controlled by law. Lastly, it is suggested that morality and especially mores, unlike law, are not subject to deliberate and rapid change.[12] This notion has been traditionally stressed by conservatives anxious to limit the legislative urges of radicals. It has come to appeal to liberals, again, one suspects, in order to limit governmental action—not necessarily radical action, of course. One cannot forebear to mention that this notion is plainly false. In an age of concentrated propaganda, morality and mores *are* subject to quick and deliberate change. The morality of large numbers of Germans surely underwent extensive and rapid changes during Hitler's regime. In fact, every one of the suggestions that treats law and morality as two separate blocks of rules that are just "there" to be identified can be shown to be too narrow—to have excluded some moral possibility or historical manifestation. This is true even of the fundamental distinction, on which most separations ultimately rely, between the internality of morals and the externality of law.

To understand at all the emphasis on the internality of morals one must remember traditional Christian morality, from which it is derived and which alone makes it intelligible. To speak of this internality as if it were an obvious psychological or social fact is absurd and has strange results in practice. For orthodox Christians, now as ever, the most extensive category of human failure is sin. A sin is not just an injury to another person. It is a rejection of God. It may be a purely internal act which may lead to no change in external behavior. Secondly, there is immorality. Every immorality is a sin. It is an act that rejects God and God's law by failing to fulfill one's obligations to His creatures. There can be immorality even in acts directed at oneself primarily, such as suicide, but most immorality obviously involves a rejection of God by injury to another person. Immorality can—and Christian adherents to Thomism insist that it must—be further divided into private and public forms of immorality. On the whole there is now a general agreement among American and English thinkers of this school that only the public forms of immorality ought to be made crimes—that is, punishable by law—as a matter of political convenience, since the disadvantages of interfering with private immorality appear to outweigh any possible gain. There is no categorical, absolute objection to making private immorality subject to punishment; this is regarded as a question of practical prudence. What *is* absolutely rejected is any attempt on the part of the law to punish sin, or indeed to concern itself directly with man's relation to God.[13]

Internality, as distinguished from privacy, refers to sinfulness in general, but not to that part which expresses itself in external behavior, not to immorality. Since St. Thomas' day natural law theory has been perfectly clear about this. The trouble is not theoretical but practical. In fact, governments throughout history have been busily doing God's work for him. The history of the criminal law is the story of "the protection of God's interests." [14] Primitive governments used to punish sins in order to prevent divine punishment, and they regarded the expiation of sin, the elimination of taint, as a communal responsibility. When civil courts took over some of the jurisdiction of ecclesiastical courts, they aimed at the same thing, without perhaps being aware of it. In any case, punishing sins has been the preoccupation of the criminal law, whatever theologians may have said about the matter. As long as men regarded crimes as sins, even if practical social values were to determine what sins were to be punished, this was not so utterly intolerable. The real transvaluation of values did not come with St. Thomas, however pragmatic his political philosophy may have been. It came when Europeans in large numbers ceased to believe in sin altogether. It is since then only that the punishment of sin has come to be an utter outrage. That explains the unanimity in emphasizing the immunity of internal acts from law. That, too, explains why internality is emphasized so much as the distinct, non-legal aspect of morals. Unfortunately it is a distinction that is perfectly meaningless unless one believes in sin, and it is not of primary relevance even if one does believe in sin, except for purposes of keeping the "powers that be" away from one's soul. For practical purposes, even among Christian natural lawyers the relevant distinction is whether immorality is private or public. The great problem of our age, moreover, is not the persecution of sinners but the ideologically inspired repression of moral dissenters.

To be sure, the internality of morality is not an idea limited to those who believe in sin. The morality of motives or of conscience also asserts that the distinguishing mark of a moral act is that it is prompted by the right motive and nothing else. Motives, moreover, are internal, while laws can claim to control only external behavior, which is a matter of outer conformity. The rightness of the motive, however, depends upon its conformity to universal moral principles. The relation of internal motives to these is, thus, analogous to the relation of sin to God, and the reason for keeping the hands of the law out of both is the same. To T. H. Green, for instance, it seemed both futile and tyrannous to legislate such morality, since it is by definition an inner act, as is the acceptance or rejection of God for the Christian.[15] The effect of the morality of motives is obviously to extend the scope of individual autonomy. By doing away with the subdivisions of traditional moral theology and by making internality the identifying mark of the moral act, the morality of motives greatly limits the sphere of morally permissible external pressure upon the individual, whether such pressure be educative or coercive. That is why it is one of the preferred moral theories of classical liberalism from Kant to T. H. Green. Only utilitarianism can rival its popularity among men of liberal convictions. Internality is thus relevant to only *some* moralities, not to morals as such.

The main trouble with the ethics of sin and the ethics of conscience is that their origins and purposes, theological, philosophical, and social, are rarely remembered by those who still adhere to them. This is especially true of those writers on criminal law who insist that criminal responsibility must be justified in terms of the freedom of the will—who claim, in other words, that only those actions which were freely chosen by the individual may be punished. That is to them the moral justification of criminal law. What, however, is meant by the freedom of the will? It is not a psychological theory of human conduct. Rather, it is an account of man's relation to God. Man is free to sin, to reject God, even though he is the creature of God who is omnipotent. It explains why sin is possible at all. In the case of the ethics of conscience it explains moral irrationality, the possibility of not doing what reason tells one to do even though reason is universally valid, self-evident, and ultimately guaranteed by God. In neither case does it say anything about why and when society should take action against its deviant members. It does explain why God may be injured and men err. Unless one really believes that public authorities ought to act as God's agents or that they represent the voice of universal reason, free will is irrelevant to the theory of criminal punishment. Yet the justification of criminal punishment as limited to freely willed actions is often professed even by people who regard morality as a matter of community values.[16] In this case one is faced with the proposition that community values have the same status as God. There is almost no idea more horrible to contemplate in the modern world, in which, after all, large numbers of people care neither about sin nor about motives, and where those who claim that they do often do not know what they are talking about. This does not mean that the term "voluntary" has no place in criminal law, if one means by a voluntary action, whatever its motive, one that was not performed while the agent was being coerced by others or was mentally deranged, nor was done accidentally or when the agent was totally incapable of appraising the facts of the situation in which he found himself. These and similar qualifications can be defended on several grounds. One may argue that the effect of law that emphasizes personal responsibility in this way is to educate self-reliant citizens. One can say that these negative extenuating circumstances increase the security and freedom of the individual by making the conditions of criminal responsibility clear and explicit. In any case, no resort to the morality either of sin or of conscience is required.

This review of the origins and fate of the idea that morality is essentially something internal is not meant to defend or to criticize either Christian moral theology or the morality of conscience. It is merely meant to show that this idea has a place in only those two systems of moral thought. It is not even politically very relevant to one of them, Thomist natural law, which makes the distinction between sin and public immorality very clear, and which has consistently denied that sin as such is the concern of the criminal law. As a way of classifying morality and law this distinction will simply not do, because it excludes far too many types of moral theory. Thus it is an exhortation, not a description. Yet ultimately all the schema of differential characteristics come down to this—that morality is internal and law external. As such, they are insufficient as classifications. The ideas that inspired them have even ceased to be adequate defenses for moral freedom; for the freedom that is to be defended is not just that of the inner man in his relation to God or to eternal principle, but the freedom to profess moral views that cover a far wider range of moral and political attitudes. From the point of view of liberalism, at least, it is diversity that is to be cherished, and tolerance is to be practiced in the interest of social freedom—not only the freedom necessary for faith in God and adherence to universal maxims of morality, which is what the sacredness of internality is meant to secure.

Thus, neither as classifications nor as ideologies of freedom are the differential characteristics a great success. Their moral partiality is understandable among those who really believe that evaluation and classification must not be separated in an harmonious order. This is permissible within their own system, in which the empirical is merely the accidental and contingent and not the real object that is to be classified. As a non-evaluative classification, however, the system of differential characteristics is absurd. To fulfill this function it would have to be applicable to every conceivable form of morality and every known system of law. At the very least it would have to cover the major ethical and legal systems that have appeared in the course of history. In fact, it does nothing of the kind. The only morals covered entirely are the ethics of conscience, and the only political systems envisaged are those that recognize the separation of law and morals, of the secular and the divine, and of the coercive and the educative. In fact, however, there are several moralities which are completely incompatible with the traditional scheme, and some which would reject the very idea of separation altogether. Consequently, there can be no way of dividing law off from morals in general without first selecting one set of moral and political values as the only valid one. From the historical point of view, no less than from that of the neutral analysis of normative discourse, such a procedure is clearly unjustifiable. The entire distinction between inner and external action is, for instance, quite meaningless to those who measure the value of an action in terms of its consequences and not in terms of the motives and intentions of the agent. For the ethics of consequences, motives are merely one aspect among several that give an action its total character and effect. This is, moreover, the role that they do, or at least should, play in "matured systems of law." If, as in the case of utilitarianism, the end of morals and law is to be identical, the need for differentiation also disappears altogether.[17]

The ethics of consequences is not the only one that does not fit into the traditional pattern of differential characteristics. A morality based entirely on custom, on tradition, would be similarly indifferent to the contrast between inner and external action. No theocracy could possibly accept the notion of any sort of separation of law and morals, nor could any of the various theories of the educative polity, of which Plato's *Republic* is the most enduring model. For none of these can personal choice be regarded as the core of morality, least of all when opposed to objective demands. The possibility of a conflict, moreover, is denied. It certainly is not graced with any of the approbation implicit in the morality of conscience. Nor does ethics always have an individualizing tendency; this is particularly unlikely among its most legalistic forms, such as that pictured in the Old Testament. These examples hardly furnish a complete list of exceptions. They only point to some of the historically most important ones, but they do demonstrate the inadequacy of differential characteristics as a system of classification.

For those who do not wish to commit themselves to an essentialist position, but still require some firm line to be drawn between law and morals, there is another alternative: sanctions or modes of enforcement. Purely formal analysis has always relied upon this as *the* dividing point. The advantages of this notion are obvious. It is flexible and open-ended, in that it does not specify the content of any kind of morals or law, but only supposes the most general social character of both. It does not even say anything about the desirable limits of one in relation to the other. Though this does not imply indifference to the problem of governmental power, it does make many liberals uneasy. Few theorists have spent more effort than Bentham, for instance, on weighing the exact minimum of public pressure necessary and the maximum of private regulation possible in a perfect balance between law and private ethics. Even so, the more liberal among his admirers have worried about his sweeping rejection of motives and intentions in his calculations of the exact amounts of pain to be distributed where punishment was called for. This was not because they wished to return to the morality of conscience, but because they saw a threat to individual freedom in the uncertainty and incalculability that might follow if extenuating circumstances were ignored in punishment. If accidental and unintended acts were not treated as less punishable than premeditated ones, the individual's ability to predict the action of public authorities would be decreased, and his freedom as well; for he could never be quite sure when he was in danger of committing a crime.[18]

The reason why enforcement is inadequate as the sole distinction between law and morals is not, however, that its indifference to inner states may justify unduly extensive, severe, and unpredictable punishment. It is, rather, that it provides no real standard of distinction at all. It is both in substance and in its historical origins a denial of higher law theory, rather than a genuine attempt at providing a classification. As such it is more a counter-ideology than anything else. Its main purpose is to insist that law is *not* to be identified by its goodness but by some morally neutral standard, such as the fact that it is enforced by someone. The identification of that someone has proved rather difficult. Since the notion of sovereignty lost any concrete political manifestation with the disappearance of absolute monarchs, it has become a mere tautology: the law is what the sovereign says it is, and the sovereign is he who says what the law is.[19]

Its successor, Kelsen's "basic norm," is afflicted with the same deficiency, but being totally impersonal it is not meant to be more than a logically necessary hypothesis.[20] Even as such it is too limited a notion. In concrete terms it presupposes the modern centralized state. It is an aspect of only stable, matured legal systems, where one enforcing agency that is accepted as *the* public authority can be identified at any given point. However, even under these conditions the usefulness of this definition is limited. The lawyer in his practice may find it serviceable only to the extent that he is concerned with keeping his clients out of jail, but most of his time is spent in keeping them out of troubles that involve enforcement by way of sanction only very remotely, if at all. For the purposes of pure formalism the notion of law as sanctioned norms might prove adequate as long as it really remained perfectly pure, that is, totally abstracted from history. The difficulty is that no legal theory, indeed no theory concerned with social institutions, can remain quite that pure, for even the purest of pure formalists agrees that law is a form of social control. However, if he thinks that it is possible to define social control in terms of one formal criterion, such as governmental enforcement, he obviously does not know or care much about social control. What matters is not the possibility of enforcement, whether immediate or remote, but the conditions under which it takes place. Enforcement is not a reified entity that has a tangible structure. It is a series of events and actions taking place under various circumstances which alone can define its character. Of these, "who" is neither the only relevant nor the most relevant question. That is why pure definitions are rather an avoidance of descriptive classification than a contribution to it. Sanctions and enforcement are such vague notions as to have very little concrete meaning. What gives them their character in any given time and place is intangible, depending upon the attitudes and relative positions of both the enforcers and their subjects. The character of those doing the enforcing and the views of those to whom the sanctions may apply, no less than the degree and form of organization among the enforcing groups, whether governmental or private—all this is inseparable in actuality from any system of enforcements. It is not "there"; it is a series of shifting relationships.

If the definition, "Laws are rules that can be enforced," is inadequate in itself, it also involves difficulties in defining morals. If there is any attempt to specify the sort of pressure that is distinctly moral, it is bound to lead to great partiality. No number of paradigmatic cases can exhaust the variety of the history of human morals. This only illustrates again the difficulty of a positivism which insists on treating law and morals as social phenomena but tries to escape from history into formalism. After all, people have tried to enforce almost every conceivable form of behavior by an inexhaustible number of means. There are, moreover, some societies in which all rules are subject to only one type of enforcement. To repeat, what is the difference between law and morality in a theocracy? One need think only of Calvin's Geneva or of the codes in *Leviticus*. Were there no morals here or no law, since nothing was potentially without sanction from one source, and one only? Again, in modern, complex societies it is by no means clear that the sanctions exercised by large organizations—such as huge business enterprises, or even great universities with their inner disciplines, their plant and campus police, and hierarchical organization—affect the individual in a manner totally distinct from his relations with governmental officialdom. Indeed, in highly legalistic societies, where children's secret clubs, no less than great political parties, have rules, settled procedures, and identifiable agents of enforcement, the individual may not find the law the chief source of restraint. It may not even be a clearly distinguishable source of restraint in its effects upon his daily life.

This argument is not meant to support that theory of pluralism which claims that organized government is, or ought to be, just like any other group in society, and that only its monopoly of military force distinguishes it from the lesser associations. To begin with, monopoly of violence hardly explains anything about the actual conduct of government in a constitutional democracy. No monopoly of violence ever got a single bill through Congress or Parliament. It is, however, clear that modern governments fulfill functions and enjoy an authority unlike that of any other group of men in society. Above all, our attitudes toward governments differ radically from those toward other organizations. What is at stake here is that, first of all, governments do many things other than legislate, adjudicate controversies by judicial proceedings, and enforce such decisions. They do things which have no connection with law but which certainly involve social control and social direction. Secondly, there are nongovernmental organizations which do perform legal functions, even if the number of people affected by them is less extensive. For purposes of legal theory, the real distinction is not between governments and other agencies that enforce legalistic policies, but between legalistic and nonlegalistic modes of behavior, thought, and social policy. A theory that distinguishes law and morals in terms of pressures applied to gain conformity and then divides these pressures into official and private ones is, therefore, historically too selective.

To avoid any sort of commitment to social reality, formal theory may simply choose to leave the question of morality open. The corollary of "Law is a sanctioned norm" is, "Morality is anything not so sanctioned." This, of course, says absolutely nothing about morals. Such a stand can be justified by a

theory of extreme moral noncognitivism, a position which
Kelsen, of course, accepts. This too, however, is only one moral
theory among many. For purposes of classification it will not
do, since it does not say what morality is but what it is not.
And this indeed is its sole ideological function, its reason for
existence. It is not a theory of law or of morals. It is a denial
of natural law cast in grammatically positive propositions.
Therefore it says nothing directly about morals except that
morals belong to the private sphere. The existence of such
privacy, one might add, is not itself an historically self-evident
fact but an ideologically inspired hope. Behind the entire view,
moreover, lies the least defensible notion of classical liberalism:
the identification of privacy, freedom, and choice with the
nongovernmental, while sanctions and force are entirely identified with governmental action. Only this rather simple view
of society and of the informal sources of oppression could
inspire such a theory of enforcement. Beyond ideology, the
elimination of content and quality has little to recommend it,
nor has the entire separation of the formal from the substantive. The latter is, indeed, the creation of the medieval scholas-
tics, whose reputation for historical sensitivity and descriptive
talent has never been high. For the historian, circumstances,
responses, content, and form are not so readily separated, nor
is any non-ideological intellectual purpose fulfilled thereby.

Whatever the differences between positivists and natural
lawyers, both are agreed that some system rigidly separating
law and morals is necessary. Both agree, moreover, that this
is possible because two different bodies of rules are there and
that clarity or virtue or both are mortally endangered by a
failure to keep them apart. To this notion every classifier,
whatever his other ends may be, is thoroughly addicted.
Explicitly or implicitly, moreover, both agree that morality is a
matter of rules. That, however, is by no means obvious. It is an
assumption that arises from the fundamental failing of legal

theory to take full account of the actuality of human diversity in matters of moral belief and political ideology. The morality of rules is, in fact, only one among many. To be sure, this has been one of the dominant moral traditions of European society. It is no less true that the greatest of our moral philosophers— St. Thomas, Hobbes, and Kant, to name but a few—have defended the notion of morality as rules deduced from prior rules, even if on very different grounds. Lastly, for all those who cherish the belief that a stable and decent political order is one committed to liberal values, to a morality capable of rational justification, and to a logically consistent system of rules, legalistic morals must seem the only morals worthy of recognition.[21] Unhappily they cannot be said to be the only ones that exist. Even within the traditions of social morality there have been at least two patterns: that of obligation—of rights and duties clearly resembling law—and that of service and mutual aid. In any case, social morality is not the only one. The morality of the "inner light"—the morality of sentiment, of authenticity, and of self-realization—has always had its advocates even in the most legalistic societies.

All the irrationalist moralities, the various moralities of the heart, begin with a denial of the value of rules and rule following. Here, whether it be sincerity or self-expression that is sought, one thing is certain, that adherence to principles or to rules is rejected. The ethics of rules and obligations overlooks the saint and the hero.[22] This sort of morality is, moreover, likely to be not only anarchistic in general but specifically anti-legalistic. The ideal society is the face-to-face friendship group for the tender-minded among these "impulse and instinct" enthusiasts, while the rule of supermen is the ideal of the more tough-minded and extravagant. In either case the impersonal element in legalistic morals is discarded. To be sure, in practice the inner call, if it is not the call of the blood and of violence, often tends to be fraudulent. The patron saint of the morality of the heart is probably Tartuffe. That the morality of "her life was wicked, but her heart was pure" is likely to nauseate intelligent adults is equally certain. However, that does not alter the fact that in our literature particularly it has played an enormous part and that many of us have in our adolescence experienced its undeniable attractions.[23] It is "there" no less than the ethics of rules and obligations.

These somewhat repulsive examples are not the only non-legalistic morals available to us. There has always been a tradition in Christianity that has identified legalism with ritualism and has rejected both. In Eastern Christianity this is especially pronounced. It was one of Leon Petrazycki's greatest merits as a legal theorist that, as a Roman Catholic and a Pole teaching in Czarist Russia, he was so much aware of the significance of nonlegalistic ethics. As an advocate of liberalism and an admirer of Western European political life he was, of course, anxious to promote the legalistic ethics upon which he felt they, as well as the general standardization of conduct required for commercial progress, depended—a view which Max Weber was developing at the same time. It is not so important that he recognized that legal development and liberal politics depend upon citizen types who insist on their rights, rather than upon humble saints; it has, after all, been often remarked that from the point of view of legal values Shylock's insistence upon his rights is worthier than Portia's plea for mercy.[24] What is more important is that Petrazycki saw that the real social distinction was not between law and morals but between legalistic and nonlegalistic social values. In nonlegalistic morality "dueness" has no place at all, and claims and counterclaims, rights and demands are not to be made. It values only a mystic authority, self-abnegation, and "turning the other cheek," which stand in contrast to the legalistic ethics of rational obligation. In fact, to be taught to demand one's due, one's rights, in the nursery is the first step in a continuum of social attitudes, of which bringing suit in court is merely one expression.[25]

It is not wholly without interest that Petrazycki's fellow countryman and near-contemporary, Malinowski, adopted a very similar approach to legal phenomena. In describing the legal institutions of the Tobriand Islanders he noted that in spite of the lack of courts of law and of any comparable machinery of enforcement, there did exist a sense of obligation and of duty to honor specific claims which amounted to an operative civil law.[26] Whatever the merits of this view from the standpoint of anthropology may be, it does point to the need for flexibility in distinguishing law from related phenomena, especially among people whose social life does not resemble that of modern Western Europe and America. We need not insist with Petrazycki that the term "morality" ought to be limited to the sphere of "autonomous," other-worldly, self-imposed duties. In terms of his own views, in fact, it makes more sense not to draw a strict line at all, but to speak only of degrees of legalism and of interacting standards and modes of conduct. As cultural phenomena inseparable from legalistic religion and ethics, legalistic political institutions and the lawyers' law cannot be treated as external events. Law and legality become part of the daily experience of the individual and part of his moral and social life. There is every reason to believe that the activities of lawyers, law courts, and other public agencies tend to reinforce the superego, especially when punishment is being administered, and that the values sanctioned by the law are internalized so as to direct and mold our moral personalities.[27] There are, in short, interactions; there are no simple divisions of cause and effect, of inner and external action, or of enforced and unenforced norms. From the sense of obligation felt in games, to courts of law, from a conscience that respects rights to a religious vision of a just and judging God, one observes a psychic whole of which official law is only a part. Once we think of morals, mores, and law as rules, law—in the sense of the official, politically sanctioned norms of matured legal systems—is merely a highly formalized kind of legalistic morality and behavior.[28] Private values and public standards are not so readily separated, unless one's mind has already been made up in favor of one true morality and one true system of legal norms and institutions, and "knows" which stands above the other.

It is, above all, when we examine systems of legalistic morals, that is, our own major tradition of moral reasoning, that the profound similarity of legal and moral thinking emerges. The extent to which moral theorists lean upon legal analogies is itself very revealing. The widely held theory of two types of rules, for instance, is closely patterned upon the distinction between legislation and adjudication. The value of a system of rules as a whole, or of a practice, is said to lie in its utility—in the fact that its authority rests on its general acceptance by society in order to give stability and predictability to conduct. This corresponds to legislation.[29] On the other hand, the worth of individual actions, like that of judicial decisions, does not have to be proved anew on each occasion. Their value rests on being consistent with established norms. To the individual, moreover, these are no less an objective, external "given" than are legal rules. This similarity of moral and legal reasoning is not in the least altered if one substitutes validation by inherent "fitness" for a utilitarian theory. The search for consistency, for regularity, in morals takes the same form as in legal thinking.

On the level of moral and legal experiences, as distinct from theories of evaluation, things are not so simple as in theories of ethics. However, that is true of law courts too. The experience of conflicting obligations is not only our most common moral, but also our great judicial, problem. It is less a question of what is *the* consistent rule to be followed in this case than of which of several equally valid courses of action one is to take, or which of several equally applicable decisions one is to make. The point here, however, is that both in theory and in daily experience the structure of legal and moral reasoning is identical as long as rules reign. When one turns to a phenomenological approach to morals, the resemblance to law becomes very evident. This, of course, may be due to the chief weakness of phenomenological accounts of moral or social experience: their subjectivism and narrow cultural scope. It is just because of such parochialism that the most extensive American attempt at a phenomenology of morals presents a picture of moral life that is profoundly legalistic.[30] For the individual, moral experience here is not a matter of doing what comes naturally, of spontaneous response to some inner urge, but it is an external demand, and, as such, objective. Whatever we may hold to be good, goodness is independent of our inclinations. The typical moral act, moreover, involves appraising a situation and deciding what rules apply to it. It is even suggested here, as it has also been by many American lawyers, that the real difficulty in deciding lies not in choosing the right norm, but in finding out just what the facts of a given situation are. To this one might well object, in both cases, that our estimate of a situation is never really a mere matter of settling facts, but from the very first includes evaluations, interpretations, personal preferences, and judgments. A situation calling for a decision is already the mental construction of the observer, rather than something that presents itself to him "there" and ready-made.[31] However, what matters here is that the issues are the same, whether moral or legal judgments are to be made. In each case the act of deciding implies estimating the character of a situation and following the rules applicable to it. This, at any rate, is the paradigm in both cases, even when duties to ourselves are involved. The value

placed on impartiality is, lastly, supreme.[32] The impartial
observer is the hero of moral theory, as the impartial judge is
the very embodiment of justice.

In view of these considerations it seems impossible to treat
law and morals as separate psychological blocks. As parts of
a single cultural pattern they resemble each other far too
much. This conclusion becomes particularly evident when one
places a work such as Professor Mandelbaum's on the phenomenology of morals beside Cardozo's phenomenological descrip-
tions of the process of making judicial decisions. There is less
standardization and less institutionalization in the case of
morals. There may be less certainty and more flexibility;
the act of choosing may well be more difficult and painful, but
it is not fundamentally different from the experience of rendering judgment according to law. This is all the more true
where the value of rules is seen to rest in their social usefulness.
It has been said that even Jehovah's gift to Israel did not tie
the people to the Covenant only because God was the giver,
but because the gift was something, indeed everything, they
desired for themselves as a society.[33] The more legalistic the
orientation of a people the more deeply will it think in identical ways about the good, the socially right, and the legal.
Justice will be the supreme value at all times.

With all this in mind it would be best to stop classifying
law and morals as blocks and to treat them instead as a continuum. The real difference is between more and less legalistic
ethics and political institutions, not between law and morals as
such. This approach would help us understand the conditions
under which law operates as a form of social control, or fails
to do so. Since it is the positivist's claim that this is the real
object of his labors, there is no inherent intellectual reason
why he should not desert formalism and turn his eyes toward
the world about him. That is an unlikely prospect, however,
because the ideological functions of formalism would not be

fulfilled by such procedures. It would mean abandoning the idea of a specifically juristic point of view, and the possibility of a distinct legal science. It would also leave the question of the scope of law, the question of what should and what should not be enforced, in an exposed position as an open question of political preference. Even if the hostility to natural law should abate among positivists, in all likelihood they would not give up formalism.

As for the natural lawyers, it is obvious that on grounds both metaphysical and ideological the rigid classification of law and morality will be maintained, no less than the belief that they intersect. To judge law in terms of morals, for natural lawyers, makes it imperative that the two be presented in this way. The treatment of morality and law as a cultural continuum would not serve that purpose in any respect. It belongs to a different realm of discourse altogether. It is, however, unacceptable to the natural lawyer on grounds other than its irrelevance to his main concern, for it obviously accepts the diversity of moral and political traditions and beliefs as something given. It would indeed be disingenuous to pretend that it does not spring from a positive preference for such a state of affairs. Now the whole aim of natural law as a political ideology is to overcome diversity. It is fundamentally an ideology of agreement. As such it is evidently incompatible with a theory that puts considerable difficulties in the way of its chosen task. The belief in tolerance as one of the greatest social virtues, and as a necessity in a pluralistic society that wishes to remain free, is not altogether compatible with legalism; for the need of agreement that natural lawyers stress is an expression of the legalistic ethos, since the type of agreement demanded is adherence to certain universally valid *rules* that are "there" for all the rational to see. That rules are "there" is in any case what is meant by objective ethics, of which natural law is the most enduring and prevalent form.

As such it is both the most intense expression and the main support of legalism at every level of social life. If a regime of rules impartially administered, if law as such, is an institution designed to create social security and a certainty of expectation, then the perennial function of natural law is to provide a similar security and certainty in our intellectual and personal lives. It need not, and often does not, wish to resort to repressive measures to achieve its ends. Natural law has plenty of very liberal adherents. It does, however, put the chronic dissenter beyond the pale of moral acceptance, and it looks upon diversity, and the conflicts and disquiet that it may create, with a very jaundiced eye. To those who regard the quest for moral certainty as in itself undesirable and who fear the kinds of repressive behavior to which it might give rise in a pluralistic society, natural law will, inevitably, be an unacceptable ideology.

### NATURAL LAW AND LEGAL IDEOLOGY

In all fairness it should be noted that the multiplicity of values, both in political and in moral life, has come to be a source of anxiety among many liberals no less than among traditionalists. It is, of course, true that natural law and absolutism in morals have long been identified with that conservatism which shrinks from social experimentation and tends to regard controversy as the equivalent of disorder, and all as supreme dangers. However, liberalism today has itself ceased to be radical, has lost most of the momentum of a militant faith, and indeed has begun to see its days of glory in the past rather than in the future. Moreover, its alliance with moral relativism was only partly a true meeting of minds. To the extent that tolerance is the very marrow of the bones of liberalism there was a genuine meeting point. But when "speech is not an absolute" any longer, as was so bluntly demonstrated by Chief Justice Vinson in the *Dennis* decision—when the absence of rigid political standards leads to the restriction of individual freedom as a primary value—then many a liberal finds himself alienated from his erstwhile associates.[34] Only negatively, only in opposition to that moral self-assertion that expresses itself in repression, had the alliance really flourished. As a consequence of this, no less than of liberalism's general defensiveness today, liberals have again begun to look upon natural law theories with considerable interest and affection. Indeed, several attempts have been made in the past to exploit "the natural" as a basis for liberal values. Natural rights are the obvious example of this. And what liberal does not sooner or later yearn for them? These, however, as has often been noted, do not yield a theory *of* law so much as a theory *against* law as part of an undifferentiated mass of governmental evils. Even without attempting an exhaustive inventory, one can see many liberals in search of a natural basis. Theories of resistance to totalitarianism, of individual self-fulfillment, of political and legal progress, and of international brotherhood have all in some way come to look for acceptable versions of natural law, often now called by some other name. These efforts, however, remain open to all the criticisms that have been raised against natural law theory in general—above all to the objection that it is simply an ideology of agreement, and as such not altogether compatible with that form of liberalism which regards diversity and tolerance for diversity as the principal conditions of freedom.

There have also, of course, been other, less obviously ideological, reasons for reconsidering natural law. If at present it is mainly a response, both liberal and non-liberal, to totalitarianism from abroad and at home, there are also purely theoretical reasons for it. The entire isolation of jurisprudence from social theory has become increasingly uncongenial to many lawyers. The most common suggestion made for the sociological or philosophical salvation of legal theory is either a return to natural law thinking, even if under some new name, or the discovery of a philosophy that would accomplish the intellectual tasks which natural law once fulfilled.[85] The trouble with these hopes is that they are rendered vain by the number and variety of natural law theories, no less than by the many functions such theories have had. In fact, natural law is a name for an enormous range of political ideas, many of them not at all directly relevant to law or legal thinking. If one element unites all "natural values," it is that by diverse means they seek unity. All ultimately are ideologies in favor of agreement.

Now legalism and the acceptance of common rules do depend upon a degree of agreement, which explains the perennial attractions of natural law theories, but this in itself is scarcely enough to justify returning to natural law thinking or treating it as a model for legal philosophy. If natural law theory often has had the merit of being frankly ideological, of openly taking a stand on such broad political issues as the limits of political obligation, the sources of authority, the rights of man, and the "true" moral basis of political and legal action, it has also been logically feeble, ambiguous, and often so narrowly committed to a specific economic and social program as to be of no lasting interest or value. At the other extreme there have been natural law theories which are mere hostile reactions to relativism or positivism. They insist that a natural system of values does exist and that we must believe in "natural right," but they never state just what these values specifically are. All we are told is that unless we abandon skepticism and believe in "political truth"—in a single, universally valid, natural system of social norms—we are doomed. This is natural law without content, in contrast to natural law which is merely another political platform.[36] What is needed, we are told, is a return to the "tradition of civility," to a common universe of intelligible discourse, to an agreement that "we hold these truths" and that we have some conception of the "public good" or the "national purpose." That all these certainties are clear and present is usually followed by a lament that, for all their self-evidence, they are totally disregarded and rejected in the present age. This tends to give much natural law writing a mildly schizophrenic tone.[87] Natural law is "there," and yet it is not "there." However, the issue here is that whatever may be the emotional pleasures of insisting upon the identity of "is" and "ought," of the faith in values that are immanent in nature and self-evident to all who truly try to recognize them, this is not an attitude which in itself has anything to contribute to legal theory, beyond pressing it into the service of a crusade against all doubters as such, or of a specific political and religious party.

The accusation that natural law theories are political ideologies is not, however, as fatal to them as is often supposed.[38] If it is meant to strike at their pretensions to universal validity and self-evidence by showing up partiality, it is a valid charge. But if it is meant to imply that natural law theorists are committed to specific sets of political values and that, in their legal thinking, law is identified with these, no abuse at all is involved. Natural law theories make no false claims to neutrality, and to say that they are ideologies is merely to say that one does not like them. It is, indeed, the greatest merit of natural law theory that it assumes that law must be examined in terms of a comprehensive political theory. It is the nature of such political theory which is really at stake. That is why liberals especially, sensing the hostility to diversity and so to tolerance and freedom which is at the bottom of much natural law theory, have tended to use the term "ideology" as one of scorn. In fact, the positivist liberal, the pure theorist, is no less committed to an ideology, and his claim to offer a universally applicable scheme is no better than that of his opponents. The question is, rather, what *sort* of ideologies have been covered by the term "natural law"—not the mere existence of ideology, which is no failing in itself. The second issue is what relation, if any, these ideologies have to legal phenomena and to other competing political faiths. Lastly, one must ask oneself why natural law appears to be an ideology which, in spite of devastating criticisms, is never completely obsolete, and why, without ever coming really alive, it nevertheless is in a permanent state of revival.

One of the delights of those who do not happen to be partial to natural law theory is to sit back and observe the diversity and incompatibility among the various schools of natural law, each one insisting upon its own preferences as the only truly universally valid ones. There have by now been a sufficient number of listings of the contents of typical natural law theories to make a new one superfluous.[39] A far more fruitful approach is to inquire into the functions that natural law has fulfilled in the history of political ideas. Here three main categories emerge. Natural law has provided a rationale for transmunicipal law, for a rational ethic to justify government and the legal order in a Christian world, and lastly, for the rights of man.[40] Of these three only the last two can be said to be "higher law" theories—standards according to which actual political practices may and should be measured and judged. As such they can provide justification for either obedience or disobedience. However, not all natural law theories are concerned with a higher law prescribing the extent of political obligation, nor are all higher law doctrines rooted in the idea of values immanent in nature. Moreover, not all natural ethics are legalistic. On the contrary, there are some which positively reject law on moral grounds.

There is also considerable ambiguity in the meaning of the word "natural" as used in moral and social philosophy. The natural may be the normal, either in the sense of the usual or of the potentially best in human behavior and development. The natural may be identified with the historical future or with the universal characteristics of man or with his rational end and function in God's created order. This last meaning of natural, the ontological-teleological conception, is not only the most enduring and popular basis of natural law theory; it is also the one most offensive to all those who reject essentialism in philosophy. On the part of those who support it, it has encouraged the habit of abusing opponents. To the true natural law enthusiast the skeptic is unreasonable and talks nonsense.[41] The chances of his being wicked into the bargain are very high. In fact, there appear to be only a few supporters of the traditional doctrine who seem to have noticed that many nonbelievers live decent lives and are neither imbeciles nor habitual moral delinquents. Indeed, it might be well to observe at this point that skeptics tend to be immune to the greatest of all modern social vices—political fanaticism. On the other hand, it is an equally gross psychological fallacy to impute a preference for political absolutism to those who believe in natural law.[42] Another strange practice that emerges from this is that, although an ontological conception of natural law can clearly be neither proved nor disproved by reference to historical fact, to what people have actually said and done, its supporters have never abstained from pointing to the beneficial historical consequences that its prevalence will have, and to the disasters that its rejection must entail. We are told that an acceptance of natural law will make us "both prosperous and free," because it alone can offer us a middle station between extreme individualism and authoritarianism.[43] And we are perpetually warned that a failure to believe in natural law is directly responsible for totalitarianism, though how such an assertion is ever to be made susceptible to historical proof is obscure, particularly when the chief villains include such notable liberals as Justice Holmes, John Dewey, and Max

Weber.[44] Indeed, one of the greatest self-inflicted weaknesses of natural lawyers is their inability or unwillingness to understand their opponents. Thus an American teacher of moral theology assures us that modern positivism teaches that "only civil law makes things right or wrong" and that this is a totalitarian notion.[45] That certainly is not what Austin said, nor is it the position of his contemporary followers. In fact, it is not the doctrine of such revolutionary totalitarians as the Nazis or Communists. To say with Father Murray that secularists hold that civil law is not subject to judgment in terms of ethical canons is simply to refuse to listen to what one's opponents in fact do say.[46] The consequence of this is only to enhance the natural lawyer's moral anxieties, and lead him to call for a return to natural law as a pressing necessity. It does not incline him to be more exact about either the disease or the nature of the cure.

One question raised by all these considerations is, "Just what does natural law contribute to politics in general and to law in particular?" If, as some of its most distinguished exponents have declared, its contents are those of the Decalogue, then it has no specific political meaning beyond exhorting even rulers to cultivate the private virtues. But if the natural law has something to say on every aspect of life from birth control, sterilization, euthanasia, and parental authority to the right party to vote for in an election, it is clearly a comprehensive political ideology. It is a total design for living, both private and public. In fairness it should be noted that the scope of natural law is a moot question among its adherents. It is also uncertain to whom natural law is addressed. Originally it was designed to direct rulers, and this is still its aim for those who believe that private citizens must obey established governments since rebellion is always worse than misgovernment. However, in recent years, partly as a response to democratic influences and partly in the face of the rise of totalitarian governments, natural law has been presented as a guide for all citizens. Nothing else, it is said, can help the individual resist tyranny or tell him exactly when he ought to do so.

What are the advantages of natural law as a doctrine of resistance? Is it really a matter of supreme importance whether men decide to disobey because they can say, "This is non-law, for it is incompatible with the higher law of nature," or because they prefer to say, "This is a law, but I regard it as thoroughly bad and mischievous in its likely results"? As a point of historical and psychological fact it does not seem to matter much. If, as is clearly implied, resistance here means a decision to reject an entire political regime, not just this or that demand of an otherwise acceptable government, it does not really alter the case. Why it is felt that a higher law is needed to justify resistance is not, however, difficult to understand. It is linked to the subject-ruler relationship of our monarchical past, in which authority was sanctified and resistance required more than a merely pragmatic justification. To this view Christianity and its version of natural law contributed much. In its perennial concern for civic peace and unity as the supreme social good it still does. It also assumes that there is an authority, either ecclesiastic or at least among "the wise," which has the office to interpret these higher obligations, to know when they conflict with political rules, and to say what is to be done at any given time. These circumstances alone give the idea of natural rules *against* evil rulers the semblance of law. If, however, we refuse to invest governments with some inherently sacred claim to our allegiance, with authority above and beyond their pragmatic value (and, alas, their overwhelming strength), then the need for a higher law justifying disobedience, partial or complete, is not necessary. That is why a positivist attitude, linked to a utilitarian view of politics, has never inspired Englishmen or Scandinavians to an excess of political submissiveness or to an uncritical acceptance of "the powers

that be." On the other hand, where an inclination to treat law
as analogous to military orders prevailed, positivism could be
used to rationalize subservience to tyranny. In the case of Germany, however, one ought never to forget other ideological
considerations. Its official classes, especially its judiciary, were
not induced by positivism to accept and apply the law of the
Weimar Republic. In fact, they sabotaged it with no legalistic
compunctions. Positivism was only invoked to rationalize their
far greater readiness to comply with Hitler's New Order.

These considerations in themselves raise some doubt about
the necessity for a natural law or any law to resist tyranny.
What is needed is a critical and independent attitude among
citizens in general. The truth of natural law as a theory of
morals, of course, is not affected by these pragmatic considerations. However, the case for natural law as a theory of resistance is today urged not in metaphysical but in psychological
and historical terms. Without natural law, its supporters claim,
the individual is helpless before the law, with no stable principles to help him make up his mind. Natural law supports
him by offering him guidance instead of leaving him alone
with nothing to rely on but his own moral resources. It may,
of course, be questioned whether it is the function of legal
theory to make such decisions for us. However, as the case
is not put in normative terms it need not be answered thus.
The sole question is one of historical and psychological facts.
Has natural law in fact helped people to resist tyranny? Was
natural law, in fact, what caused them to do so? The answer
is, on the whole, negative.

In the wake of the celebrated Remer trial a number of
eminent German theologians (both Protestant and Catholic),
historians, and jurists joined to consider the entire theory of
the right of resistance. All of them admired the conspirators
of the July 20th movement. Yet in the end even the natural
lawyers among them agreed that ultimately no general for-

mulas applicable to all circumstances were available. Some acknowledged from the first that this was a decision for the individual conscience; others saw more definite justifications. However, none offered anything so specific as to be a real guide to the individual, even though all recognized the need for such guidance.[47] In the end all would have had to agree that "the dilemma between conscience and social order no theory can solve. If it pretends to do so, it will merely repeat abstract, empty formulae, which, devoid of concreteness, merely veil the impossibility of squaring the circle."[48] In short, natural law does not really offer the potential individual resister anything beyond what he already has—the prospect of making an awful choice.

When one turns to the historical claim that natural law has, in fact, inspired resistance as nothing else could have, the picture is again far from clear. Atheists, relativists, communists, socialists, and liberals, no less than committed Christians, were to be found among the resisters to Nazism. They were inspired by as many ideologies and as many moral beliefs as the diverse modern world has to offer. In many cases what counted most was concrete political experience in a liberal and democratic society, not ideology (whether natural law or something else). Here one thinks especially of the Danes and the Dutch. Looking at the problem from the viewpoint of the individual who asks, "What should I do?" it is clear that there is no moral authority simply "there" to decide his case for him. What he is faced with is the difficult choice among a variety of equally valid obligations—to his family, to his friends, to his associates, to his profession, to his countrymen, and to his political convictions (to name but a few). Neither our conscience, our superego, our capacity (if any) to predict the results of our action, nor any moral law can deliver us from the actuality of inner moral conflict, created by a multitude of valid claims. Not least among these must be the purely practical consideration that in certain technologically highly developed societies resistance to government may have become utterly futile. For the present, however, the main issue is that what is involved is not a confrontation of law and morality at all, but a choice between competing moral values and a decision to resist or obey an entire political system, whatever part legal activity may play in it. In this situation natural law has, in fact, been singularly unhelpful. Natural lawyers differ among themselves as do other men in any concrete situation. Their unanimity, the alleged source of their strength, is limited to the incantation of generalities. To promote "the common good," to do what "the public order" requires, or to resist when it is clear that these are being destroyed reflects a view of society as an integrated whole. At best these phrases are reminders of the moral unity of smaller and more simple societies; at worst they reduce to mere platitudes the infinite difficulties of those who must face the prospects of contemporary tyranny.

Moreover, on the subject of our more commonplace moral difficulties this theory of obligation has nothing to say. Once the "basic norm" is valid, once the obligation to obey a political order and the legal system within it is accepted as a natural one, there is no more to be said. As long as subordinate rules are formally consistent with superior norms, as long as they issue from "legitimate" authority, there is nothing more to say. This is the root of that very perversion of legalism which has always been able to find some legal justification, and thus a claim to obedience, for any regime. This mentality, which has often been falsely ascribed to positivism, actually is common to all formalisms, including that of natural law. The effect of natural law theory that sees in the act of legislation the one point of intersection between law and morality may in fact stunt the critical faculties of those who would prefer, like most of us, to avoid trouble at any cost. This is not surprising, for it is a theory that has its origin in an age when there was a premium on obedience to some authority or other, rather than on moral and political self-reliance. The actualities of moral and political life are, however, a matter of limited choices—of specific decisions made by legislators, administrators, judges, and citizens within a political system—and here again it is not a matter of "to be or not to be" moral, but of which of several claims one shall honor.

Do the immigration laws of the United States have a greater claim on one's allegiance than the members of one's family who are not eligible for a visa? The Chinese, Italians, and Jews have not found it easy to answer this question with a simple yes or no. Moreover, the deeper their affection for "God's country" the greater becomes their sense of duty to bring their relatives to it. Every member of a legislative assembly, and every public official, must face conflicting but valid demands made upon him by diverse groups and by the voices of conscience and of public necessity. An English judge is said to have remarked that some of the most cruel things he had ever seen were mere enforcements of rights granted by valid contracts.[49] That does not diminish a judge's obligations to enforce the common law, to maintain the security of expectations, and to regard "fidelity to law" as a claim prior to that of occasional and, perhaps, erratic mercy. To all this, natural law as a theory of political obligation has nothing to say. In fact, it is a theory that hides the facts of moral life in the interests of false comfort; for, once we have a legitimate government we have no moral worries, and there is always a rule to tell us not only when a government is or is not legitimate, but also exactly what we are to do about it. Far from explaining the relations between law and morals, this is merely an instance of legalistic morality in its most rigid form. In sum, then, natural law is no great help to potential resisters—a failing it shares with all other general prescriptions which try to deliver men from moral conflict.

Historically there is only one version of natural law which, until the nineteenth century, did serve as a powerful inspiration to rebellion. That was the theory of natural rights, which, as has often been noted, was a radical departure from the traditional doctrine of natural law. The claim of "the poorest he" to participate freely in government was, in the English Civil War and in the Revolutions of 1776 and 1789, the very heart of revolutionary ideology. It was also the basis for constitutional governments, which were designed to break the vicious circle of oppression and revolt by providing means for peaceful social change and the free expression of political opinions and interests. Increasingly, however, utilitarianism replaced natural rights as the philosophical underpinning of those constitutional governments which were successful going concerns, and this with no loss of liberty at all. Later revolutionary movements, when they did arise, depended on collectivist ideologies even more remote from natural rights theory than utilitarianism. The contemporary claim for natural law as *the* doctrine of resistance, also, is not based on natural rights thinking. This is scarcely surprising, since resistance is urged, not in the interests of liberalism or constitutional democracy, but solely as a protest against the inherent immorality of totalitarian regimes. Moreover, the call to resist is not addressed to the victims of such governments. Now natural rights was the doctrine of those who felt that their social claims were being ignored, and who justified rebellion because they had been deprived of what, under the higher law, was their own. That might well be the feeling of the inmates of concentration camps, but no one is suggesting that they hasten their death by resisting. Natural law, like all other calls to stand up to totalitarian government, is addressed to those who by acquiescing to totalitarian policies can lead quite tolerable lives. Natural lawyers argue that if such people really believed in natural law they would not behave in this immoral fashion but would actively oppose governments whose policies conflict grossly with the higher law. It is an appeal to the leaders within communities—socially well-placed men like those of the July 20th movement—not to the helpless victims who have been herded to their doom. Natural law is meant to put some steel into the moral veins of those who protect themselves by supporting or quietly accepting totalitarian ideology and government, not to those whose rights have been destroyed along with their very lives. Natural rights are, thus, not the significant issue when resistance to totalitarian regimes and immunity to totalitarian ideologies are at stake. Only the notion that the acceptance of a universally valid higher law is the necessary and the most effective counter-ideology to totalitarianism is in question now. Natural rights have simply ceased to play a significant part in political discourse, except as a very minor part of that current form of natural law theory that regards the belief in a higher law as such as a political necessity.

The shortcomings of natural law as the higher law that fortifies resisters do not touch on the logical and ideological problems inherent in the ontological conception of the natural. As Professor d'Entrèves has noted, this must be treated as a "take it or leave it" proposition, about which it is too late and too pointless to argue. Some issues are not negotiable for either side. In the words of Jacques Maritain, one must simply "take it for granted" that there is a human nature that is the same in all men and that this nature is "an ontological structure which is a locus of intelligible necessities" that gives man ends "which necessarily correspond to his essential constitution." If one cannot take this for granted, one is simply doomed to talk nonsense.[50] Even without the implied obloquy, it is clear that the most eminent of contemporary natural law theorists regard the ontological view of human nature as something that must simply be either accepted or rejected, not as something that one can rationally debate. In this, surely, they are perfectly right.

There are, in any case, many non-ontological moral theories which propose to evaluate legal and political life by confusing "is" and "ought." That we ought to pursue "the greatest good of the greatest number" because we are beings who always choose pleasure over pain is one of them. What is more important is that the confusion of "is" and "ought" which the word "natural" invites has been exploited by totally nonlegalistic, indeed antilegalistic, ethical theories, which have, nevertheless, been received with delirious enthusiasm by traditional natural law theorists, as well as by others. The ideological hunger of the present is at no point more evident than when the most conservative persons embrace the psychological theories of Erich Fromm—not because they accept his radicalism in politics but because he gives them "scientific" blessings, a kiss from the enemy camp of materialism, for the identity of the good and the natural. Here the mental luxury of certainty, of feeling that what ought to be must be, overrides every substantive consideration, and no one seems to have noticed that it is done in a spirit that is as hostile to liberal politics as it is to legalistic ethics.

The end of ethics has now become "positive mental health"; the aim of politics, the "sane society." Now health, whether mental or physical, has a far less controversial sound than goodness. It is not only universally desired, but it seems objective in an empirical sense. Or so it would appear. In fact, the "sane society" is built on "normative humanism" which rejects all "sociological relativism," and "science" will find "universal criteria for mental health" as well as support for "natural values." When we look at these natural values they turn out to be highly selective, even though we are assured that they correspond to the tenets, not only of the "Judaeo-Christian

Ethics," but indeed to those of all the wise men from East and West of all times. Natural and universal as mental health turns out to be, it is decidedly antilegalistic. "Fairness" as a value is rejected as part of the "sick market personality" which demands only impersonality. Mental health requires relationships based on love. This, we are assured in advance, will be the finding of science. The certain result of a "correct description" of human nature will show it to be something that *is* "common to the entire race," as well as what it *ought* to become, if it ever becomes truly human. (What it is now is not clear.) This will be possible only after a total social and political revolution, and will be realized in the "face-to-face" group organized according to the principles of "humanism and socialism," free from any coercion, in which the members live in a "natural harmony." [51] Now this is nothing very new. It is the cooperative commune of traditional utopian literature. The appeal to science to discover true human nature beneath the conventional, historical, and actual rests on the same act of faith that all natural law theory rests on. What separates it from that great tradition is its radical rejection of legalistic ethics in favor of a morality of spontaneous love. Curiously enough, lawyers and sociologists in America have found this a truly acceptable version of the law of nature, even though, far from offering a synthesis of law, morals, and ideology, it is a simple rejection of law. It is partly the prestige of psychology—the magnetism of the word science, however much abused—and partly the projection of the unity of "is" and "ought" into the future that gives this conception of the law of nature its undeserved popularity. [52]

The notion of a natural law based on a human nature conceived not ontologically but historically and psychologically as something to be realized in the future is surprisingly popular in America today. It reveals a faith in the inevitability of political progress that has become relatively rare as an explicit

doctrine. It is a higher law doctrine, moreover, in a fairly restricted sense only. It serves as a measure and guide for positive
law, but it does not invalidate the arrangements of the present
absolutely; it only aims at changes in the future. Thus Professor Northrop has suggested that law must take its content
from "the living law," that is, from "the inner order of the
behavior of people in society." In short, law ought to follow
custom, assuming always that custom provides simple, un-
ambiguous legalistic directives. Even if this were possible it
would seem very conservative. However, it is not possible,
since custom or the living law itself is measured by the "is"
of future living law. The "ought" of the present can be seen
in the future presumably only because the future is superior
to the present, and the present to the past.[53] Thus, too, Professor Paul Weiss insists that is and ought are irreconcilable
only to those for whom the present and the future are rigidly
divided off from each other. The future, he holds, calls us to
a "law of civilization" that is even more universally valid, less
parochial, and "higher" than natural law.[54]

On a more modest scale Professor Fuller speaks of positive
law as moral because its history is that of a "collaborative
articulation of shared purposes." [55] It seems that he can see
the goodness of the legal order without reference to any social
history apart from the progressive evolution of the law itself
toward perfection—to what it ought to be. To make sense at
all, this formulation of the identity of "is" and "ought" must
suppose that legal progress is part of a general social progress
and that the value of the purposes it articulates is due to their
contribution to society as a whole. It is because law, presumably, is at any time moving in step with history that the future
"ought" is already immanent in the present. But Professor
Fuller sees the progress of the law as an independent growth.
The isolation of law from history, the notion of an integral
legal history apart from that of society in general, is in itself

one of the great oddities of legal theory. It has, as will presently emerge, served many functions. In this case it is meant to prop up natural law. However, most natural lawyers tend to reject it. As a rational, objective ethic, natural law cannot allow itself to be reduced to any form of historicism.

Psychology and history are not, however, the only "sciences" to have been exploited in order to provide an unshakable foundation in nature for legal values. Anthropology, more than any other social science, has been used to create a picture of mankind united in one nature, and, potentially at least, sharing one world and one set of political and legal values. Now one-worldism is no doubt an estimable sentiment, and it is a necessity we cannot escape in any case. The day when the European world was the only one that really counted is long past, and it is not surprising that some ideological adjustments are being made in response to the unavoidable and all too obvious facts of contemporary life. How sensible these alterations have been is, however, an open question. That natural law thinking should be drawn into this area of intercultural political thinking was surely inevitable. It is, after all, as a basis for international cooperation that natural law theory has fulfilled its longest and most honorable function. If Professor Weiss's "law of civilization" and the anthropological search for a common human nature display an hostility to parochialism, to ethnic pride, and to cultural autonomy which is clearly the product of the post-colonial era, and if Professor Northrop's supra-ideological system of international cooperation is a response to the Cold War, all are adaptations of an ancient program.

Its first appearance, in fact, came in Roman natural law thinking. Except for the Stoics, this was not of the higher law variety. It offered rather a rationale for a technique of governing an empire composed of the most diverse peoples. To lessen their differences and bring them back to their common

humanity was the main task of the law of nature. Unlike similar attempts made in later ages to appeal to a common reason
and higher morality above ideological and cultural conflicts,
the Roman lawyers appealed to the lowest common human
denominator, the most simple inclinations of mankind. It was
thus seen that human nature provided a basis for the application of at least some rules to the most vital social relations. For
it was from the very nature of things that the possibility of
fair judgment between commensurable human entities seemed
to emerge.[56] To believe that this was not only feasible, but
even morally necessary, was of course very convenient for
those seeking an imperial ideology. Surely it was also one of
the most monumentally successful theories in practice. The
efforts of contemporary anthropology, though far more sophisticated, will probably not do quite so well. The stated purpose of much of the study of the social institutions of primitive
peoples is to discover what is universally human. However,
the end impinges heavily upon the ethnological accounts, and
we are constantly asked to believe that primitive law, especially, is essentially like that of "matured legal systems." The
ubiquity of legal life is then taken openly or implicitly to
demonstrate the possibility, and indeed the likelihood, of a
universal system of law.[57]

This anthropology of uniformity is partly a reaction against
the ethnology of the last century which, eager to see both
historical progress and European superiority in everything,
overstressed the distance between the civilized and the primitive. Anthropologists no longer look down upon primitive
men. The liberal rejects pride as a remnant of colonialism; the
conservative may see in primitive communities those very
habits and beliefs which he misses in the urban world of in-
dustrialized societies. In their separate ways both have lost
that perfect confidence in the achievements of European civilization. After two world wars and all that they entailed, it is

hardly surprising. Along with this change in ideology, the "functional" approach to the study of both developed and undeveloped society has also, perhaps inadvertently, contributed to an attenuation of the sense of difference. Not only does the primitive society become a simple paradigm of all societies, the "case" in which universal social patterns are most easily discerned, but the idea that every social institution, custom, and regularity is to be seen in terms of its "function" in maintaining the system tends to reduce differences in content by dwelling on similarity of form. Not only is every society treated as a whole, but each of its parts is seen in terms of the role it plays in integrating all the parts of this whole; and, seen in this way, one rule or one custom or one order is formally much like another. The neutrality of this method is, moreover, severely strained as function insensibly becomes purpose, and approved purpose at that. The train of argument tends to run thus: All men have rules to follow; these rules have the function of maintaining society; men in all societies aim at an integrated social life; this shows that a common human nature and common human purposes and aspirations exist and are manifest; therefore, a universally valid order of moral and political norms is not only possible, it is something men really want. The concentration on primitive law is thus far from accidental. It is the inevitable focus of that ideology which seeks one world under one law.

There have, however, always been some very real problems in studying primitive law. On one hand primitive societies appear to be highly legalistic in the sense that religion and custom are strongly ritualistic—a matter of strict rules to be punctiliously observed. But the prevalence of tight definitions and reified conceptualization in modern jurisprudence has made it difficult to apply the concepts of Western law to the institutions of primitive society. There is, of course, no obvious need to do so. A scale of degrees of legalism and a flexible typology of legal and political ways would have served the purposes of clarity very well. However, since the wish for common elements, definable in universal terms, was never far below the surface, such a procedure was not followed. If it had been really understood how incoherent is the reality described by such terms of Western legal discourse as "civil law," "public law," "crime," "tort," and "contract," and how large a part historical accident has played in deciding what actions and rules belong in each category, there would have been less agony expended in squeezing primitive legal ways into these fortuitous classifications.[58] However, those who were determined to reject the nineteenth-century notion of primitive man ruled by the dead hand of custom felt that nothing less than the full complement of Western legal institutions and concepts must be ascribed to him. In these circumstances the only hope was to employ the most abstract formalism that legal theory could devise, to find a set of categories so totally devoid of any specific content as to be applicable to all social institutions from the most primitive to the most overdeveloped. Here the schemas of Hohfeld and Kelsen have proved very valuable indeed.[59]

Law as a conscious shaping and sanctioning of mores could be said to exist wherever politically organized society could enforce rules, and wherever direct, organized, definite social action could be observed. The presence of courtlike institutions as the test of whether law existed or not was rejected as too confining. The use of "socially approved force," without any examination of what "approval" meant in the general confusion of function and purpose, was taken as sufficient proof of legal life. It is not, of course, self-evident that institutions for the expression of overt consent are necessary for legal life anywhere. However, if it is assumed that this is the case, social approval cannot be inferred from the simple fact that rules are followed and enforced and are fulfilling their integrative function. In any case, the habit of analytical jurisprudence of identifying any government with law, and both with enforcement, has been transferred to the study of primitive society in order to show that here, also, law exists, and that it exists just in the same way as in "matured legal systems." Nowhere has verbalism triumphed more completely over the true task of description—that of qualifying and differentiating.

To agree that law exists universally, as do a sense of right—of legal obligation—and a notion of crime, would seem quite enough in the way of seeing uniformity among men. However, more recently there has been at least one effort to go beyond these ambitious aims.[60] Any regular institution for the arbitration of disputes in any society is now treated as a court. Even in the absence of the means of keeping records or determining rules, the application of "precedents" and of "legal rules" to similar cases by a chief and his counselors is regarded as possible, and, indeed, very similar to the procedures of the judiciary in the West. Indeed, it is even taken to prove the existence of a jurisprudence. Now all arbitration does involve reference to some common standards shared by those involved. The question is whether the mending of family disputes by tribal chiefs in terms of the morally most desirable solution in an African face-to-face society, with no signs of moral or intellectual diversity, is in any way like the judicial process of overdeveloped areas. Is the fact that different words for "law" and "morals" exist in tribal language enough to prove that the difference between the two is understood to have the same meaning in this familial group as in the legal ideology of an urban society? Is the mere fact of arbitral activity enough to prove that legal and political institutions quite like those of the West exist? Does America really resemble a political order in which the attitudes of superior and inferior within the primary family group are identical with those that prevail among the chief, the notables, and the rest of the tribe? What

is a court without a legal profession and forensic skill? What
is a criminal law that is not separate from religion, and a civil
law which appears to deal almost exclusively with family
quarrels and which is flexible and informal, as it must be in
view of its function? Are we really to draw lessons about the
universality of legal values from this, and even to copy the
individualization and uncertainty of law that this absence of
rigidity among the primitives demonstrates?

There is no place where the notion of degrees of commitment to legalistic values and procedures would have been more
appropriate than in the study of primitive institutions. The
insistence on identity of institutions and attitudes, as a matter
of fact, was dictated not by the evidence but by ideological demands—by the wish to see a single human nature operating not
as an ideal but as a universal fact, and manifesting itself in
broadly uniform social ways. And it is taken for granted that
without a fundamental likeness between men there can be no
peace among them. If this is a generous approach to international understanding and law, it is doubtful how well we
are served, either by so obvious a torturing of the evidence or
by an outlook that places such a premium on human uniformity. All ethics and politics that rest on a conception of a single,
uniform human nature, whether it be an ontological, historical,
or potential nature, are ideologies of agreement, and as such
they are opposed not only to a world in which moral diversity
flourishes, but also to that ideology which cherishes this variety
as the true expression of individual freedom.

From this by no means exhaustive survey of current types
of natural law thinking it emerges that it would be entirely
erroneous to impose simple political labels on natural law as
such. What the various forms of natural law share is a longing
for unity, for a less complicated and more organic sort of social
world. What is wanted is a world in which it would be easier
to be certain about "the public good," and one in which peace

would be more than the bare absence of physical violence. Revulsion against the condition of the contemporary nation-state and the international politics of the present has caused people of the most diverse political views to accept natural law. There are Thomists who are very conservative and others who are radical; some are authoritarian, others very liberal. To these must be added the various non-Thomist natural lawyers. There are those who see in nature a traditionalist ideal, and others who find in it the hope for a radically altered social order. Some see in it a more rigidly legalistic system, others see the natural society as one of spontaneity. Clearly, natural law is not a simple ideology. Nothing more should be imputed to it than a concern for agreement as an end in itself. That is, in any case, its great source of appeal.

The need for agreement is intimately related to legalism, though it is by no means alien to many other moralities. Legalism, both in theory and in practice, does not just pre-scribe unity; it presupposes a degree of agreement; for legalism is the morality of rule following. Now rules are clearly not just any casual "ought" statements. They are norms that are ex-pected to endure for some length of time, that are meant to apply to groups.or to whole classes of individual persons, and that are, in the main, accepted as binding for one reason or another. All this necessarily implies a considerable degree of agreement among all concerned, among the framers, the ad-ministrators, and the followers of rules—among judges and judged. It means stability and it means common views. With-out them there can be no functioning judicial activity, no legal order. That is why natural law has always been a philosophy congenial to judges. It guarantees the possibility of an imper-sonal administration of rules. It is in any case the theory that has been built into the judicial systems of European countries. Historically the two are coextensive. To those who wish to preserve them and who are sworn to maintain their functions natural law may not always be appealing on metaphysical grounds, but in that case they will hasten to find some substitute for it. When they recognize this as impossible, they may well become disoriented and incapable of maintaining the integrity of inherited institutions. More usually, however, a satisfactory version of natural law can be devised so that judicial poise may be maintained.

### THE IDEOLOGY OF AGREEMENT

The most interesting thing about natural law theory and its replacements is their indestructibility. Their endurance cannot, moreover, be ascribed simply to the well-known survival power of the Roman Catholic Church. Natural law has also been built into the judicial systems of most Western countries. It is, finally, as a guide to legislation, whether monarchical, parliamentary, judicial, or administrative, that it has fulfilled its greatest function. The belief in an objective common good has remained very powerful, and this is not surprising; it certainly makes the responsibility of deciding less onerous if one can believe that there are prefabricated rules waiting to be recognized and followed in legislation. There is, indeed, every reason to believe that the several revivals of natural law thinking in the twentieth century have all been part of more general ideological movements in favor of unity, and of wider searches for political values transcending those of the competing groups. The first revival in Europe before the First World War was at least partially a defensive reaction to the socialist doctrine of inevitable class war, as well as to parliamentary party fragmentation.[61] The present revival in Europe seems to represent a search for *some* set of values in a situation of more or less complete political apathy, where people are haunted, nevertheless, by memories of fascism and prospects of Soviet penetration. In America the recent successes of natural law theory are surely part of the general cry for "national purpose," for a "united moral front." To this must be added the native passion for ever more "consensus," and an implicit belief in "a common good" or "the public interest" towards which the nation is perpetually moving. In all these cases, whether it be a simple appeal to "political truth," to the common good, or to "social solidarity," natural law has played its ideological part, as it would wherever unity has, for some reason, come to appear a vital political need and agreement has been treated as an end in itself. In response to the continuing appeal and even intellectual respectability of such attitudes, the liberal heirs of Austin are bound to renew their determination to keep law and morality apart. Professor Hart is at his best when he is brilliantly demolishing the views of those who, like Justice Devlin, defend legislated morality. That, after all, is the *raison d'être* of analytical positivism.

The various ideologies of agreement now current are by no means all genuinely higher law doctrines. On the contrary, some display an extraordinary pseudo-pragmatism. It is, for instance, Justice Devlin's contention that society will fall apart unless an accepted morality is enforced by the public authorities.[62] Even without the threats of the Cold War, which have stimulated the "need for values" and the call for a national purpose in the United States, it is here argued that, not only does *a* notion of morality prevail in England, but that social disaster must follow any failure to give it the backing of coercive legislation. The tricky question of who really knows what is moral is answered by referring the doubter to "the man on the Clapham bus" whose moral attitudes can be taken as representative of all England, or at least of all of England that matters. Here one is in the presence of the mythical "average man," whose uses have at last been discovered by conservatives. The unquestioning mind is taken as the best index of public opinion, morality is then identified with this opinion, and the survival of society is made to depend upon its being the sole guide for public policy, with no further need to check the facts of the case. That tolerance and freedom might also be values, that the moral successes of public enforcement remain dubious, are matters which do not even seem to occur to this type of mentality.

What is taken as axiomatic by Justice Devlin and his American counterparts is that freedom cannot be the basis of legal justice.[63] The distinction that is never made here is not the one between law and morals, but the one between educative and legalistic moral and political values. The argument is always presented in the form of a rather self-evident proposition: that no policy is totally value-free, that the enforcement of *some* morality is inevitable, and that those who deny this fact in order to defend moral freedom are either foolish or wicked, or both. The point is well taken but it hardly meets the issues, for freedom and diversity are values, too, and individualism and impersonal justice are types of morality as well. To defend them is not to deny the obvious—that, whatever "society" does, it promotes some set of values. However, the defenders of the "man on the Clapham bus" not only are urging upon us a very specific and narrow set of norms; they are doing it in order to bring conformity into a pluralistic society, and under the false pretense of defending moral values against the amoral. It is, of course, true that in supporting tolerance and skepticism liberals have often pretended to be "value-free," and so, to a degree, they are responsible for these rather devious intellectual exploits on the part of the defenders of a common public morality and of "political truth."

Even if, as in the case of Mr. Berns' defense of legislation to suppress pornographic reading matter and films, it is claimed that repression is likely to be ineffective in stimulating virtue, this is only regarded as a secondary consideration. The primary one is the absolute necessity of having one standard of moral

rectitude both recognized and officially endorsed. Justice Devlin, indeed, never seriously considers the question of whether,
even from the Clapham bus fellow's point of view, there
might not be practical advantages in restraining one's desire
to give one's sense of outrage a legal expression where homosexual acts between consenting adults are involved. After all,
there might be moral advantages in leaving people alone,
especially where sexual habits are involved. In America recent
experience with the forcible breeding of loyalty in the hearts
of the citizenry has evidently made even some supporters of
legislated virtue more cautious about persecution as a means
of creating civic goodness. Nevertheless, it appears that most
remain deaf to Judge Learned Hand's reflections on the
failures of crusading politics, and Judge Parker, no doubt,
speaks for a substantial part of the American public in insisting
that both the wickedness of and the popular disgust aroused
by homosexuality are such that a model criminal code ought
to penalize such conduct.[64] Mr. Berns is less specific. For him
it is not belief in the superiority or prevalence of one standard
of virtue or, as he would have it, "natural right" and "true
political knowledge" (the content of neither of which he ever
reveals), that is in question here. It is neither the existence nor
the content of a given morality that is ever seriously discussed.
The only point of passionate concern seems to be that one set
of values, and one only, must be valid and that public authorities have not only a right, but a duty, to support it—if necessary, by repressive means. To Mr. Berns the greatest danger
lies in the Supreme Court liberals' denial that any one moral
standard exists or should be enforced in America today. The
declared preference for diversity and the open condemnation
of uniformity through legal repression are what disturb him.
For him it is a simple either-or matter. Either one defends
political truth, or one is against moral conduct. That, in fact,
no absence of values is involved or even possible, but that it is

a question of degree and method of governmental activity in favor of either repression or tolerance does not occur to him as a possibility. That to promote freedom is also a moral decision strikes him as absurd, because clearly in his mind tolerance and the positive encouragement of immorality are identified. The obligation to believe in "natural right" (never specified) is primary; freedom of choice is secondary. Here the true villain is not the man who commits an illegal or evil act, but the liberal who refuses to accept a single scale of values or who rejects legal action as a means of habituating men in the practice of true goodness. It is not an issue of the relation of crime to sin or of law to morals, but of the defense of the emotional and social pleasures of a perfect moral certainty supported by every organ of public authority, as against the spirit of doubt and the conditions of life in a highly civilized society, in which a multiplicity of opinions is sure to prevail. The anxiety of the elite that possesses "true political knowledge" or of the "man on the Clapham bus" is understandable; it is, however, in itself no argument in favor of laws and judicial decisions which rely on a myth of moral uniformity or which pursue an ideology of agreement-at-any-price.

The idea that law exists in order to impose agreement is the counsel of despair, since there is no pretense that agreement in fact exists, even though this is considered very desirable. The more optimistic view, and the one more likely to serve as a substitute for traditional natural law theory, is that agreement, in fact, exists either actually or potentially. This future-looking view has a particular appeal in America, just as the theory of progress still serves as a form of natural law thinking here. Thus, even so emphatic an opponent of ontological natural law as Professor McDougal sees in the notion of "human dignity in a free and abundant society" the goal toward which all mankind is striving and which can, therefore, be used as a standard for measuring every law and every social institution.[65] Here, as a matter of observed fact, we are told, are the values we all unambiguously and uniformly agree on and ardently long for. It is thus only their actual realization that lies in the future. Agreement on an operative ideology is already with us. To this one might well raise three objections. First, even if everyone did agree on this formula as the sole basis for law, the mere fact of agreement is not, in itself, proof of its value. Second, this is so vague a notion as to have no concrete meaning in any specific situation; if it were made to have a concrete political application, all agreement would evaporate. Last, even in its present all but meaningless form, it is not really universally appealing. If the abundant society means the "affluent society," it is certainly not acceptable to all.

Another American variant of natural law thinking replaces the "wise men" of the traditional doctrine with "experts" who bring agreement and certainty based on "facts." This is particularly evident in the various writings of the radical "realists" of the New Deal era. While all such American "realists" were by no means radical, "court-centeredness" being perhaps the only common denominator among these diverse writers, the movement as a whole was united in at least one other way: it wanted to get away from both natural law and analytical jurisprudence. In the end, however, the radical exponents of the realist doctrine, who found their "cause" in the great Court fight and the creation of the quasi-judicial agencies, did emerge with only another form of natural law doctrine. At first sight they seem an astonishing group, indeed—unlegalistic lawyers, even anarchists. This is, however, only a superficial view. To be sure, all of the New Deal realists were united in one belief: the "basic myth" must go. The basic myth was that judges find the law "there" rather than make it.[66] This was, of course, the judicial rationale for holding New Deal legislation unconstitutional, and that is why it was obnoxious. The realists, however, did not stop with exposing the "symbols" or "rituals" which the basic myth perpetuated. The legally most sophisticated among them, Jerome Frank, went on to urge that "certainty," the very aim of legalism in general, ought to be abandoned. The desire for certainty was merely an infantile yearning for a father-figure, projected onto the social scene. Society did not need certainty; it needed change, and experimentation.[67] The person to give that was the fully mature judge, self-conscious after a psychoanalysis, meting out justice in accordance with Erich Fromm's notions of social sanity. Law is still what the judges make it. What they make, however, is not really law, but a series of disconnected individual decisions, tied together by what Frank was now to call, with some qualifications, natural law.[68] With these notions in mind, the judges should abandon certainty of expectations as their social objective and as a pretense. Instead, they should openly aim at making each litigant who appeared before them a happier and better man or woman.[69]

Not surprisingly, while English lawyers can explain American realism as a response to the incoherence of the American legal system with its fifty-one separate legal systems, its often unprofessional, elective lower-court State judiciary, and the legislative power of the Supreme Court, they have been apparently incapable of grasping its general purposes.[70] They can understand realism's court-centeredness, but not its social aims. Surely nothing can exceed the sheer incomprehension of Professor Hart's suggestion that Jerome Frank's "gnawing problems will drop away if [he ceases] to ask 'what is law' . . . and asks instead 'what sort of statement is a statement of law.'"[71] Taken at its face value it would seem that Professor Hart is offering linguistic analysis as the best road to social reform. In fact, he is not even aware that social reform was Frank's aim. It does not even seem to him possible that a legal theory should concern itself with the social consequences of law. That is the job of politicians and moralists, but never the task of legal theory. Law is "there," to be analyzed. That too, of course, hides a social preference, the belief that certainty in law is the best guarantee of individual freedom.[72] In any case, quite apart from the general rejection of formalism by American philosophy and political thought alike, logical analysis was the last thing that Frank needed. He was perfectly clear that the legalistic demand for certainty inevitably favored conservatism, and Frank wanted social change, and he wanted it quickly. What is far more astonishing than his New Deal enthusiasm is the extent to which his thinking remained faithful to traditional American jurisprudence. Indeed, his thinking was *more* court-centered than that of most other American lawyers. Whatever law was to be, the judiciary was going to make it.[73] If there was to be reform, the psyche of the judges would have to be altered. Of general historical development, of social changes and stabilities in the nation as a whole, one hears almost nothing. Psychology, especially Freudian psychology— always appealing to American liberals because of its immense individualism—was preferred to any sort of economic or historical analysis.[74] The psychoanalyzed judge would "cure" society in accordance with its real needs and would, presumably, be able to count on the agreement of his fellow-citizens and "patients" to this end.

Some New Deal lawyers, unlike Frank, in their hope for a benevolent ruling class did look away from the courthouse. Indeed, they went beyond Jeremy Bentham's hope of abolishing lawyers. Anarchism, so distasteful to the utilitarian tradition of English radicalism, managed to find its way even into legal minds in America. Thus Thurmond Arnold, after exposing the purely ritualistic and "symbolic" fictions of law that is "there" and of adversary proceedings, suggested that courts be entirely abolished, to be replaced by a benevolent and competent ruling class, open to the spirit of experimentation. Perhaps law might still be needed to protect the weak and oppressed, but, beyond that, "curing" conflicts should be the job of a socially scientific elite endowed with all the virtues, including "opportunism." [75] One does not really have to wonder who *his* father-image was. The same suggestions were offered by Professor Rodell, to the applause of Jerome Frank. Law was a "high-class racket," "a hoax," "streamlined voodoo," and "word magic." [76] Humane arbitration and psychiatry were to replace civil and criminal law respectively. Welfare, humaneness, and efficiency are not "symbols." Without further definition they are "real." The law, on the other hand, is a matter of rules, and rules are words, and words are not "real." Ideas when conservative are symbolic; when radical they are "actualities," to be fashioned by expert hands. It all sounded very revolutionary and radical, and many people were quite frightened by it. They need not have been. "Sentimental anarchism," in the contemptuous words of Morris Cohen, is all there was to it. [77] When Veblen observed that "lawyers are exclusively occupied with the details of predatory fraud," he was objecting to a fraudulent and predatory society. [78] The realists never went beyond the details of judicial life, not even to its basic ideas. Indeed they did not really abandon legalistic morals and politics; they only wanted a few "experiments," and new "experts" and "doctors"—wise men all—to bring harmony and agreement to public life.

Without ever giving up his belief in the advantages of making judges dispense "law" in a ruleless, uncertain, and individualized way, Frank, quite inconsistently, eventually came to champion "certainty" after all. Perhaps he came to realize that "faithfulness to uniform treatment is one of the values to be looked for and weighed." [79] Perhaps he realized that consistency has valuable consequences too. What drove him, immediately, to rehabilitate certainty as a value was the charge that the new regulatory commissions, and his own S.E.C. in particular, were arbitrary and ruleless. To this charge he replied that the courts, in fact, were less capable of providing certainty, because they had no means of establishing the facts upon which to base decisions. Unhampered by antiquated rules of evidence and juries, and staffed by experts, the regulatory commissions gave really sounder, more just, and more certain decisions, because they knew the facts. Expertise in the facts, in short, was the best means to legal justice as well. From "rule-skepticism" Frank moved on to "fact-skepticism," which allowed him to salvage all the legalistic values without having to abandon his war against the traditional court system.[80] And in fact the passion for this sort of "scientific" expertise rests on quite the same ideological presuppositions as most American natural law theory. It assumes that there is "a public good" which a wise man—now an "expert"—can discover and to which all must agree as a proved necessity. It is "there," as the law was "there" for the old courts. The "public interest" replaced the existing rules of law—that was all. To some of the anarchists the "thereness" of the public good meant that social "doctors" were to replace courts entirely, but the idea of facts applied by politically independent experts is ideologically the first cousin of traditional legalism. The realists were lawyers too, even if temporarily radical ones. The expert was expected to apply facts to settle conflicts in precisely the way that judges addicted to the "basic myth" applied rules. The neutrality of expertise is not different from that of the idealized bench. Both demand a politically antiseptic atmosphere in order to deliver decisions that are inescapable by virtue of their rational necessity. That had been the idea behind the "Brandeis brief" all along. The truth, nevertheless, is that no amount of facts, however accurate, yields a decision or an agreement. The weight of facts is even less likely to convince disappointed claimants of the validity of decisions than the weight of precedent that supports judicial opinions.

One must, moreover, ask the most difficult question: expertise in what? Is not expertise as formal a notion as that of rules of law? Is there an expert in the "public good"? What facts will automatically tell an expert where the public interest lies, and convince those who must follow his decisions? The radical lawyers never made it clear. Their ideological capital was, in fact, too much like traditional legalism for that. Expertise was indeed only the perfection of judicial virtue that had eluded the old bench. Certainty and flexibility as needed were revealed only to the objective mind of the expert. As such the content of expertise was as vague as the wisdom of the Stoic sage and indeed as that of all natural law. This, like its belief in an objective public good, put the realists squarely into the natural law tradition, all the failings and attractions of which realism also shared, in spite of its valiant efforts to rise above all traditional types of jurisprudence. Once the New Deal had won its victories, realism as a legal theory became as formal and general a theory of law as any. It stood for nothing concrete, as was inevitable. Once the public good, to which all wise men must agree, ceased to have the specific content it had acquired during the crisis years of the early New Deal, it became only another term for the natural law, and as such was quite without a social direction.

The problem of vagueness is one that assails all the ideologies of agreement-as-an-end-itself, and this is not surprising since the agreement is fictitious. It depends entirely on not being put to the test of any specific, concrete political or moral situation in which a decision must be made. It is this circumstance which makes the hope of those who, like Felix Cohen, think that "value clarification" is itself a helpful device for diminishing conflict in morals and law seem totally unfounded.[81] To be sure, there are many disagreements which are due to misunderstandings, but this is not true of all by any means, and it is perfectly possible that clarification would only sharpen

them. Apart from the classification and evocation of moral
attitudes as exercises in their own right, there are no particularly important political and legal advantages to be gained
from heightened self-consciousness. The only half hidden
belief that compromise and consensus would automatically
flow from clarification has no real basis in experience. The
entire intellectual history of Europe, in fact, argues against it.
Behind all these programs, whether pragmatic (as in the case
of McDougal and Felix Cohen) or not, lies the same urge
which animated that "most philistine of all philosophic
schools," the Stoics, to evade conflict and to gloss over the
reality of human diversity.[82] The fault lies in the enterprise
itself, in trying to find too solid, too certain, a basis for law
and morals.

The demand for an unshakable foundation for law is hard
to resist, because it is the legislators and judges themselves who
press it upon the theorist. It is probably quite true that the
greatest advantage of scholastic jurisprudence was that it presented the judiciary with a fairly precise set of rules to follow
in case of doubt.[83] It is this appeal from the bench and from
politicians that has, as much as anything, inspired the con-
tinued call for either a revival of natural law or some replacement. If natural law was a doctrine of reconciliation in the
seventeenth century, if it could supply a basis for international
and even domestic law and order after the ideological passions
of the Reformation, could not it, or something like it, fulfill
the same function today? After all, this also is an age tired of
ideological warfare. Is this not, therefore, the right moment for
a constructive, common ideology of agreement? Such, at any
rate, is the feeling of those who think that a deontology or a
science of axiology could be devised now, to provide a basis
for post-ideological politics.[84] Here there is no longer an
appeal to ontological natural law; this clearly would be too
controversial. The foundations of deontology are to be in the

realm of the actual. "Can we agree that certain things are binding?" we are asked, for what matters is the agreement. If we can all agree, then "is" and "ought" are reunited, for whatever is universally regarded as obligatory, as an "ought," will actually be made so. The logical jump at last ceases to have any ideological or political importance; for in this case the logical problem is probably secondary. Create agreement and the issue will die. Here, as in the case of the champions of "political truth," we are never told what we are to agree on, or what the values are which we are to support. What is asserted is the necessity of agreement-as-an-end-in-itself, as an independent value. It is true that as far as content goes there is no longer any political ideology involved in all this. All that remains is the bare insistence upon the rightness of belief, the need for agreement, and the difficulties and feebleness inherent in doubt and ethical pluralism. What we have here is natural law without any content whatsoever—a scheme of values that is not even vague, it is totally empty. It is, because of this, all the more revealing, because it shows the intellectual and emotional predisposition at the core of earlier ideologies. Both for practical political reasons and for private satisfactions there is a simple will to believe in at least the possibility of a universal code upon which one can rely whenever the prospect of making a decision has to be faced. Nevertheless, it ought to be remembered that, in any society where moral diversity exists, agreement-as-an-end-in-itself can only be achieved by totalitarian methods, and that from Calvin's Geneva to Nazi Germany and Soviet Russia the price of unity has been very high and the moral returns very low indeed. In any case, what on earth is so impressive about agreement and unity? When we are told that we need—all the millions of us—a national purpose, that even a "damnable ideology" is more effective than none, we may well ask, "Why?" and

"Effective for what?" Why do we need an "identity" as a people? Just what means are to be used to achieve it?[85]

The answers to these questions bring us right back to the problems of the legislator, especially the judicial legislator. All judges must sooner or later legislate—create rules either unconsciously or openly. The codes of several European countries directly provide for this possibility, and in the United States it is an accepted aspect of every stage of judicial activity. From Austin to Gray, moreover, writers on jurisprudence have urged judges to face the facts of life candidly, to accept the responsibilities the community has placed upon their shoulders, and to make rules that seem to them useful and intelligent. To the judge, however, these are frightful occasions.[86] By training and professional ideology he is tied to a vision of his function that excludes self-assertion and places a premium on following existing rules impartially. His natural impulse is to find a rule at any cost, or at least to assimilate his decision to a rule as closely as possible. He may even openly evade responsibility. Most likely, there will be a plaintive call for *some* rule, *any* rule, even if statute and precedent have failed, from society or from the specialists and experts in the field of social life into which the awkward case falls. Either he will convince himself that some set of social facts, some set of expertly developed "is" conditions, yields a rule for him automatically, or he will appeal to a higher law, or he will rely on what he hopes is the view of the majority of his fellow citizens. In all three cases it is obviously of great importance to him that the rules he relies on be based on universal agreement among either the experts, the wise, or the whole people. Otherwise the rule becomes a mere opinion, possibly just his own—a thought he does not wish to entertain. This explains such exercises as the Brandeis brief and Chief Justice Warren's citations of psychological texts in support of his decision in the segregation case. Here the professional expert is used to supply a basis for a new rule. The revival of natural law thinking in code countries before the First World War was certainly due in part to the situation created by narrow and dated codes and, in France especially, by a parliamentary system too immobilized to be able to introduce necessary legal reforms. Just because the spirit of codified law tends to enhance the legislative inhibitions of the judiciary even more than is usual, the demand was mainly for rules immanent in the law itself, or at least in its spirit or in the society out of which it grew. In the United States the extent of judicial lawmaking is both greater and more frankly recognized than anywhere else. Nevertheless, this does not mean that our judges like the system. It is well known that Judge Learned Hand and Justice Frankfurter have expressed a deep aversion to the notion that even in constitutional questions the courts take any legislative initiative. Preferably they should rely on the legislature to have the last say whenever possible, and when that has failed they should place their trust in community sentiment.

This last notion, that there is a stable community sentiment and that the judge may and should rely upon it rather than upon his own conscience and intelligence, is politically most dubious. It leads right to that pseudo-democracy of agreement among Clapham bus riders which Justice Devlin proclaimed and which from the liberal point of view is thoroughly dangerous. It is, of course, only fair to emphasize the difficulties of the American bench, which is faced with the democratic faith in majority government as well as with legislatures that regularly pass the moral buck to the judiciary, which can look forward to nothing but abuse whatever decisions it may choose to make. Is it really necessary to ask the federal judiciary to decide what constitutes a "good moral character," as the naturalization law does now? Is mercy-killing immoral under all circumstances and thus a disqualification for citizenship?

Judge Frank suggested a poll among the "ethical leaders" of the nation—shades of the Stoic wise men! Judge Hand could have relied on his own conscience, which was a guide the community might have been perfectly willing to accept, but in the end he chose to follow what he regarded as "generally accepted moral convention current at the time."

The difficulties of judgment do not stop there. How, after all, does Judge Hand know what the conventions are, even if it is agreed upon that they are to guide him and his fellow judges out of their perplexity? Surely a "best guess" as to community sentiment is not good enough. A more accurate assessment is needed, and one at least has been offered: the best way to find out what the community thinks is, after all, to ask its members. The only way truly to gauge community sentiment in regard to what the law ought to be is to poll the community. It is this obvious step that was, in fact, taken by a team of scholars in Nebraska who constructed and used a questionnaire to discover how people felt about the current laws on parental authority. While the pollsters admit that majority feeling is an arbitrary way of settling community opinion, they accept it as the democratic basis for judicial legislation.[87] Considering how often American courts, and especially the Supreme Court, have used the "higher law" or their own vision of the Constitution to defeat the projects of democratically elected legislatures, this general concern for democracy is understandable. It is, after all, just what troubles Justice Frankfurter and Judge Hand. The issue here, however, is whether direct democracy achieved through polling and the open circumvention of the legislature and electoral process, without the controversy and exchanges of views that elections and public debates involve, is the answer to the judicial quandary.[88] Is it not a way of establishing agreement, both by the inherent character of polling through a uniform questionnaire and by elimination of public discussion? Is this really more democratic than allowing the judiciary to follow its own preferences? Certainly it is not more liberal. It is rather a search for the lowest common denominator of social morality, that part which, as Justice Devlin admitted, expresses only disgust and indignation. As such it is a form of moral obscurantism intolerable to any liberal or sensitive person, whether he be a natural lawyer or a positivist.[89] Moreover, the judge who falls back on this or on some vaguer estimate of community sentiment is legislating no less than he who uses another standard. The judge, the legislative representative, the administrative official, or the private citizen cannot avoid deciding, and often deciding without any support from nature or society. Much as all might long for agreement, for an end to doubt and multiplicity, there is no way of evading the actuality of diversity. That this makes it impossible to have a theory of the relations between law and morals is the equally certain intellectual consequence. However, the demand for such a unified theory has its roots in the very ideologies which set a premium upon agreement as a social end. When both the possibility and the desirability of this policy are discarded, it becomes a matter of the relations among types of morality, types of ideology, and types of government and law. Of these, legalistic morality and law form a social continuum, united by their common end—that rules are to be followed. Rule following may be more rigid among the official guardians of the law than in daily life, but legalism as a social ethos is clear on the main point: it is following rules, pre-established, known, and accepted, that gives actions their worth in every case.

Rules to be followed must be there, and this, as we saw, means a degree of agreement. However, obedience to rules and the belief that rules are "there" presuppose agreement; they do not in themselves create it. On the contrary, rules are exclusive: either they *are* obliging or they are *not*. And so legalism may in practice make people especially uncompromising, for it has nothing to say about the relationship between incompatible systems of rules save that one set must be binding, in which case the others are not really rules. Natural law has always been perfectly candid about this. Positivism, to the extent that it is a formal theory, however, is in its own way also a theory of agreement, to a limited degree. It does not, as natural law does, concern itself directly with the conditions of social unity. These are simply put between brackets as a question irrelevant to legal science. Law is sealed off from the world of conflict, lifted out of the sphere of social dispute. The legal system is "there"—a body of accepted rules. Professor Hart's obsession with games as the paradigm for legal activity is very revealing in this respect.[90] Law is thus pictured as a matter of combat, but one in which both "teams" accept the rules as a matter of self-evidence. Otherwise it would not be a game. If one player lifts the chess board and hurls it at his opponent, he is no longer playing chess; he is not playing at all. This is what legalism must assume: certain basic rules are there to be followed, and if someone refuses to follow them there is nothing more that can, formally, be said about it. Unhappily, perhaps, law and legal systems are not games but social institutions, and they do not exist in the social vacuum of a game of chess. The behavior of men involved in social conflicts and the conditions under which these may, and may not, be resolved by appeals to rules simply do not resemble games. Not only does no system of law or morality known to history have such a simple inner consistency and symmetry, but all are perpetually challenged by other sets of rules, or by social preferences and policies that are fundamentally unlegalistic. Direct bargaining, splitting the difference, direct coercion, or propaganda not only compete with legalism, they also provide the conditions within which it exists socially. Unlike games they cannot be isolated, nor do they have simple purposes, a clear beginning, or an end.

The argument between natural lawyers and positivists is thus essentially a family quarrel among legalists. That is, perhaps, why outsiders find it often tiresome. Both agree about the necessity of following rules but differ about what to do when a conflict between rules occurs. However, the question of choosing between sets of rules is one of great practical importance to those who exercise judicial functions, perhaps more so than the occasions when there is a normative vacuum. The judge who in delivering a decision that he regards as morally unsound says, "This is a court of law, not a theological seminary," is not morally stunted. Rather, he is living up to a moral ideal, that of "fidelity to law." In these and similar expressions of the judicial creed, the judge is making a choice of political values, a choice usually in favor of stability, of predictability, of narrow interpretations of statutes and precedents, of the separation of the judiciary from the policy-making departments of government, and of an impersonal administration of legal rules. What he is defending is the typical judicial ethos, as well as a very specific conception of how a legal system should operate and what it should accomplish. It is a position that is not, however, necessary or self-evident. Indeed, it is bound to conflict with other equally powerful social and political preferences. The only reason why this is not always obvious in theory is that as a matter of political faith, though not of consistent practice, most people in "mature legal systems" approve of this judicial stance and accept it as natural. In fact, they regard it as a necessary part of legal justice.

This admirable restraint of the judge, this impersonal, neutral submission to the rules that are "there," does not, always, lead to approbation in practice. However much neutrality may be admired as a personal attribute of judges, it does not yield socially neutral results. Those who feel offended or injured by an impartial decision will not be in the least reconciled to it by the judge's fairness. To them the decision will still appear "unjust," because it does not conform to their system of moral rules. If they happen to believe in natural law they not only will declare it to be morally obnoxious, but will very likely condemn it to grammatical death through definitional execution. It will be said not *to be* a legal decision at all, implying both that it is undeserving of existence—that it is nonexistent, that it is something else less sacred than a legal rule—and that, in any case, one need not obey it—or at least one need not positively feel obliged to obey it, even if, to avoid "scandal," one does conform. The positivist will approve the stance of the judge, without, however, advising the citizens of their duty to obey or defy the decision.

This has recently been made very plain in a debate between Professors Hart and Fuller,[91] for they at least were clear that fidelity to law was the issue between them. One of the subjects of disagreement was the right policy of courts in regard to a woman who had denounced her husband to the Nazis and so caused his death. Both Professors Hart and Fuller agreed that retroactive judicial decisions are, on the whole, undesirable, though both seemed to feel that if a retroactive statute had been passed by the Bonn parliament this would have been far less disturbing. It is, of course, true that almost any new law upsets someone's expectations based on existing rules, but it is difficult to see why legislative retroactivity is any better than judicial, unless one has a strong prior notion as to the ends and functions of the law courts. Professor Hart clearly has made a choice in favor of security of expectations on the part of individuals, of as small an area of judicial discretion as possible, and thus of the least possible amount of judicial legislation. While it would have been more candid to say,

"This is what I prefer courts to do," rather than, "This is what law is," his stand is clear. He thinks that courts are most likely to achieve justice by fidelity to law, even undesirable law. Professor Fuller, however, feels that justice is not done unless the "inner morality of the law" is preserved, even at the cost of the retroactive punishment of those who contributed to its destruction, since totalitarian politics are so incompatible with law that they may be combatted even by departing from what would, ordinarily, be sound judicial practice. In short, there are at least some political values which are not only prior to fidelity to law, but which make the latter possible in the first place. The odd thing is that for some reason Professor Fuller feels that these values are immanent in the law as such and that law is not law unless they are present. Now this definitional self-insurance is not really necessary for his position. In fact, it destroys it. It is quite enough to say that the possibility of formal justice itself is not independent of other political values, and that it cannot prevail under all political conditions. Moreover, it is also true that fidelity to law is never fully achieved but only approximated, that judicial legislation is inevitable, and that, since judges must sooner or later make a choice among different social values, they should promote justice by favoring those social policies which make the operations of an independent judiciary and the autonomy of the legal system possible. In both cases there is, lastly, an implicit assumption that justice is something that can be understood apart from law.

The issue is whether law can be defined so as to exclude justice or not, or at least whether its partial inclusion commits one also to a notion of a morality inherent in law. Professor Hart is ready to agree that a legal system implies that general rules must be applied equally to like cases, but he refuses to go on to demand that only morally good general rules be applied or that the application of general rules is bound to bring goodness or a "good order" with it, and it is this last point that Professor Fuller insists on. If the latter had said that legalistic morality and social procedures are the best kind and that the courts of law operate so as to produce this ethos—that law as an historical institution contributes to a morally superior society—he would have been intelligible. If he had argued that law acts as a conservative influence in society implementing established rules and expectations, he could speak of it as guaranteeing a good order, once he had made it clear that this was his notion of social goodness. In neither case, however, would this allow him to speak of the law as a closed-off unit, as a discrete entity with its own self-contained, inner morality. As long as he speaks of this order as good in itself because of its inner consistency, with no reference to its social context, he cannot escape from the obvious criticism that regularity as such is as compatible with the most wicked policy as it is with the best. Such consequences are, however, inevitable as long as the lawyerly habit of treating law as "there" prevails.

Whatever their disagreements, both sides agree that justice is a matter of the equal application of rules. The pursuit of rules—pre-established, known, and accepted—is the end, moreover, not only of law but of all legalistic morals. It is this common aim that makes law and legalistic morality not separate entities but a single continuum. And the name of that continuum is justice. Rigorously applied in courts, more compromisingly in daily life, the virtues of acting according to rules may be practiced in varying degrees of intensity, but the cast of mind, the moral attitude, remains constant. As such it is but one morality among others. It is this circumstance that legalism in its exclusiveness finds so difficult to accept and so impossible to adjust to—in theory, no less than in practice. That is why legalism is so drawn to ideologies of agreement; for justice presupposes rules and rules depend on agreement, and this is inescapable in every sphere in which legalistic morals operate—at home, in groups, in legislative chambers, and in courts of law. It is the very condition of justice. It is also the policy of legalism. The pursuit of justice is the aim of legalistic politics, both domestic and international. To understand both legalism's view of politics and its relations to policies other than its own, one must first consider the notion of justice and then see what the single-minded devotion to that virtue entails.

# PART II

# *Law and Politics*

## INTRODUCTION

Politics is treated in legal theory in much the same way as are
morals, except that here there appears to be virtually unanimous agreement that law and politics must be kept apart as
much as possible in theory no less than in practice. The divorce
of law from politics is, to be sure, designed to prevent arbitrariness, and that is why there is so little argument about its
necessity. However, ideologically legalism does not stop there.
Politics is regarded not only as something apart from law,
but as inferior to law. Law aims at justice, while politics looks
only to expediency. The former is neutral and objective, the
latter the uncontrolled child of competing interests and ideologies. Justice is thus not only the policy of legalism, it is treated
as a policy superior to and unlike any other. All this more than
merely encourages legal theory to present law in a decidedly
apolitical manner.

The following pages are, therefore, devoted to a criticism
of the legalistic approach to politics. First there is a discussion
of the notion of justice in general, and especially its central
place in legalistic thought. This is followed by a critical
analysis of legalism in international politics as displayed in the

theory of positive international law. To be sure, international law is not the only field in which legalistic politics operates. It can also be observed in the theories that express themselves in domestic legalistic politics—in the struggles over constitutional and administrative law in Britain and in the United States, for instance. Here, however, the political history of these countries would have to be considered in detail. International law is not the expression of local political conditions and histories, but a transnational intellectual enterprise. It forms an integral part of all legal theory now, as it always has. It is thus one of the great examples of the political implications and, indeed, weaknesses of legalism as a policy and an ideology.

The rest of the discussion of law and politics is concerned with a lengthy analysis of political trials, especially the great International Military Tribunal at Nuremberg. This too is a chapter in the story of legalism as an ideology and of the policy of justice, for it is here that this policy is most starkly confronted by political aims different from, and often opposed to, its own. Political trials reveal the intellectual rigidities and unrealities of legalism as no other occasion can. Here its inability to recognize its own social functions, both in their greatness and in their limitations, is fully revealed. What lawyers say and do in the course of political trials must, thus, be investigated if one is to understand legalism as an ideology and to overcome its conceptual narrowness, without impinging upon its undeniable social value. The great paradox revealed here is that legalism as an ideology is too inflexible to recognize the enormous potentialities of legalism as a creative policy, but exhausts itself in intoning traditional pieties and principles which are incapable of realization. This is, of course, the perennial character of ideologies. It should not, however, in this case, lead one to forget the greatness of legalism as an ethos when it expresses itself in the characteristic institutions of the law.

## JUSTICE: THE POLICY OF LEGALISM

What, then, is justice? It is, Professor Hart has written, "the most legal of virtues." Surely he is right. Justice is a personal attribute—*habitus animi,* in Cicero's words.[1] As such it is one virtue among many. For legalistic ethics, however, it is the pinnacle of goodness, the epitome of morality. It is the sum of legalistic aspirations. In an individual it implies fairness, impartiality, a disposition to give each man his due—in the faith that a system of rules ascribing what is due always exists. Justice is the commitment to obeying rules, to respecting rights, to accepting obligations under a system of principles. It is the individual's consistent adherence to the morality of rule following in a moral world where right and duty are the dominating issues. On the other hand, the ethics of love, of service, of aesthetic enhancement, no less than those of instinct and of "supermanship," can only treat justice as an inferior attribute and an unworthy end. There is, of course, the possibility of totally redefining justice, as Plato tried to do in the *Republic.* Here the educative polity in pursuit of harmony was termed just, in opposition to the legalistic politics of "dueness" which was rejected as inferior. To do this, however, justice must be identified with insight into moral truth in the individual and with social harmony in collective life. Now these may indeed be far more important than dueness under a system of rules and they will conflict with it, but, on the whole, justice as an identifiable quality has usually been associated with the latter. It is Aristotle's discussion of justice, not Plato's, that has become the paradigm for all subsequent discussions of the subject. Throughout all the wrangling about the source and content of just rules, one thing has at least remained stable—that following rules impartially is a virtue. For those who do not accept the morality of rule following, justice is simply not a moral good, or at best it is only a very subordinate one. Romantic and mystical morality do not aim at justice, which is to them confining and cold; neither do other forms of irrationalism, especially those that glorify violence. The "grand" ideologies of the present century have no use for justice. All of these points of view, in short, are radically opposed to justice and to the morality that makes justice its highest good.

If, among the partisans of justice, the duty of sticking to rules is not a source of disagreement, the content of the rules is. That is why justice is a personal attribute, not the effects of such an attitude. Justice is not a specific social result, even if legalistic morality creates a whole ideological climate, a way of thinking about society, and expresses itself in specific social institutions—the legal system and the courts of law, most obviously. For a social action to be termed just, however, one must first agree that it is in conformity with one's system of rules, and since in any conceivable modern society there are always several competing systems of rules, it is not possible to say that any rule or act as such is just. It is, however, possible to speak of the justice of the men who make decisions, whether these be personal or public. Men who try to apply rules impartially, whatever the rules may be, are just. They are the heroes of legalism. Only one aim, one habit of mind, is constant in all the possible occasions when justice is demanded: namely, that a general rule be applied to an individual instance. Justice has been called a "quasi-morality" because it is not a virtue that is always relevant or valued. In personal relations it has not always been rated very highly, even by people of a legalistic bent of mind.[2] Charity has usually been conceded to be not only superior to justice but incompatible with it. In any case, even within a generally legalistic society, justice must constantly compromise with other moral values and policies.

Not only is justice but one personal virtue among others; its comes into play at all in only two specific instances: when rules concerned with the distribution of powers among individuals are involved, and when adjustments of conflicting claims that arise under any system of such rules are made. At the least formal stage this implies what Aristotle called distributive justice, the process by which scarce goods, both material and intangible, are meted out among competing groups and persons according to whatever notion or notions of merit may be accepted. At the commutative or more institutionalized level justice is the maintaining of this system of distribution in individual cases. This scheme is, however, never even approximated, because at any given time there are several competing notions as to just who merits what in the first place. Nor is there ever a simple process of deductive reasoning from general distributive rules to individual decisions. On the contrary, the complexity of each case involves new distribution, a change in the balance, a choice of values each time.

If the rather limited character of justice is recognized, then the distinction between "formal" and "substantive" justice tends to fade. To pursue impartiality, fair-mindedness, an impersonal state of mind, the self-control to recognize and curb one's prejudices—all this surely is qualitative, a matter of content and character. Since all this is done in the service of only one ethical ideal and since this ethical ideal includes the formal attributes of law, the distinction becomes insignificant. It is not true that "giving each man his due" is a totally meaningless formula; it implies a precise end, it aims at a certain type of character. It is only meaningless as a prescription for specific actions. It is more than "You ought to do what you ought to do," but it does not tell us what in any given instance we ought to do. That will depend on what is meant by "merit" in the first place, and that is, of course, what most ethical and political disputes are about. In any case, however, the man who is determined to honor claims made under a given standard is just, though he may be neither kind, generous, nor amiable. To offer a more elaborate definition of justice is merely an effort to hide the real conflict about the nature of merit. To insist on formulas other than "what is merited or due" is to extend the meaning of justice in such a way as to make it a compatible part of any type of morality, even the most unlegalistic kind. Neither operation seems particularly necessary. This becomes evident when one analyzes the major formulas offered to supplement dueness or merit as a criterion.[3] "To all the same" merely implies that men qua men all merit an identical portion of pains and benefits. "To each according to his work" identifies merit with an individual's productivity or contribution to society rather than with his simple humanity. "To each according to his need" means that all men are entitled to a certain minimum of the scarce goods available to the members of society and that this claim must be honored before any other rewards or penalties may be distributed. "To each according to his rank" identifies merit with social position, presumably established on an hereditary basis of "blood" or surname, or on success in winning popular acclaim or political power. Lastly, the formula, "To each what the law attributes," gives priority to merit as defined by accepted political authority. To say, "To each according to his merit," is thus not to set up an alternative formula, but merely to state what the common element in all the others is: it is justice itself. What true desert is, what should be regarded as meritorious, no man can tell another. It is even uncertain whether justice deserves our approbation. Even if it does, this impartial blaming, praising, rewarding, and punishing of specific acts may be carried out for very different ends. Some see them as "fitting" responses which we simply know to be necessary, others regard them as merely educative devices to be used in order to promote certain types of conduct.

It is because we cannot possibly expect to agree on what we ourselves deserve and on what is owed to others (because each person is likely to suffer from moral conflicts, from being torn between different standards as well as different inclinations) that we constantly feel that injustice is being done even by those who accept the legalistic ethos. Even the most impartial and fair-minded people, and especially those who are in a position to impose political or judicial decisions upon us, will seem unjust sooner or later. Even when the rules to be applied, the nature of merit, are not challenged, no two cases are really so alike that equal treatment under a rule can be realized to everyone's satisfaction. That is why just behavior does not necessarily lead to results recognized as just by those affected. There is bound to be too much disagreement to make justice perfect in practice, too many mutually exclusive standards to make justice either a simple or a clear policy. Within a system of rules and among those who accept that system as binding upon themselves the just decision will be accepted as such. Outsiders will see it in a different light.

To say, however, that justice is primarily a personal attribute that can be recognized in an individual, apart from the actual rules that he applies, does not mean that it is not relevant to social action. The pursuit of justice does in fact express itself in specifically legal institutions of which the courts of law are the most characteristic, but which can be found in more or less systematic, courtlike institutions in many organized groups. Judgment between opposing claimants according to established rules is something that most societies know in some degree, and the difference is thus one of degrees of legalism prevalent and the extent to which it finds institutional organization, both governmental and private. The advantages of thinking of law in terms of degrees of legalism is very evident here again. The policy of justice is to intensify legalism in political life by promoting the institutionalization of the administration of justice. Its social aim is to resolve as many social conflicts by judicial means as possible; for there are degrees of legalism in the political life of highly legalistic societies, no less than in those in which this is a relatively weak ethos and which have only primitive legal institutions and ideas. The judicialization of all political processes has its promoters in all countries with deep legalistic traditions, though not in societies where legalism is feeble. At the most extreme level it means that all political issues ought to be solved by courtlike procedures. In a far less institutionalized way people call for justice not only when they want the prevailing rules changed in terms of some other ideology, but also when they want the existing system of rules applied more rigorously, more impartially, more "judicially," and over more extensive areas of social conduct. These perfectly obvious observations only point to the way in which justice as a moral attribute expresses itself more or less intensely in characteristic institutions and policies. However, this does not alter the fact that justice as such is ultimately a personal trait, a form of individual conduct, the highest expression of legalistic values.

In practice, however, the policies of justice must constantly compromise with other social demands. For instance, there can be no perfect justice in wartime rationing because individual exceptions to the distributive criteria are bound to be made in response to practical needs and moral demands other than those of justice. Children may have none of the merits that entitle them to special rations, sick children least of all; however, it is not a concern for the future generation but an instinctive protectiveness that causes us to increase their share beyond their due. It is not enough to say that since children form a recognized category of beings there is no injustice so long as all children are treated alike. That issue arises only when an exception has been made in favor of children. The decision to apply a standard of dueness to children that is not based on the prevailing scheme of merits is itself based on considerations of values other than justice.

It might be suggested that political or ultimate social justice lies in giving their "due" to all conflicting moral and political claims and ideologies whether they be legalistic or not. There is no need to doubt that the realization of personal justice is infinitely more likely in a society which thus honors freedom and equality. However, the three are not, for all that, identical. Justice presupposes an identifiable rule and the disposition to follow it. It is a state of mind no less than a policy, and as such it is the thread that ties legalistic morals, legal institutions, and legal politics into a single knot. As this is not the only possible virtue or policy, it should not be identified with other moral ends. Yet this is constantly done because justice is a term of universal approbation and has therefore been tagged on to every conceivable program and social aim. As one consequence we are faced with all kinds of justices—political, social, and natural, to name but a few. Political justice is in fact usually freedom, especially the possibility to effectively press social claims and interests. Now this is surely a condition for the realization of justice. How is one to get one's due if one cannot hope to stake a claim? However, it is not, in itself, justice. Social justice usually means equality. Now legal equality, implying that rules be applied alike to like cases, is only another term for justice as an attitude. There is, moreover, a degree of equality beyond this that is implied in the practice of justice. A person who is regarded as subhuman or so inferior as to be an object of solicitude or at best of training, who is felt to be irremediably immature, cannot be said to have anything due him, nor to be capable of making valid claims. Such permanent disability puts a man beyond the purview of justice. For a racist, Jews or Negroes are subhuman and thus clearly not fit for justice, even though he may be a scrupulously just man in his behavior to those whom he regards as his racial equals. There is thus an intimate relation among equality, freedom, and justice. However, beyond that minimum, equality and freedom remain independent values, a way of settling what constitutes human merit rather than ascribing dueness in individual instances. Justice, as an operative private virtue, may depend upon the acceptance of freedom and equality as social values, but no purpose is served by speaking of economic, social, or political justice, beyond attaching the sacred name of justice to social ends which, however worthy, do not form a part of justice and may, in fact, come into conflict with it.

Justice, as a policy among other policies, is, in short, legalism, and as such its main rival is surely that educative, manipulative ethos which is causing so much justified fear today. It is not that legalism and law, even in the narrowest juristic sense of the term, do not educate people and do not promote specific values and ideologies, but that their method is limited, and with it the scope of their influence upon the lives of individuals. It is not true to say that legalistic societies and legal institutions—law, in short—do not mold the character of those whose behavior they control. The just character is as much, or as little, an "internal" moral attribute as any other, and life according to rules is as much a technique of social control as any. However, it will lead to different personalities and a different distribution of qualities from those of the "organization man." It is not, after all, that this human type is over-coerced or unhappy, but that his behavior is conditioned by methods and values which are not those of legalism. He is not living in a world of rights and claims, of impersonal rules to be obeyed or ignored, but of smooth cooperation and adjustment to personal pressures. On the political level it is thus the manipulative state that is the real rival of the legalistic state, and the policy of inducement, whether by propaganda or by terror and related pressures, competes with the policy of legalism. It is not that the latter does not control the lives of individuals effectively, but the policy of applying rules is limited by the procedures imposed on it by the ethics of dueness in a fashion that other ways of governing men are not. That legalism is much less than what men mean by freedom ought also to be remembered.

The claim of those who say that law cannot make men moral is thus false. The law reinforces legalistic morals and vice versa. Even if law is identified, falsely, with punishment, it affects morals. The kind of morality involved, however, is one in which a good deal of individual discretion is likely to survive in view of the ethos of justice with its procedural inhibitions and its conservatism. This is what distinguishes it from other types of political control and other ideologies which favor the total reconditioning of individuals, an aim in which they may perfectly well succeed. This is not to imply that every society may not require the promotion of values to which justice is irrelevant. In education and in educational policy justice is often a liability, as any examiner forced to mark justly knows. A career open to talent is the universally accepted end of educational policies today, but when it is administered with that impersonality which is the necessary concomitant of justice it often ends by being shortsighted and cruel. For instance, if we identify talent with academic excellence as displayed in exams or any sort of "objective" test, and if we insist that these be taken by all at an identical age and marked according to one standard, we are probably being just. We are also causing considerable pain to many children and their parents, and we are promoting a certain type of competitive personality which may eventually dominate society, and which we may well come to loathe as we find ourselves living with an elite of emotionally stunted rat racers and a mass of dim-witted inferiors who were relegated to the bottom before they reached puberty.[4] We may also waste potential talents that mature late. In short, a policy of justice in this, as in many other areas, may lead to far worse social consequences than a policy of semijustice, in which several incompatible goals are allowed to live in compromise, even though logically they are mutually exclusive. It is not wickedness that creates a multiplicity of needs and values, but the inevitable diversity among people and the complexity of the demands that a highly developed culture makes upon them. This does not diminish the value of legalistic ethics or of legal institutions. To show that justice has its practical and ideological limits is not to slight it.

It is, however, not to be expected that the extreme legalist will accept this limited view of the functions of justice. The uncompromising character of justice as a virtue militates against any latitudinarian view of social morality. Instead, legalism is apt to disparage every other type of social policy. All politics must be assimilated to the paradigm of just action —the judicial process. Indeed "politics" itself becomes a word of scorn. Direct bargaining, for instance, is often treated as a matter of disreputable expediency, a sort of ideological anarchy, hardly to be distinguished from uncontrolled physical violence. Again, extreme legal formalism puts politics in brackets just as rigidly as it does morals, for here it is not logical deduction but pure chaos that reigns. Here science cannot penetrate, nor rational order prevail.[5] Thus to maintain the contrast between legal order and political chaos and to preserve the former from any taint of the latter it is not just necessary to define law out of politics; an entirely extravagant image of politics as essentially a species of war has to be maintained. Only thus can the sanctity of rule following as a social policy be kept from compromising associations.

To subdue this irrational political world it becomes all the more necessary to insist on a policy of uncompromising rules and rule following. Either rules for their own protection must be magically lifted out of politics, or society itself must be made safe for justice by imposing a unity upon it, which will make possible a consistent policy of justice according to universally accepted rules. The first is the positivist program, the second that of natural law. Both are equally legalistic, both are the philosophic exponents of the ideology and policy of justice. To analyze both in these terms is in no way meant to denigrate the value of justice as a virtue. The entire aim is rather to account for the difficulties which the morality of justice faces in a morally pluralistic world and to help it recognize its real place in it—not above the political world but in its very midst.

### LAW AND INTERNATIONAL POLITICS

In all fairness it should be noted that legal theory and the judicial ethos are by no means the sole promoters of this notion of politics as a perpetual war. It is also the theory of that other school of determined categorizers, the "realists," who insist on the "autonomy of politics." [These "realists" are not to be confused with "legal realism."] For all their proclaimed hostility to legalism and moralism, these theorists share at least one important belief with traditional legal thought: that social experience must be neatly divided into distinct parcels. History is a matter of separate "spheres," each dedicated to some "factor": economic, legal, ethical, aesthetic, and political. Each of these has its own "laws" of operation and its own rationale. This is, moreover, not just the outcome of specialization in historical studies, of mere "tunnel" history. It is rather an ideology.[6] Its contemporary appeal derives entirely from that fact. The theory of the autonomy of politics is partly an answer to the economic interpretation of history and the ideology that inspired it, and partly a reaction against legalism in international affairs. As such, its essential ideas are very old. The new Machiavellism is a mere modernization of that peculiar manifestation of seventeenth-century rationalism, the idea of reason of state.[7] "State" has been replaced by "the national interest," but beyond that the structure of thought remains unaltered. Whatever the national interest may be, it is agreed that there are specific, rationally calculable techniques for promoting it. If the rules of this game are followed dispassionately, success is assured, just as surely as disaster will overcome those who do not follow the "laws" of politics. The greatest source of danger in this respect is ideology, which tends to becloud men's ability to assess the "objective" demands of politics correctly. The essence of ideology, moreover, is that it confuses politics with other realms of social activity. The "rules" of politics may never be confused with those of morality or those of law. What the "national interest" can be except an ideology is hard to say, but one thing is clear to realists—it must never be conceived in terms of "moral" or "legalistic" values. This was, for instance, the great sin of Woodrow Wilson, the *bête noire* of realism. To the extent that realism rejects legalism, which sees legal justice as the only way of settling international conflict, it is, of course, sensible enough. However, its animus against Wilson goes well beyond a rejection of international law as *the* sole means to preserve peace. It is, rather, a direct dislike of liberal ideology, largely because the latter failed. The urge to debunk thus becomes a psychological response to disenchantment, a tough sneer at all "cant." It is perhaps understandable, but it does not dispose of ideology as an ineradicable element of social life.

In order to preserve the "autonomy" of politics from hypocrisy, no less than from the practical dangers of ideology and, especially, legalistic morality, the "realists" have found it necessary to establish the "distinctive characteristics" of politics. How else to keep it clear of law and morality, if not by definition? The essential mark of politics is power. However, taken as a formal concept, power is meaningless. Unless it is placed within a specific historical situation it is completely unimaginable. The only occasion in which it can be said to appear in "pure" form, unconditioned by a host of circumstances, is in active combat. Here power means destroying an enemy physically or subordinating him to one's will by the threat of destruction. That is why the only perfectly clear definition of politics-as-power is that of Carl Schmitt. The "specific and self-evident distinguishing characteristic" of the "realm of politics," analogous to the distinctions of good and evil in morality and beautiful and ugly in aesthetics, he wrote, is "the distinction of friend and enemy." "The terms 'friend' and 'enemy' and 'struggle' obtain their real significance from their relation to the real possibility of physical killing," moreover. War need not always be a normal occurrence, but it "must subsist as a real possibility";[8] that is, politics is active or potential physical violence.

American realists today are, however, anything but fascists in the making. They are, in fact, despairing liberals all. They may long for a central, essential concept of politics, but not at the full price. They have therefore subdued the notion of power by extending it. Power is not just success in combat; rather, it is a universal human urge, the *libido dominandi*. Original sin is what this used to be called. The trouble here is that a universal human disposition can manifest itself in an unlimited number of ways and situations. It can appear in any conceivable human relationship. If this is what power is, then its usefulness as *the* concept defining politics is destroyed. What this shows is that the effort to classify politics fails, and fails in exactly the same way as the analogous definitions of law and morality. These contradictions of political realism are not, however, the main issue here. What does matter is that realism has served to fortify the most obdurate prejudices of political legalism, of the policy of justice.

The realistic picture of politics is, in fact, that of legalism gone sour. Realists have recognized the limitations of the policy of justice, but they have not re-examined its premises. They accept its "spheres" of social life and its view of politics. They continue to see only "politics-as-war" and may offer quasi-nationalistic schemes for coping with it, and they continue to abide by the notion that history is a matter of discrete "blocks." The block named politics is one in which power and its norms, the rules of prudence and expediency, operate. Law is the judicial order, morals the order of conscience. And disaster will hound the statesman who does not know which box is which.

What this brief review of the theory of "realistic politics" illustrates is that the formalism of juristic thought has taken root even among its professed opponents. The latter have simply applied the same type of arguments that legal theorists have used in separating law from morality to the task of preserving politics from both law and morality. The very real appeal of realism today, however, does not arise from its method. It is, rather, a deeply felt reaction against one aspect of legalism—its application to international relations. The theory of positive international law, especially as it has developed among positivist thinkers, is not only an ideological curiosity. Its influence on public opinion and policy has, at least until very recently, been quite considerable. This in itself explains the intensity of realist rancor. For the purposes of a theoretical understanding of modern legal theory, moreover, it cannot be overlooked. Nothing is more revealing of its ideological bearings.

No modern work on legal theory is complete without a chapter on international law. This is hardly surprising for natural law theorists, but it is, at first sight, puzzling in works of a positivist persuasion. For natural law thinking, international law poses no serious intellectual difficulties. Natural law theory is under no particular compulsion to prove that a *positive* international law in fact exists at any given time. All that one must believe is that there is a universal law of reason binding on all, which regulates the conduct of states as much as that of private persons. It is, as always, the same "take it or leave it" proposition. At various times, indeed, it has been the main function of natural law theory to promote rules of decency to govern the relations of states in war and peace. In the seventeenth century, especially, the great flowering of natural law theory was a response to the need for some trans-cultural and trans-religious rules. The former were badly needed to constrain the conquerors of the New World in their behavior toward the local population, which was neither European nor Christian. The latter were needed to bring some order to a Europe weary of religious war but as far as ever from religious unity. Natural law, it was hoped, might provide a common basis for conduct in both these instances, where men had to face each other simply as men, with no other common ties to bind them than the faith in a shared nature and rationality. From the point of view of natural law, the existence of rules binding upon statesmen in the conduct of international relations is self-evident. It poses no logical difficulties at all. To a very significant extent the hope for international order based on rules still rests on a belief in the validity, universality, and efficacy of the law of nature. The recent Papal Encyclical, "Pacem in Terris," is an eloquent testimony to that faith, and one shared by many who are not Roman Catholics.

The troubles of natural law in international relations are practical. They appear as soon as some political agent tries to enforce them in a specific case. This is especially true when natural law or laws are applied in the form of punitive judgments to those who do not share the belief in them. When, for example, the American prosecution at the Tokyo Trials appealed to the law of nature as a basis for condemning the accused, he was only applying a foreign ideology, serving his nation's interests, to a group of people who neither knew nor cared about this doctrine. The assumption of universal agreement served here merely to impose dogmatically an ethnocentric vision of international order. It was the claim that these universal rules were "there"—the assumption of general agreement, which was so contrary to the cultural realities of the situation—that made the application of natural law seem both arbitrary and hypocritical under these circumstances. It illustrated again the central ideological weakness of natural law in a world society that is even more complex and pluralistic than the great nation-states of our time.

If international rules are part and parcel of any theory of natural law, the same can hardly be said for a positivist philosophy of law. Given the immense care with which law is defined so as to exclude morals and to involve only a narrow range of municipal rules, it is odd indeed to find that, for purposes of international law, positivist theories, Kelsen's most of all, insist upon an all-embracing, extended definition which allows *positive* international law not only validity but a validity even higher on the normative scale than that of municipal law. The logical procedure, for a consistent positivist, is to follow Hobbes and Austin and to deny that international law is law "properly so called." Bentham, to be sure, had spoken in favor of an international law, but he, at least, had limited himself to advocating its establishment, rather than insisting upon its actual existence as a legal reality. Contemporary positivists have been less careful in keeping "ought" and "is" apart in this matter. The reasons for it are obvious enough. They lie in the ideological affinity between nineteenth-century liberalism and positivism. Peace through law is a cherished aspect of liberal ideology. Commercial relations would replace military ones, and law and commerce would go together internationally, as they do within the confines of domestic political society. For a positivist to apply a methodical analysis to this law, however, presupposes that it have at least some existence, that it be "there" in order to be analyzed in legal terms. The actuality of positive international law must, therefore, simply be posited, its validity simply assumed. This, indeed, is what happened. Moreover, the contempt for politics inherent in the policy of justice and in legalism has led to a theory of positive international law which regards the latter as not just "there," but as a veritable substitute for all other forms of international politics. That is why the modern theory of positive international law, the law of civilized nations, or, as it is now called, world law, is perhaps the most striking manifestation of legalistic ideology. Its ideological character is especially discernible because the principles of international law are not supported by effective institutions. As such, it is a program and little else. This has become increasingly evident because it is a declining ideology, challenged openly by rival ideologies. The result is that, in their views on international law, positivists are often close in their approach, though not in their vocabulary or premises, to natural law thinking. They are only less consistent. Ultimately it is the legalistic ethos that unites both theories in a common inability to adjust to the historical realities of the present age.

In the nineteenth century, to be sure, the claims for international law were often more extravagant than they are today. It was urged not only that international law was a means to peace, but that it was the only road to that end. All other forms of political action not only could be neglected; they were regarded as undesirable. To this very day Kelsen, the last to fully represent the nineteenth-century orthodoxy, still assures us that the only alternative to a legal approach is power politics among states.[9] By a legal approach he means governing the relations between states through judgments made by the International Court of Justice. If a world federal state is to be established, as he argues it must be eventually, the first step must be the setting up of an international judiciary. Without a tribunal to give objective, impartial decisions as to whether law has been violated, "any further progress on the way to the pacification of the world is excluded." [10] The legal approach to the reorganization of the world must precede all others, even the economic, because all our problems are due to war or fear of war, and only an international court with powers of compulsory jurisdiction can prevent war.[11] How the decisions of this tribunal are to be enforced in the absence of executive authorities is not clear. The assumption, in Kelsen's case, is that it will inevitably be set up.

In this respect the older views of Oppenheim are even more illuminating. For him international law did not just exist to regulate politics; its ultimate end was to replace politics altogether.[12] No writer maintained the legalist view of the opposition between adjudication and politics, law and violence, or law and compromise more rigorously. Law is indeed not only superior to politics; its "essence" is independent of it, a self-generating system in which principles are derived automatically from one another. It is here, usually, that the leap from history into formalism occurs, and here Kelsen has remained faithful to the old view. Though he is capable of recognizing that law is a political force, too, as when he claims that "the idea of law is stronger than other ideologies," he offers no more proof of this proposition than did Oppenheim.[13] The consideration that Nazism and Fascism prevailed in the very heart of the most legalistic culture throws enough doubt on this notion to make reference to unlegalistic, non-European societies unnecessary. In fact, however, Kelsen saves himself the trouble of historical reflection by retreating into formalism. "Law is its own creation," as rules generate rules, nationally and internationally.[14] There is a "basic norm," the customs of international society, which is "the law-creating fact" and which enjoins that "states should behave as they customarily behave."[15] From this all treaties, conventions, and the norm *pacta sunt servanda* are derived in a "dynamic" process of autogenesis. Not only do rules create each other, they create all political institutions. Law "creates a monopoly of force" within states, creates centralized authority there, and must be expected to create these internationally as well.[16] Indeed, it is a logical necessity. That is, of course, where the fallacy becomes evident, because the word "create" is simply being misused to becloud the issues. Rules *validate* other rules; they *create* them only in the sense of giving them their binding character as part of a legal system. Rules lend authority to other rules and in that sense create them—that is, give them their character as legal rules rather than mere advice. Validation, however, has nothing to do with historical creation. A higher rule justifies a lesser one, it does not generate it historically. Autogenesis as a purely formal term is simply transferred to the realm of historical genesis, to causality. Alas, rules do not cause other rules to be made or obeyed. Law does not by itself generate institutions, cause wars to end, or states to behave as they should. It does not create a community. Only the disingenuous misuse of the word "autogenesis," allowing as it does the confusion of the validation of rules with their historic causes, origins, and force, can permit anyone to believe that law will create world society through operative judicial tribunals.

The ideological backbone of these ideas can be readily found, in nineteenth-century liberalism, in its least convincing aspects. Its origins lie in the belief that state and society are not only separate entities, but that the former is a festering sore on the healthy body of the latter. It is a view that derived its validity from the identification of the state with the traditional military aristocracy and with monarchical absolutism. By the latter part of the last century only liberals of the Spencerian dispensation still expected that the state would disappear as the vital powers of society asserted themselves. Even they believed less in its likelihood than in its desirability. In any case, with the passing of monarchical and aristocratic domination the disappearance of the traditional state receded as a primary concern of liberalism, while it came to cope with the new political threats of democracy and socialism. Only in the realm of international relations was there no re-assessment. The reasons for this are not difficult to understand, because neither in theory nor in fact did the relations between states seem to have altered very noticeably. The concept of sovereignty, reinforced by nationalism, the fact that military and diplomatic office remained in the hands of the more aristocratic members of society and that even their non-aristocratic colleagues quickly absorbed their basic attitudes—all this combined to make Europe seem internationally much as it had always been. One could still hope that trade would replace war and that politics would be eliminated by law, because these hopes, no longer relevant to domestic politics, still found their justification in an unreformed international world. Here is one of the great examples of the creative interplay of ideology and counterideology. It was thus entirely possible for Oppenheim to identify war, expediency, and compromise as part of a traditional political world which would be replaced by an international community held together solely by the rule of law expressed in adjudication. He thus compared war to duelling, as something difficult but not impossible to outlaw gradually. The analogy is interesting because it shows how much war was identified in his mind with the remnants of the aristo-cratic ethos.[17]

For Oppenheim even that pinnacle of international legal enterprise, the Hague System, was only a first step, because it provided for a court of arbitration as well as for a strictly judicial tribunal. To set up *ad hoc* machinery for arbitral settlements was at most a first, and temporary, step in a sys-tem of strictly judicial settlements of legal disputes. Only a full court, on the model of domestic courts, would do, because arbitrations "have in view compromise, rather than a genuine settlement of law." In short, not only the politics of violence but the politics of bargaining and compromise must go—but not to be replaced by legislative or executive authority, which were also unnecessary. It would be a truly voluntary society, "agreeing" and not "decreeing" law. Such, too, was Judge Kellogg's view. The Permanent Court would put an end to "splitting the difference" in compromise agreements.[18] At the present time most world law theorists concede, regret-fully, that arbitral institutions and the generally less legalistic and flexible approach of the United Nations system must be accepted as an unavoidable concession to political necessity.[19] Arbitration is not downgraded as radically as it was by Oppenheim, significantly, because it at least preserves the core of legalism, a settlement by an impartial third party. When it comes to directly negotiated settlements, however, the tolerance of the orthodox comes to an end. Negotiations are not interested in justice but only in peace, they have none of the certainty that law gives, they drag on interminably and tend to give the stronger power an unmerited, "undue" advantage. Above all, where "force and dictation are out-lawed," adjudication is the only appropriate procedure.[20] In short, there is a limit to the amount of politics that law can endure. Indeed, even the most perceptive of all writers on

international law, Charles de Visscher, who has done more
than anyone to explain that international law is itself a
policy, depending for its success and failure on other political
developments and ideologies, cannot help speaking of "the
distorting action of politics on international law."[21] What
he means is that in a world of conflicting ideologies the idea
of law, of maintaining established expectations, has become
obsolete if not impossible.

The question, retrospectively, is whether it ever made any
sense. That this idea continues to win adherents is, however,
more than an anomaly. It is a serious political obstacle to any
concrete action in international politics, for the liberalism of
yesterday is the conservatism of today. The idea that all international problems will dissolve with the establishment of
an international court with compulsory jurisdiction is an
invitation to political indolence. It allows one to make no
alterations in domestic political action and thought, to change
no attitudes, to try no new approaches and yet appear to be
working for peace. No wonder that the leadership of that
citadel of American conservatism, the American Bar Association, has of late enthusiastically embraced the world law
movement.[22] Domestically this only requires repeal of the
Connally Amendment, and not on the grounds that this
would diminish American international freedom of action
in any way. On the contrary, it is explained (and quite rightly, as it happens) that without costing us anything in terms
of sovereignty or domestic policy, this move will bring us
prestige and an occasional award in a suit with smaller nations. For the rest, the world law movement demands only
international meetings of lawyers and support for scholarly
research.[23] The first object of research is to codify *existing*
legal rules. From then on it is hoped that study will reveal
the common core of all existing legal systems of the European
and non-European peoples, which will be codified into a

new world law. As is well known, codification is the stabilization of existing rules. As is equally well known in all political systems, research or the calling of commissions of inquiry is the most common substitute for action and decisions that might entail inconvenient changes of mind or habit. One is painfully reminded of the jibe of the early depression years, "Another commission is Hoovering over us." The program of the A.B.A. is little else. Seemingly so much more up-to-date and enlightened than the old isolationism, it is, in fact, only a respectable gloss for the old ideology. It is a substitute for foreign policy, for taking a stand on issues, for thinking about international relations. By concentrating on an aim that is unrealizable in the foreseeable future and that demands nothing in the way of political action beyond research and statements of principles, it gives the appearance of having a purpose without having one. Ultimately, moreover, this is as true of those who merely want to codify existing international law and promote the jurisdiction of the International Court of Justice as of those who propose extensive changes in the rules. Those who demand this, in the interest of underdeveloped nations, do so with the analogy of domestic legislation inspired by either Keynesian or more radically socialist economics. These radical steps, by no means entertained by the A.B.A. idea of world law, would, however, really alter nothing, for the changes affect only the rules, not the political realities that make such rules recommendations at best. As far as the A.B.A.'s type of world law is concerned, it is worth noting that it has so far said nothing in favor of American action on the Convention on Human Rights. It is not that such conventions can do much, but the silence of the A.B.A. is significant in demonstrating the quality of its passion for world law. It is, like all noncontroversial legalistic politics, essentially verbal. In reality it is, as legalism must be, a defense of the *status quo*.

What gives this "crusade," now as ever, its plausibility is the idea that law is "there," ready to be found. Custom, usage, conventions, and treaties provide a complete system of law, analogous to municipal law. Formally, lawmaking is the same in both cases, a matter of autogenesis. Both are gapless wholes since, logically, once there is a tribunal it can always derive a rule from another more general one, and, in any case, what is not forbidden is permitted, in law. The law is, then, formally there. In principle, this means that international law is, formally if not in content, identical with municipal law.[24] Indeed, "from a formal standpoint we have attained a universal legal order with surprising ease."[25] It only remains, it is said in an aside, to create the political reality to fill the form. This, however, is no great problem. The main thing, in the words of Kelsen's spiritual heir, H. L. A. Hart, is that it is not "fundamentally impossible" to oblige states by rules of law—in a formal way only, of course.[26] This formal perfection of international law as a legal system serves as a proof of its "reality." It thus appears to answer the common objection that states are, after all, not individuals, and that perhaps it is not convincing to treat their disputes as simple *lites inter partes* under municipal law. Legalism, however, as an ideology consists essentially of an effort to see all situations of conflict in terms of this classical image of a lawsuit. The age of absolutism, when classical international law was born, gave this image some basis in historical reality. The quarrels of monarchs were quarrels between individuals over marriages and real estate. Today no one can honestly pretend that the state is anything but an aggregate of institutions and not an individual. Some writers find it possible to shrug this circumstance off by saying that domestic law also deals with groups—to which one might reply that courts often do this badly, precisely because they insist on treating them as individual parties. Moreover, the nation-state is not limited like other groups. Whatever distinguishes the nation-state, however, from other groups is said, in the words of Scelle, to be merely an "historical-political accident" which is of no legal significance.[27] As long as aggregates can formally be treated as individuals, their historical and political character does not matter. What matters is the formal, conceptual possibility. It matters because without it the faith in the primacy of legal justice, as the sole road to peace, cannot endure. In the eyes of a skeptical observer, however, the enumeration of "the specific characteristics of law" to cover, formally, both munipical and international law, provides only "material for pleasing prodigies of juristic reasoning" as they divert attention from the actualities, which are "dismissed as irrelevant to legal science."[28] To accept that, however, would force one to de Visscher's sad admission that the international community is only a "potential order in the minds of men."[29] That would mean recognizing international law as an ideology and not as an established fact—a recognition that no ideology, by definition, can yield.

To supply formalism with some basis in historical reality requires something more than the juggling of the word "autogenesis" in order to make validation appear equivalent to legislation. This need is filled by a theory of history. For legalism, like all ideologies, has such a theory. Simply stated, this is the belief that law has an integral history of its own, that it follows a definite pattern of evolution, and, above all, that its laws of growth can be understood without reference to the history of the societies in which law exists. After all, it is law that "creates" communities and states. In its most sensible version the integral history of law is really the history of the legal profession, which in view of its long and identifiable existence in European history can be a fit subject of sociological and intellectual history. That was certainly a part of Savigny's concept of historical jurisprudence, and it was the entire substance of Max Weber's.[30] However, in Savigny's, in Sir Henry Maine's, in Sir Paul Vinogradoff's, and, since then, in Roscoe Pound's writings, there is to be found a far less convincing theory. It is the outcome of seeing law as "there," as a whole—even if, as all historical and sociological jurisprudence admits, a changing, evolving whole. Sociology and history are here integrated into legal conceptions. After a quick look at general historical "influences" on law, general political history is conveniently bracketed, and the development of legal principles and the work of courts are presented quite autonomously.[31] It is not a matter of seeing law as part of the history of society; rather, history and sociology are absorbed by the closed world of law to give it *its* history as it already had *its* logic. This integral history of law is not, moreover, just a matter of "tunnel" history, that awful child of specialization. It is ideological history in the service of legalism, especially in its excursion into the international world; for it is only the belief that law has its *own* history, that follows its *own* stages of growth, which makes it possible to speak of international law as "primitive law."

The formalists, in theory so hostile to all historical jurisprudence, are in fact happy enough to borrow its central conception when it suits their purposes. In the present cases, it is very necessary to prove that international law exists in the absence of a community and of legislative or enforcing agencies. International law is, we are told, merely in a primitive stage of development where self-help prevails, as in the remote past of Europe.[32] Alternatively it is said to be in a period of "transition" common to all legal systems in times of rapid change.[33] Others see it as comparable to the earliest stages of the common law in England.[34] Even those who recognize the awkward fact that what made primitive law primitive was its being part of a primitive society merely think it "paradoxical" that international law should remain primitive in a world where everything else is highly civilized.[35] The point of insisting on the primitive character of international law is, of course, that its development through the other set stages of legal history is then inevitable. Law having its own laws of growth, primitive law is bound to grow into mature law, moving step by step to its predetermined end in a predetermined pattern of progress. The faith in progress as a law of history is, indeed, the last of the many fatal contributions of liberalism to legalistic ideology. Given this hope, the only task ahead is that of legal craftsmanship— the formal perfection of the rules.[36] In vain is the warning that "the lawyer's craft can never supply the wanting social and political basis for an effective legal system."[37] The inevitable requires only that we adjust our minds to it. It does not demand political decision or action. That may be left to history, a history in which principles will replace men.

The intellectual fantasy which has been pictured so far refers only to general international or world law, which sees the replacement of politics by law as the solution to all the problems of international conflict. It has, obviously, nothing to do with particular international law or with those international rules which all nations find it easy to accept, since they do not concern subjects under dispute. The regulation of postal communications is the obvious example of the latter. The various institutions, adjudicative and administrative, set up under various multi-lateral, intra-European treaties are examples of the former. These, however, have grown up without benefit of much ideology. They do not make eternal peace their aim and, indeed, may not contribute to it.[38] This has been the ambition only of general international law and its offspring, the Hague System, the League of Nations, and the United Nations. Indeed, as far as judicialization is concerned, the United Nations has not followed in the ideologi-

cal footsteps of its predecessors. In recognizing that the public
and publicized nature of judicial ways of arbitrating disputes
only hardens the bellicose arteries of the contestants, it has
preferred secret mediation efforts. Its meager triumphs have
been in "not quite pacific settlement and pacific non-settle-
ment." If it has "forfeited justice to order," no one need
complain so long as it has brought order. The legalistic approach to peace yielded only principles and rules, not security
of expectations among states, nor a legal community. If the
U.N. is to be more successful, it will not be by following that
path, but by treating each conflict as unique.[39] This in itself
constitutes part of a general decline of legalistic ideology in
international affairs. The non-European nations often regard
international law as guarantor of the *status quo,* as indeed
all law is. For them that means that it is essentially a relic
of the colonial age. In this feeling they are joined by many
repentant Westerners who, however, see this as a defect in
the present rules of international law, rather than as an inherent weakness of the basic formal structure, or principles,
of international law in general.[40] Even if the representatives
of some of those nations that have no legalistic native traditions should come to view international law with as much,
or as little, favor as their European opposite numbers, there
remains the ideological rejection of international law by the
communist world. Here again it is not a matter of rejecting
all principles of legality in international life. There is said
to be a law of socialist states. It is, however, a radical rejection
of all traditional international law. This, moreover, is not
just due to the general Soviet belief that all law is subordinate
to the political and ideological ends of states rather than
above them, as traditional legalism claims.[41] It is a far more
serious matter than that. As long as communism has any
pretensions to being a world revolutionary movement, it cannot possibly accept as binding rules that aim at preserving the

established order among states and their governments. Even if legalistic values—"socialist legality"—come to play a greater part in East European domestic government, it is ideologically impossible for communists to accept obligations imposed by an international system which they are dedicated to overthrowing.

The ex-colonial and Soviet statesmen are not alone in their lack of interest in international law. There is a considerable body of public opinion in liberal constitutional states that has lost its enthusiasm for international law as the road to peace. Moreover, it is not only nationalists, chauvinists, and political "realists" who have come to reject international law, although its orthodox adherents invariably claim that super-patriotism is its sole ideological opponent.[42] In fact, however, since the 1920's there has flourished in Scandinavia a school of "realists" who, although thoroughly democratic and devoted to international peace, have relentlessly attacked the influence of international law thinking on international relations.[43] One may guess that, partly as a result of their neutrality in the First World War, they came to reject the Versailles Treaty, and the punitive policy which it covered with legalistic justifications, sooner than most observers. Partly, their early experience with the legal controversies that inevitably attend the establishment of a welfare state may have given them an insight into the limitations of the policy of justice when it collides with other social ends. In any case, for some forty-odd years there has been a responsible body of legal opinion that regards international law as a dangerous superstition and its main advocates, Oppenheim, Kelsen, and Scelle, as mischievous hypocrites who have nothing to contribute to a lasting peace. The substance of these objections to international law was that, in its treatment of states as individuals who were the subjects of rights and duties under law, it exacerbated rather than lessened conflict. It tended to make the "righteous" state feel its "due" was a matter of justice, and so prevented all possible compromise. It led victors, such as those at Versailles, to exact compensations analogous to damages suitably awarded in a private lawsuit, and to feel perfectly justified in inflicting suffering on the defeated population in the name of justice, of dueness. The result of this spurious use of false analogies could not be peace. While this criticism was as correct in its prognosis as it was in its diagnosis of the intellectual flaws of international legal theory, it was inadequate in calling such theory merely hypocrisy. Ideology is rarely a mere matter of lying. If it has that function in actual political combat, it is not such a simple matter for its proponents. The great authorities on international law, who have held it up as the road to peace, were not hypocrites. They have never had either the motives or the character for that. It is not true, or even relevant, that statesmen such as Woodrow Wilson were hypocrites because the results of their policies and their announced ends and ideals failed to correspond. Ideology is a way of understanding the world, whatever may come of it. It is, in this case, a matter of projecting, with perfect candor, legalism onto the world scene. Just as domestic politics is seen in terms of legalistic categories, so is the international world.

The problem, therefore, is not hypocrisy, nor even just international law as such, but legalism as a whole, as a comprehensive view of man and society. As a part of the liberal ethos legalism has only proved itself a liability, preventing liberalism from facing up to the realities of contemporary politics. Liberalism, in turn, has often prevented legal thinkers from arriving at a clear view of the limitations of legal government. Not that the two are inseparable by any means; on the contrary, legalism is apt to be conservative. It is liberal theory that needs to free itself from the illusions of "the rule of law" ideologists. As for legal philosophy, both natural law and positivism, its main task is surely to recognize the narrowness of its outlook and its remoteness from the political realities of the present century. The first step is to acknowledge that law is a form of political action, among others, which occasionally is applicable and effective and often is not. It is not an answer to politics, neither is it isolated from political purposes and struggles. Above all, it is not something that is "there" or "not there." Rather, like any form of political belief and behavior it is a matter of degrees, of more or less, and of nuances.

There is no situation in which these ideological habits of legalism are more openly confronted by competing policies than in the course of political trials. Both in accepting and rejecting political trials legalism strives valiantly to distinguish itself from "mere" politics, even such politics as might well serve the future development of legal institutions and values. That is why an examination of both what was said about, and said in the course of, political trials and, also, of what *might* have been said more suitably, must form an integral part of a full view of law as a part of politics.

### POLITICAL TRIALS: POLITICS WHAT?

Anyone who asserts that justice is a policy and that the judicial process is not the antithesis of politics, but just one form of political action among others, must expect to meet certain outraged accusations. The most usual of these is the charge of "Vishinskyism." [44] Someone is sure to say: "If you claim that law is but a type of politics, that it serves political ends, are you not suggesting that law is merely the instrument of the ruling class, to be used by it as it sees fit to promote its own interests?" The answer, of course, is that there is politics and politics. No class theory of politics is implied by the notion of law as a political instrument. Indeed, since the political function of law becomes particularly apparent in the pluralistic and constitutional political order of America, where class domination is relevant neither in theory nor in practice, it is clear that the ideology of ruling classes and the recognition of the law as politics are entirely separate and unrelated notions. The Vishinskyan theory acquires its concrete meaning only when one remembers that it refers to the role of law in a totalitarian system, where it is used as a relatively insignificant means of promoting a single ideology and of maintaining the power of an unchallengeable ruling class. Precisely because legalism has little to contribute to an ideology of permanent revolution, law as an institution can play only a minor part in a political world where terror and propaganda predominate as instruments of social control. It is when one analyzes the ideologies and regimes which are incompatible with legalism that one recognizes the extent to which law is both the expression of and participant in another sort of politics. The question, in short, is not, "Is law political?" but "What sort of politics can law maintain and reflect?" Law as a political instrument can play its most significant part in societies in which open group conflicts are accepted and which are sufficiently stable to be able to absorb and settle them in terms of rules. As an instrument of terror, of coercive persuasion, and of revolutionary re-education, it is all but useless. A trial, the supreme legalistic act, like all political acts, does not take place in a vacuum. It is part of a whole complex of other institutions, habits, and beliefs. A trial within a constitutional government is not like a trial in a state of near-anarchy, or in a totalitarian order. Law, in short, is politics, but not every form of politics is legalistic.

There is another argument, however, that is likely to come from a liberal critic, which raises more serious issues than the indiscriminate cry of "Vishinskyism." How is one to distinguish that abomination, the political trial, from due process of law, if all legal decisions are said to express political values —are policy decisions in individual instances, rather than direct emanations from the law? Must one not stick to rigid distinctions between law and politics if one is to isolate and condemn the political abuse of the judicial process and, indeed, of the very spirit of the law? The answer again must be that there is politics and politics. It is the politics of persecution which political trials serve that is the real horror, not the fact that courts are used to give it effect. There are occasions when political trials may actually serve liberal ends, where they promote legalistic values in such a way as to contribute to constitutional politics and to a decent legal system. The Trial of the Major War Criminals by the International Military Tribunal at Nuremberg probably had that effect. To be sure, within a stable constitutional order political trials may be a disgrace, a reversion to the politics of repression, but it is not the political trial itself but the situation in which it takes place and the ends that it serves which matter. It is the quality of the politics pursued in them that distinguishes one political trial from another.

General jurisprudence is, quite naturally, concerned with the characteristics of "normal legal procedures." This, as well as the ideological propensities of modern legal philosophy, makes this theory quite irrelevant to such a marginal area of judicial life as the political trial. Nevertheless, just because political trials fall outside the range of easy legalistic generalizations, they often bring some of the most important theoretical issues to the surface. A review of some of these thus offers, not a practical illustration of the difficulties raised by such general legal theories as analytical positivism and natural law, but an additional set of conceptual perplexities created by legalism as an approach to politics. It does so precisely because it is here that the legalistic view of politics is most clearly challenged by other political objectives and convictions.

The main difficulty in pursuing the policy of justice is not that it has nothing to contribute politically. To the extent that it may reinforce legalistic values it is often very constructive, as it was at Nuremberg. That is, however, not the way in which its adherents conceive of their ends. In its exclusiveness, justice as a policy tends to ignore all other political ends and the very social circumstances which condition its effect and even its possibility. Formal justice depends for its social impact upon the total political environment in which juridical actions occur, and its functions cannot be understood in isolation. Yet isolation from politics is its first ideological demand. For example, the principle of legality in criminal law is certainly a primary value of legalism—perhaps its greatest contribution to a decent political order. It cannot, however, in and of itself create such an order or even maintain it. It enforces persecuting laws as readily as any other kind. Formal justice can, moreover, render such laws respectable in the eyes of liberals anxious to avoid conflict. "He had his day in court; he was not *really* persecuted," they can argue, and congratulate themselves on the procedural perfection of formal justice. In such circumstances legalism offers a destructive temptation to liberalism. On the international level of politics a single-minded pursuit of a policy of criminal justice has even graver defects. Since, for justice, law must either be "there" or "not there," it becomes necessary to pretend that a legal system analogous to a well-established domestic order exists. In the case of three of the architects of Nuremberg that meant a system such as prevails in constitutional democracies. That was the first fiction. It led to others, and to a greater concentration on charges which could be squeezed into the mold of municipal law (such as waging aggressive war) than on novel but politically more important charges, like crimes against humanity. An effort, ultimately not successful, to revive the law of conspiracy was made, because a legal peg analogous to a domestic law seemed necessary in order to deal with the Nazi movement as a whole. History had to be tortured throughout in order to reduce events to proportions similar to those of a model criminal trial within a municipal system. The future was not altogether ignored, but it was seen, characteristically, as the future of law only. The contribution of the Trial was to be made to the future of international criminal law. It was to be an act within a legal system enhancing the strength of that system. To think of either the immediate political needs or the ideological impact of the Trial on Germany would have been to descend to mere politics. Nevertheless, it was these and these alone that justified the Trial. The possibility that in an ideological vacuum the Trial might strengthen the very values upon which legal systems and the principle of legality depend was not one that the lawyers who conducted the Trial were willing to discuss. What would domestically, in Britain or the United States, have been a dilution of legalistic values, however, was in a totally different social situation a positive ideological contribution to legalism. It was a legalistic way of coping with violence, vengeance, disorder, and even the future of German politics. To measure it in terms of law and non-law was only the ideological necessity of a rigid policy of justice blind to the actualities surrounding it. As such the Trial was a tribute both to the intellectual limitations of legalism as an ideology and to the real political value which legalism has in practice, even if it refuses to recognize this clearly.

If one thinks in terms of legalistic politics rather than of law and non-law, one can also recognize that there are trials to which legalistic standards are totally inapplicable because none of those participating in them have the slightest use for legalism. This was certainly the case in the Moscow Trials and their subsequent counterparts, as well as in the various Nazi and Soviet "people's courts." What occurs in the course of these proceedings has nothing to do with justice. Their end is elimination, terror, propaganda, and re-education. In terms of these ends they may or may not be effective. They are part of regimes that have already abandoned justice as a policy, and our judgment of these courts must depend on our view of the ends they serve, not of their "betrayal" of justice, since the ideologies which inspire them are profoundly unlegalistic and indeed hostile to the whole policy of justice. From a liberal point of view it is the repressive character of these regimes that matters; from a legalistic view it is their rejection of legal justice. In either case it is not the trials particularly, but the entire structure of such governments, that is objectionable. To study the judicial performance of such regimes without reference to the ideological and political system of which they are a very minor part makes even less sense than it does in constitutional regimes. In the latter, legalism and juridical institutions form at the very least an important, indeed a primary, ideological and institutional aspect of political life as a whole. Yet the analytical equipment of the legal mind, accustomed to working within a system of positive law, induces lawyers to think of law as "there" or "not there" at all times and in all places, rather than in terms of degrees of legalism in the politics of complex social orders. The natural law theorist should, ideally, be equipped to deal with legalism in nonlegalistic political environments, but in fact he is not. Having uttered his denunciations he has fulfilled his ideological function. In any case the historically minded student of legal phenomena has received no help from traditional theory. That is why a review of political trials from an historian's point of view may prove illuminating in showing some of the limitations of legalism both as a policy and as a method of evaluating political action. Legal theory is not only to be found in the books of academically inclined lawyers. It is also reflected in the course of judicial proceedings, especially in the unconventional cases, such as the significant Supreme Court decisions or great political trials. These, to be sure, are exceptional events, but that is precisely why they evoke more conscious and articulate theoretical reflections from those who participate in them. A critique of contemporary legal theory would therefore be incomplete if it were limited to academic jurisprudence. Many of the deficiencies of legalism that emerge there can be observed in the course of the great trials also.

What, after all, is a political trial?[45] It is a trial in which the prosecuting party, usually the regime in power aided by a cooperative judiciary, tries to eliminate its political enemies. It pursues a very specific policy—the destruction, or at least the disgrace and disrepute, of a political opponent. To regard this as the essence of politics one would have to accept Carl Schmitt's friend-enemy definition in its crudest form. In fact, however, there are political societies in which political persecution and political trials are rare and constitute an insignificant part of politics. So the political trial can hardly be said to reflect the essence of politics. There is more to politics than that. Secondly, one ought not to exaggerate the importance of political trials, for all their spectacular fascination, in societies where the politics of persecution does prevail. These trials amount to no more than the "frosting on the cake" of perpetual purges.[46] What distinguishes most, though not all, political trials is that they scorn the principle of legality, which, ideally, renders criminal law just. To some degree most political trials follow Goebbels' famous dictum that trials should not begin with the idea of law, but with the idea that this man must go.[47] The judge will be subservient to the prosecution, the evidence false, the accused bullied, the witnesses perjured, and rules of law and procedure ignored. This is, as it were, the classical model of a political trial, whether for constructive treason or ideological deviation. It is, at least in theory, perfectly possible to have trials for political offenses which do not resemble this model but which are ordinary criminal trials. It is not true that all trials for treason or espionage are political in the sense of being simple persecutions dressed in judicial robes. Nevertheless, the sound instinct of the Founding Fathers in defining treason very restrictively in the Constitution was based on the knowledge that in practice opposition and treason will not always be delicately distinguished.[48] No less a consideration is the difficulty of maintaining judicial calm when the deepest political passions have been aroused.

In an age of ideological warfare it is inevitable both that political persecution will occur and that political trials of varying degrees of fairness will follow. Nostalgia is, however, out of place on this score. Political trials have been endemic in our civilization. The intellectual history of Europe opens with the trial of Socrates, and we have been trying real and fancied traitors and subversives ever since. There never was a golden age in which governments refused to persecute anyone, though there once was a hope that we would reach that end. It is not a hope one can entertain today. On the contrary, we have come to a point where we may be grateful for the possibility of giving the persecuted at least the benefit of a fair trial; for we live in a world where many acts will be punished without trial, and where there will be convictions for acts never contemplated or performed. Yet it is also true that the inner procedural fairness of some political trials can lull us into forgetting the main issue: Should there be any trials that aim at the elimination of the politically obnoxious? Does the legalistic method justify the policy? These questions are by no means capable of general answers. It is sometimes even true that persecution by nonjudicial devices can be justified. Thus impeachments (even if they were common) could be judicial processes, but they are left to legislatures. A trial for "attitude crimes" committed during the German Occupation was something no self-respecting court would handle in the Netherlands, but somewhat less formal bodies did—again, perhaps, justifiably.[49] For the liberal, troubled by political trials, there are always two questions. Is a policy of persecution being pursued in these trials, even the fair ones, which endangers freedom? Secondly, is the trial a fair one, and hence a contribution to the legalistic ethos, assuming that the object of prosecution is a justifiable one? Ultimately it is the political results that count. For a liberal the fairness of a trial is part of the end, to the degree that legalism is an aspect of liberal politics in constitutional regimes. The fundamental value, however, must always remain the prospect of a tolerant society.

### THE SPIRIT OF POLITICAL JUDGMENT

Since mankind's talent for mischief is known to be infinite, calling forth all the inventive ingenuity of the race, there are as many kinds of political trials as there are persecutors. To set forth a complete classification of types of political trials is therefore hardly possible. Like all political actions each one is to some degree unique. Only a very general view of common sorts of trials for political crimes can, therefore, be offered. What kind of criminal justice is involved here, first of all? Clearly justice in criminal law does not mean the same thing as in private law. Who can be said to be getting his due? Unless one believes in an injured deity or in unavenged ancestors who demand their due by way of retribution, no one can be said to get anything due him. The community may be protected; that is a general result, one hopes, of criminal law, but it has nothing to do with getting one's due in a specific case. The criminal may be said to be getting his due in that "he has it coming to him"—so much and no more. This means that he is being tried for an act which the law has declared to be a crime when performed under specified circumstances, and that he is shown by a court to have, in fact, committed the crime. The principle of legality—that there shall be no crime without law, and no punishment without a crime—*is* criminal justice. In limiting both crime and punishment by a system of rules, this policy aims at protecting individuals against arbitrary governmental action. As such it is a very negative notion of justice, though one of infinite value. Only if one is prepared to abandon legalistic values, replacing the idea of criminality by that of disease, and punishment by medical cure and "re-education," can this justice, the principle of legality, be ignored on moral grounds.[50] Political trials are not defensible on such grounds. They simply tend to circumvent the demands of legality.

What the principle of legality demands is a law and also an act made criminal by law. In political cases either one or the other or both may be lacking, as often as not. Most often the act is missing; since persecution aims at preventing future dangers, either criminal acts will be falsely charged, or legally innocent acts will be misinterpreted so as to seem criminal. There are thus three possibilities. The judge may be totally hostile to the accused, and evidence presented by perjured witnesses may be used, which will result in a purposive miscarriage of legal justice. This may be done in accordance with the wishes of a regime, or simply on the initiative of an individual judge. The former is, of course, far more frequent. In either case the law declaring an act to be criminal is not affected; it is the acts of the accused that are willfully misinterpreted or invented. In the age of absolutism, there was at least an effort made, by hook or by crook, to prove that the accused *had* done something in the past. In the age of ideology, "historical responsibility" suffices—that is, not past actions, but future, potential, as yet uncontemplated acts can be used as a basis for imputing present criminality. The first possibility, then, is that there is law, but no criminal act. The second possibility is that there is no law which designates the actual acts performed as criminal. Laws may be invented on the spot or drawn by analogy. Rules may be so vague (or judicial interpretation makes them so vague) that virtually any public action can be construed to appear criminal. That is the story of "constructive treason." The last and third possibility is that there are both law and action. This is the case when espionage or treason statutes, restrictive in scope and interpretation, are applied in the normal course of criminal adjudication. It may also be the case with sedition laws of a more expansive but not really vague sort, objectionable as these may be. In short, there are in the usual course of affairs three sorts of political trials. Either law is lacking, or an act is lacking, or both are present in a trial that comes very close to an ordinary criminal trial, even though elimination of a specific sort of political enemy is the aim.

There is, however, a very rare situation in which there is no law, no government, no political order, and people have committed acts so profoundly shocking that something must be done about them. That was the setting of the Nuremberg Trial of the Major War Criminals. Here there was indeed no law, but there was a surfeit of action. However, what tends to distinguish all political trials, even those most similar to ordinary criminal cases, is the difficulty of blending them into a continuous process by which one case can be more or less assimilated into a pattern of similar cases. The sense of regularity which comes from merely adding one decision to a host of apparently identical ones cannot be maintained, for what can be ignored in cases of murder and theft is unavoidably clear in political crimes. Each one is unique, because political interests, actions, and circumstances, and especially attitudes toward them, change more rapidly and are subject to far

greater conflicts of opinion than are cases involving acts that
are and have almost always been regarded with fear and outrage, such as private murder. Only treason, of all political
crimes, comes close to being an ordinary crime in these respects, and even that may soon cease to be true. In any event,
the articulation of political opinion, of opposition, the character
of the persecutor no less than of the persecuted, and the way
each "looks" to different segments of the population vary
almost from case to case, and certainly from decade to decade.
As a result, even formally just political trials will rarely seem
so. That does not mean that these sporadic judicial actions are
indefensible, as the Nuremberg Trial of the Major War
Criminals may show. [Hereafter this will be called the Nuremberg Trial for the sake of brevity, but only in referring to the
I.M.T. trial, not to subsequent American-sponsored trials at
Nuremberg.]

Precisely because at least part of the Nuremberg Trial can be
defended on political grounds, and even in terms of legalistic
political values, though not of legalistic ideology as a whole,
it serves to illuminate many of the deepest perplexities presented by all political trials today. Since the issues raised were
faced with greater intellectual clarity at this, the first of the
postwar international trials, and at its counterpart in Tokyo
than at any of the subsequent trials of minor figures, there
seems to be no reason for considering the latter. They did not
produce anything of political interest comparable to the discussions that occurred in the course of writing the Charter.
Their main value lies in the historical facts about Nazi government which they brought to light, not in any theoretical issues
that were involved. The only important question they raised
was whether more simple administrative purges would have
been politically more effective than trials in dealing with some
of the lesser figures of the Nazi regime. As for the Eichmann
case it, too, does not really create new problems for legal

theory. Eichmann, alas, was always a Jewish problem. Once he landed in Jerusalem his trial became an issue of Jewish politics and interests, both in Israel and in other Jewish communities. From the nonlegalistic political point of view one must judge the trial in terms of its political value or, rather, values as they appear to the various, conflicting groups of Jews. To one who admires President Ben-Gurion's policies, clearly the trial was an asset. To those who have a different vision of Jewish political life, it may not appear so. It must, however, be treated in terms of the totality of political possibilities, not as a simple question of its adherence to "law" or "non-law," though this, of necessity, was the position of all the lawyers in Jerusalem, as it was of those in Nuremberg. The theoretical problems being the same, however, there is no need to consider any international criminal trial other than the first and most generally interesting ones that immediately followed the Second World War.

The Nuremberg Trial of 1945 was not remarkable only because it was something entirely new in the history of international law. It was a great drama in which the most fundamental moral and political values were the real personae. Emotionally and philosophically it confronted every thoughtful individual with the necessity of making some clear decisions about his beliefs. For persons of liberal convictions and a strong commitment to legalistic politics it was a genuine moral crisis. How many were really sorry to see the Nazi leaders punished? Not many. Was it just a matter of uncontrollable revenge? Or was it also true that this Trial, unlike many subsequent Occupation trials, did serve a politically justifiable end in a fitting manner? The argument suggested here is that as far as the Trial concerned itself with crimes against humanity it was both necessary and wise. It cannot be claimed that this was a trial comparable to those held under more stable systems of law. It was, rather, a legalistic means of eliminating the Nazi leaders in such a way that their contemporaries, on whom the immediate future of Germany depended, might learn exactly what had occurred in recent history. Precisely because of the traditional legalism of Germany's professional and bureaucratic classes, evidence presented in this way, and judgment delivered upon such deliberations as the Trial offered, could be effective. There is a great deal of reason to suppose that the Trial did in fact reinforce the dormant legal consciousness of these classes, which is more than can be said on behalf of its grandiose claims to revolutionize international law, or of the various schemes for the re-education and democratization of Germany. The main point here is to show that it is practically of great importance to see legalism as a matter of degree, to recognize that there are lawlike political institutions and legalistic politics which are not just "illegal," but rather form a continuum consisting of degrees of legalism. To do this one must step outside the haven of traditional legal theory and ideology to see what legalism as a policy can and does do where there is no legal system to be dissected. Just as mere analysis has nothing to say about the political functions of trials within legal systems, so it can only shrug off a trial in which the validating of legal norms in terms of other legal norms is futile. Yet this may well be the occasion of a genuine triumph for legalism as a social policy.

In fact, neither natural law nor analytical positivism had much to offer in dealing with these actualities. Natural law thinking played no part at Nuremberg, where every effort was made to build on the fiction of a positive international law envisaged as analogous in its formal structure to the legalistic image of municipal law in matured systems. At Tokyo natural law was, indeed, introduced, with very unfortunate results. It produced a notable outburst from at least one Asian member of the Tribunal, who did not hesitate to reveal the cultural narrowness, ethical dogmatism, and historical emptiness of the ideology of agreement. Both Trials are therefore perfect illustrations of not only the theoretical and historical limitations of these theories, but also of their political disadvantages in a world too diverse and untidy to fit their neat categories of thought.

That there was no political system resembling that of nation-states within which judicial institutions exist was clear enough. The Nuremberg Trial took place in a social vacuum. There was and is no system of international criminal law, just as there are no international community and no international political institutions to formulate or regularly enforce criminal laws. The U.N. was not even a going concern at that time, and its existence since then has not contributed anything to creating those social conditions on which criminal law must rest to be effective. For a lawyer this circumstance creates a great difficulty, given his tendency to think in either-or terms of law or non-law. If the principle of legality, the existence of prior law, alone can justify a criminal trial, then the Trial was simply unjust. In order to evade that conclusion some lawyers either invented law on the basis of analogies drawn from their vision of municipal legal systems, or pretended that an international law in the form of custom or accepted usage did exist. The opponents of the Trials had little difficulty in exposing the feebleness of such rationalizations, nor were these necessary except as exercises in legalistic ideology. It is hopeless to try and squeeze this Trial into the pattern of trials held under a continuous, regular system of adjudication and law enforcement. However, as political trials go, it had an advantage that many a domestic political trial lacks. At least the accused were not being eliminated on vague or false charges. Here the facts were not fabricated as in the Moscow Trials, nor were beliefs and future acts at stake, as in the *Dennis* case. Nothing was being imputed to the accused. There was no room for speculation about mental states or potential future behavior. The Trial was a trial of past acts, concrete beyond the slightest doubt. Moreover, it was the charge, for which there was not even a pseudo-legal basis—that of crimes against humanity—which concerned itself most with past acts, and with acts that made the Trial both politically necessary and inevitable.

The Trial fulfilled an immediate function which is both the most ancient and the most compelling purpose of all criminal justice. It replaced private, uncontrolled vengeance with a measured process of fixing guilt in each case, and taking the power to punish out of the hands of those directly injured. This alone would suffice to show its enormous social value as an expression of legalistic politics on an occasion when it was most needed. When one remembers the setting in which the Trial took place, it is clear that these men had to be punished. The only consequence of officially doing nothing would have been to invite a perfect blood bath, with all its dynamic possibilities for anarchy and conflict on an already disoriented continent.[51] One need only recall that fears of lynch justice at its worst persuaded so responsible a government-in-exile as that of the Dutch to authorize mass arrests in order to avoid worse excesses. The strains were even greater in those places where the struggle between resisters and collaborators was part of a conflict between Right and Left, and where no government in exile, enjoying the loyal support of the vast majority of citizens, existed. One emphasizes the case of the Netherlands because there, unlike France and Belgium, for example, the optimum conditions for a resumption of constitutional democracy existed. Even there it meant vengeance, and on a vast scale too. The political function of criminal law is here shown to be clearly not just a matter of protecting society against its deviant members, but of protecting all the members of society against themselves, against the corrosive effects of their own passion for vengeance. To be sure, vengeance is not a moral virtue. It does not follow that its existence ought to be ignored because it is unworthy of official recognition. A criminal trial need not just be a giving way to vengeance; it is a containment of it. Without a trial, vengeance would have satisfied itself, with all the political dangers involved, especially as it became a violent part of the struggle between Right and Left. There were, indeed, many who did demand "good, clean vengeance" instead of trials. To those whom the resistance had made into professional revolutionaries, who after defeat and occupation had come to reject the entire political order of the past because it had failed them in the face of Nazism, a legalistic process of punishment seemed arid and false. What they wanted was direct action against collaborators, no less than against the Nazi leaders.[52] The political advantages of a trial that replaces the anarchic cycle of vengeance need hardly be belabored; they have been well known since the days of Aeschylus.

If the only alternatives had been a trial or uninhibited redress by the injured, nothing more need be said in favor of a trial. These two were not, however, the only possibilities. The British in 1945 felt that a political solution, that is, a quick military trial or mere military shooting of the major Nazi figures, might be best.[53] This, they argued, would satisfy the demand for vengeance without debasing the ideal of legality. A spectacular trial would look like a "put-up job," something traditionally unpalatable to British public opinion. A trial which was not part of a legal system, and thus remote from domestic principles of legal justice would, it was feared, defile the whole concept of law. However, the American argument that to eliminate these Nazis without a trial and without producing the evidence of their action would have a worse effect upon the future of law and order in Europe, and especially in Germany, prevailed. Inasmuch as Americans foresaw the Trials as a great contribution to world law they were deceiving themselves, but as far as Germany was concerned their point was sound enough. Even the critics of the Trial in Germany do not deny that the crimes against humanity were in fact committed, nor have the Nazi leaders become martyr figures.

These arguments, both for and against the Trial, are all based on its political necessity and possible future advantages. From the point of view of traditional legal ideology, they are therefore not just inadequate—they are totally misguided. They prove only that expediency, and not justice, was served, and, these two being irreconcilable, they show what a farce the Trial was from beginning to end. No principle of legality means no justice. The answer can only be that strict justice is not everything. Ironically, perhaps, a trial without law, in this instance, was still a closer approximation of justice, more in keeping with legalistic values, than any other course of action. There were other objections to the Trial, of course. One was that there should have been neutrals on the Tribunal. However, neutrality is a state of mind, and those whom good fortune had exempted from war were not necessarily more likely to be fair than those involved. Neutrality in war is a matter of luck, not of virtue. During the Second World War no one was genuinely neutral.[54] Again, those who raised a hue and cry about the Trial as a dangerous precedent, as a fearful threat to all future defeated generals and statesmen, might have remembered that neither wars nor peace settlements are precedents.[55] Each one is new and different. If the Trial had been part of an established legal order, it might have been a legal precedent, for better or worse. Since it was nothing of the sort, both the hopes and fears for the distant future of international law were groundless. The Trial was not, and could not be, a precedent, except by way of vague analogy, for the future. The danger to future statesmen and military officers comes not from the Trial, but from the sort of war which brought it about. It is ideological war fought to the bitter end by both sides that makes the elimination of the defeated leaders inevitable. This conditions both the manner in which the war is pursued and its consequences. The leaders of nations defeated in future wars will be lucky if they get a trial as fair as that at Nuremberg, indeed if they get any trial at all. It is not the Trial itself that is the dangerous precedent, but Nazism, and the total war and politics it brought to Europe.

A far more serious objection to the Trial was the *tu quoque* argument: that is, that the leaders of the states whose representatives were judging the Nazi leaders had, in the course of the war, committed acts no less criminal than those of the accused. This is a politically powerful argument. There are some very simple ways of answering this objection, but they are not adequate. One can say, if one wishes to argue in legalistic terms, that "clean hands" is an equitable principle which, like many other principles of domestic law, was not part of the law governing the Trial. To be sure, there was no established law of any kind, but that is an evasion; so is the answer that no criminal may complain that he has been punished wrongfully because other criminals remain at large.[56] That is a proper answer to a criminal who gets caught in a society where regular systems of law and law enforcement prevail. If the Trial is to be justified in terms of what it could contribute to German political behavior, not in terms of legal analogies, it is obvious that the Germans could learn nothing worthwhile from men who were superior to the Nazis only in having got away with it. This is one of the reasons why Justice Pal thought it so revolting that the Americans after Hiroshima should try the Japanese for war crimes and crimes against humanity.[57] Hypocrisy on such a scale can inspire only disgust. This was, however, not the case at Nuremberg. As far as the so-called conventional war crimes went, there was

plenty of evidence to prove that the Western Allies had committed some too. Admiral Doenitz was in fact acquitted of
having committed one such crime, unrestricted submarine
warfare, because American naval officers admitted to having
done the same thing. Justice Jackson, looking at the devasta-
tion around him in the Germany of 1945, felt that the indiscriminate bombing of cities had put the trying powers in a
relatively weak position as far as charges of conventional war
crimes went.[58]

The preference still expressed by many lawyers for the
charge of conventional war crimes is due to the novelty and
elasticity of the idea of crimes against humanity and the apparent legal solidity of the charge of war crimes by comparison.
The French representative on the Tribunal, M. Donnedieu
de Vabres, subsequently expressed his distaste for something
as foreign to legal traditions as a charge that had never even
been heard of before the Trial. In his eyes the conventional
war crimes, declared to be such in the Hague Convention of
1907, were legally far sounder. Here was all that the legalistic
ethos demanded, a written instrument of some antiquity,
known to all and obliging all the signatories.[59] The trouble
with this argument is not that it errs in pointing to the novelty
of the idea of crimes against humanity, but that it does not
recognize the reason for its sudden appearance—that fact that
the acts themselves were, as far as Europe was concerned, novel
in the extreme. Secondly, the argument in favor of the positive
strength of the Hague Convention is forced. The Convention
is obviously not a criminal statute. After all, even M. Donnedieu de Vabres himself admitted that the principle of legality
in criminal cases could not be applied to the Trial as a whole,
because the principle of nonretroactivity can only be a part of
an established legal system within a civilized and stable political order. The charges of conventional war crimes were therefore not, even in his eyes, truly legal. It must then be recog-

nized that while they were of no greater legality than any of the other charges, their political value, in view of the conduct of all the belligerent powers, was far smaller than that of the charge of crimes against humanity. The Hague Convention of 1907 did not provide any system of international criminal law to be administered by an international criminal tribunal. The Convention bears not the slightest resemblance to domestic criminal law. The relative antiquity of the conventional war crimes charges does not add anything to their legality. They declare certain forms of warfare to be wrong, but then, did anyone but the Nazis doubt the wrongness of crimes against humanity? If so, did they doubt it because these crimes were *more* horrible even than those that had already been declared intolerable? To say that the charge of crimes against humanity was unknown is therefore no argument against it. As for the legality of the Hague Convention, it is a chimera. There are no stable legal expectations apart from an established legal system in a coherent institutional order. There is no security in relying upon agreements as if they were a part of an operative system of criminal law. An international treaty is simply not analogous to a criminal law. Conventional war crimes are no more, and no less, legal than any other charge made at the Trial.[60] Only the ideological compulsions of legalism made the entire fiction of their "legality" necessary. Even if one were to accept the notion of a rigidly structured municipal law which these arguments reveal, there would be no need to pretend that a legal system operates internationally, especially in matters involving crime and punishment, in the same manner as the laws of politically unified societies.

There was, however, one thing that was quite obvious. The Germans did commit both war crimes and crimes against humanity which none of the Western Allies ever committed. Indeed, the type of war crime that was their peculiar specialty was essentially a part of all the crime which the Nazis had perpetrated since the day they came to power. The concentration camps, the shooting of civilian hostages, the erasing of villages, the forced labor deportations were all extensions of policies that began with the Roehm Putsch. Crimes against humanity were not something that the Nazis engaged in merely because they were an occupying power in hostile territory. They engaged in them because they were Nazis. Their occupation policy was only the full flowering of methods used against their domestic opponents and against non-Aryan German citizens. There was no law, no international convention, to deal with these acts, because in the balmy days of the Hague Conventions they were still unthinkable, as was the whole character of total war as we know it now. However, if the Germans were to find out what had been done in Europe during the war, and to draw any beneficial lessons from it, it was essential that the Nazis be tried for those acts which only they, and no one else, had performed. These acts, in fact, *were* Nazism. If not the Russians, at least the other three Allies could claim with perfect truth that they were not guilty of similar enormities, and that *tu quoque* did not apply to them.

There are three ways of evaluating the decisions of a court, especially in political trials. One can look only to the past, to the validity and applicability of previously established laws and precedents. This is the legalistic approach. It has been presented here with some care to show how intense the determination to preserve the distinction between law and non-law, and especially law and politics, was among the Western participants at the Trial. It meant that all sorts of illusions had to be maintained, but, in spite of so much effort, these did not hide the discrepancy between the imagined and the actual pattern of the Trial. Another way of looking at political trials would be to reject legalism altogether in favor of one of the "grand" future-directed ideologies. Instead of a concern for either the past, present, or immediate future, one can look to the remote future, to historical necessity, for a justification of decisions. Lastly, one can look to the immediate political future, to the likely results a decision will have among one's contemporaries and in circumstances that are still like those of the familiar present. This roughly is the span of our predictive powers and the range of events which we can claim to influence. Beyond this lies madness, while fixing our eyes on the past may doom us to inactivity, sterility, and, as often as not, pretense. In the Nuremberg Trial all three perspectives played a part, as will presently emerge. However, as far as the crimes against humanity were concerned, only two approaches matter, that of legalism and that which for lack of a better term one might as well call skeptical politics, which sees trials not as guarded from political life by a fence marked "law," but as part of a continuing process of political development.

The entire issue of crimes against humanity did not raise the same amount of discussion and disagreement as the other novel charge—the crime of waging aggressive war. This was true during the conference that drew up the Charter for the Trial, and subsequently. Perhaps no one wishes to appear, even indirectly, in favor of crimes against humanity. Moreover, the Tribunal, regrettably perhaps, and in clear disregard of the Charter, decided to interpret crimes against humanity restrictively, limiting itself to those committed after 1939, and so assimilating them to the less controversial charge of war crimes. In spite of this victory for the legalistic mind, the entire Trial can only be justified by what it revealed and said about the crimes against humanity. For it was this alone that did, and could, help Germany to a more decent political future. On the purely theoretical level, too, the legalistic defenses of the Trial as a whole, of the new charge of waging aggressive war, and so by inference of crimes against humanity, were hollow. Their only value was an entirely unintended one. The Trial, by forcing the defense lawyers to concentrate on the legality of both the entire Trial and its specific charges, induced the German legal profession to rediscover and publicly proclaim anew the value of the principle of legality in criminal law, which for so many years had been forgotten and openly disdained.[61]

Beyond this important but fortuitous result, the arguments of legalistic ideology had no intrinsic merit. All of them depended on treating the Trial as if it were analogous to trials held under municipal law. What made these resorts to analogy necessary was the legalistic ideology with its either-or view of law. Either a decision is valid in terms of a prior legal norm or it is not, and nothing in between will do. Either it is a judicial process or a political act, law or expediency, and again there are only two alternatives. Conformity to prior law and indifference to consequences define law; their absence would doom the Trial to the limbo of political action. If, however, one looks at law and legalistic politics in terms of degrees of legalism, of more or less, then one can recognize the political value of legalistic procedures in general and of the Trial in particular without resorting to such subterfuges. That these analogies were subterfuges becomes clear enough when one analyzes them. Thus Justice Jackson's claim that the Charter was merely a codification ignores the fact that codification presupposes the existence of laws and usages that are enforced and obeyed, and whose only defects are disorder, obsolescence, and incoherence.[62] To speak of international law as analogous to customary law is an abuse of the term "custom." Custom implies usage—continuous conformity of behavior—the total absence of which two world wars had just demonstrated.[63] To argue, as Justice Jackson did, that the Trial was part of a development analogous to Anglo-Saxon common law, which also was judge-made on a case-by-case basis without benefit of statutory legislation, is to display an utter obliviousness to history.[64] It fails to consider that the English courts were part of a relatively stable social order, that they were not *ad hoc* bodies, but a self-perpetuating corporate body forming an integral and basic part of a constitutional system. It overlooks their dependence on a host of other social and political institutions which legitimized and maintained the common law courts and enforced their decisions. As for the notion that the Trial was part of a "primitive" stage in the ever-progressing history of international criminal law, it springs from the concept of the integral history of law, which permeates traditional internationalist theory. What is astounding is that anyone should be able to discern a law of progress in operation in international criminal law right after a war which had seen in the very center of the civilized world spectacular violations of every known legal and moral norm. At best it is a testimony to legalistic optimism—and blindness to history.[65]

The truth is that all analogies drawn from municipal law, for all their tempting familiarity, are unconvincing.[66] New cases, unforeseen cases, arise within all legal systems, and the courts are obliged to deal with them as best they can. Even when all devices of interpretation and analogy fail, they are not really decided in a totally arbitrary way, because the procedures and personnel dealing with them are stable. The system as a whole absorbs the occasional case that appears retroactive, because there is nothing *ad hoc* about the courts and the general principles under which they operate. None of these conditions prevailed at Nuremberg, or at the various Quisling trials which were held at the same time in the newly liberated countries of Europe. No nineteenth-century code had contemplated the German occupation or any of its results.[67] It is indeed doubtful that legal provisions *can* be devised for events of this sort. There are no civilized responses that are fitting, and certainly no legal norms that can cope with what the Nazis did to Europe. There certainly were none, either national or international, in 1945. Just what is the proper response to Olendorf, one of the witnesses at the Trial, who proudly admitted to having participated in the killing of ninety thousand people in concentration camp and who went on to boast that those who claimed to have killed more were padding their records?[68]

If little can be said on behalf of the legality of the Trial, much can be said generally in its favor, even from the point of view of legalism. First of all, the Trial was internally fair. Each defendant had a German counsel of his own choice, the guilt of each was individually established before punishment, two of the defendants were acquitted entirely, and several were acquitted of one or more charges. It was not a rigged trial in the sense that the classical model of a political trial is. Its object in Justice Jackson's words was to "establish incredible events by credible evidence." [69] The Nazis' passion for preserving records of all their misdeeds with bureaucratic meticulousness rendered this relatively easy.[70] It was indeed the first post-mortem of a totalitarian regime, in which evidence was not only piled upon evidence, but presented in such a way that no lawyer could deny its validity. And it was to the political classes of Germany, a great part of which are trained in law, that this Trial was addressed. If one judges it in terms of its foreseeable effects upon those Germans who inevitably would and did write West Germany's constitution and dominate its political life, the Trial was not only justified, but it was the only justifiable way of dealing with the Nazi leadership. Legalism and legalistic thinking have deep roots in Germany's officialdom.[71] For all their decline during the Nazi era, remnants of them survived. There was perhaps nothing else left of Germany's more decent political traditions. It is significant that all the lawyerly comment in Germany, even that hostile to the Trial as a whole, agrees on two things— that the Trial was fair and that something deserving punishment had been committed. That something was crimes against humanity.[72] It was something of great value that evidence presented at the Trial should make minds as imperturbable as these boggle. That such men should be shaken was the best, and perhaps only, political reform that the Allies could instigate. Certainly total re-education of millions was not feasible. The Trial, addressing itself to the political and legal elite, gave that elite a demonstration of the meaning and value of legalistic politics, not only by offering a decent model of a trial, a great legalistic drama, but by presenting evidence in a way that the political elite could not shrug off. It could and did illustrate what happens when Nazi ideology replaces legalism. It also dispelled all possible belief in *Faschismus ohne Schweinerei,* which, without that Trial, might well have appealed to some. It is worth recalling here that the return to legality was what the most notable of the German resistance groups, the Kreisau Circle, had held as the most vital need. It was certainly central to the lawyers who eventually came to write the Basic Law of the Federal Republic.[73] And that document and the discussions which preceded it testify to one thing, that in so far as the Trial dealt with crimes against humanity it had a genuine effect on Germany's future leaders. In the debate on the abolition of capital punishment, perhaps most strikingly, the extent to which the facts had penetrated was revealed.[74] It comes out also in the Basic Law's ample provisions for judicial redress for all citizens. Since then, even observers who have little cause to like Germany have been impressed with the decency and even humanity with which ordinary criminal trials are conducted.[75] Western Germany is now, in short, a *Rechtsstaat.*

If one sees law and politics not as divorced but as parts of a single continuum, one can see how high a degree of legalism the Trial involved if measured on a scale of degrees of legalism. It did this because of its inner structure and its aim. What makes the Nuremberg Trial so remarkable is that, in the absence of strict legal justification, it was a great legalistic act, the most legalistic of all possible policies, and, as such, a powerful inspiration to the legalistic ethos. The point is precisely that the social value of legalistic politics is very great, but that legalistic ideology is incapable of even thinking of legal procedures in general, and of trials in particular, in these terms. The limitations of legalism as a way of interpreting the social functions of legal mores and institutions, however, do not lessen the practical contributions of the latter to political life—as judged from a liberal point of view, for instance. That is why it is quite possible to recognize that the Trial was a political one, in that it aimed at the elimination of a political enemy and of a hostile ideology, but that it need have given offense neither to legalistic nor to liberal values because of the manner in which it was conducted, the nature of the enemy, and the immediate effects of the Trial. It is, however, only because the crimes against humanity were the moral center of the case that all this was possible.

### A WAR ON TRIAL

If the Nuremberg Trial can be justified as an act of legalistic statesmanship and on the basis of its immediate effects on German politics, it is due to the revelations about crimes against humanity which it produced. For the American prosecution, however, this was not the main object of the Trial. Its real purpose was to try the Nazi leaders for having waged aggressive war. A conviction on these grounds, Justice Jackson felt, would make an enormous contribution to the future development of international law and order. It was, as such, directed at the remote future, at future generations of mankind. This in itself is a project of doubtful value. Moreover, in order to prove the charge of aggressive war, the distant past would also have to be explored, with all the difficulties inherent in attributing blame and praise for actions that have their beginnings in remote history. The result was that neither of the great ends of the Trial—its educative force among the spectators, and the rigorous attribution of guilt for specific acts—was well served. The future of international law was unaffected. The Germans, to be sure, did include provisions for the supremacy of international law in the Basic Law, as well as outlawing preparations for aggressive war. However, the future of war and peace do not depend on them alone. Moreover, the meaning of the term "aggressive war" has remained as obscure as ever, so that it is doubtful whether declaring it a crime even identifies the wars to be avoided, even if this in itself could inhibit anyone from engaging in such wars. Thus both the legalistic character of the Trial, which rested on its inner procedures and its capacity to prove that specific acts had been committed, and its possible value for the future were weakened by including this charge. The remote past cannot be legally tried, and the remote future cannot be controlled.

If no great good was achieved, neither was any harm done by the charge of waging aggressive war. Since the Anglo-American law of criminal conspiracy was also introduced, the charge might have proved harmful, but the Tribunal properly chose to interpret conspiracy very restrictively. This law, after its unhappy career as an instrument for the suppression of labor unions in the nineteenth and early twentieth centuries, does not enjoy a great reputation, even in the nations where it originated. It was foreign and disagreeable to all continental jurists. Moreover, it is, as Justice Jackson readily admitted, a dragnet device, by which individuals may be held guilty of crimes which they did not individually commit, simply by having acted in unison to promote an end itself possibly criminal, but perhaps only illegal or immoral. Its value to any prosecuting attorney is that he need not prove individual criminal intent or action beyond the act of association, once the act of association itself is recognized as a crime. To try the Nazis under this law could only weaken the legalistic value of the Trial, which rested on its inner structure. It thus became much more of an ordinary persecuting trial than it need have been. The conspiracy charge also involves a view of the past that is conspiratorial in a very different sense from the Anglo-American legal term, the technical complexities of which are, in fact, far greater than the very simple ideas which Justice Jackson presented. A criminal trial demands a *mens rea,* and there is often no *mens rea* to be found in the development of socially complex events such as war.[76] A criminal trial for waging aggressive war inevitably involves an interpretation of the past which makes it possible to point to specific persons making specific decisions which caused a war. In the case of the Nazis this did not, in fact, create any difficulties. However, the conspiratorial view of history, in its penchant for unearthing plots and secret machinations, is the very essence of the classical political trial with its simple aim of rooting out all opposition—real, fancied, potential, or improbable. Thus again the charge of waging aggressive war made the Trial seem a more conventional political trial and as such reduced its value for legalistic politics.

As it happened, the vagueness of the notion of aggressive war was not a matter of great importance at Nuremberg, because whatever definition of the term was used, or even if it was not defined at all, it was clear that the decisions and acts of the men being tried were the actual cause of the war which broke out in Europe in 1939 and of its subsequent extension into Russia. However, its usefulness to any conceivable future international law was fatally impaired by its vagueness; for, as each war is different and as the form of future wars is unpredictable, so is the character of aggression and defense. Aggression may occasionally be imputed to someone in a past war. As far as future wars are concerned, it is an indefinable term inapplicable to unforeseeable circumstances. As such it cannot influence the future conduct of statesmen, however often it may be verbally outlawed.[77] At the least, one can say that this was an effort to deglamorize war in general. However, if that has occurred, it is surely due more to the character of nuclear war than to anything that was, or could have been, said about the criminality of aggression at Nuremberg or at any trial. At worst, the emphasis placed on "aggression" may have the effect of making some types of war "defensive" in purpose, respectable, and even morally desirable. However, the distance between this outworn conception of the morality of war and the present actualities of warfare seems too great to make the survival of the theory of the "just war" likely.

The trouble with the charge of waging aggressive war at Nuremberg was not that it would have been impossible to prove. To do so, however, would have required a searching review of European history since 1919, or at least since the Nazi seizure of power. The one thing all the Allies agreed on was that they did not want that. The one thing the British had from the first feared was that if the Nazis were allowed to present their interpretation of recent history the Trial would offer them a great opportunity to spread their propaganda. Perhaps a public review of the diplomatic history of the 1930's was not welcome to them on other grounds as well. That the Russians were not interested in a discussion of Soviet-German relations in 1938 and 1939 can also be easily understood. Indeed, Justice Jackson agreed, too, that nothing could do more harm to Allied relations, or affect American public opinion more adversely, than open recriminations about who did what to whom in Europe in the interwar period. The Nazis were therefore not allowed to present their views about the causes of war. They consequently had no way of offering any defense against the charge of waging aggressive war, except to challenge the legality of the concept. It seems that the sole aim of Justice Jackson's definition of aggressive war and of his notion of a crime of conspiracy to wage such war, both of which were eventually included in the Charter, was to avoid the very possibility of any discussion of the causes of the war.[78] None in fact took place.

Why did Justice Jackson insist on including this charge, in spite of the many objections raised by the French and Russians, and in spite of his own awareness of all the difficulties it involved? Why did he feel to the very end that the outlawry of wars of aggression was the most important, enduring, and valuable result of the Trial?[79] His enthusiasm for the law of criminal conspiracy is easily understood. Unfamiliar with Europe's recent history, he was stunned by what he saw and heard, while his European colleagues, only too aware of all that had happened, were long past outrage. As a result Justice Jackson wanted to "get" the Nazis, and as many of them as possible, and conspiracy was the best legal formula to achieve this.[80] By making conspiracy to commit crimes against peace a separate crime he hoped to be able to "get" them not only for acts performed after 1939, but also for all those that preceded them. It was a simple idea, but the Tribunal sensibly enough did not act on it.

Justice Jackson's motives for insisting on the crime of waging aggressive war were more complex. His main preoccupation was to vindicate his own and Secretary Stimson's position on the Neutrality Act and Lend Lease before America had entered the war. If it could now be proved that Germany had from the first been engaged in an illegal war of aggression, then the morality and legality of aiding Britain from the first was demonstrated once and for all, and no future historian could cast aspersions on that decision.[81] This was something Justice Jackson was intent upon even before he sat down at the conference table in London in 1945. A second concern grew upon him, however, the more he realized how little he and his fellow Americans had shared in Europe's recent experience.[82] To prevent America from following its natural inclination to relapse into isolationism became his second great concern. In the end his insistence that Americans must be informed of the facts of twentieth-century life and reassured that they had fought in a wholly moral cause if they were not to forget their future obligations to maintain an international order won over, not only the French judge on the Tribunal, but even Professor Trainin, the Soviet legal expert at the London Conference. When Justice Jackson grimly assured the latter that one could not trust an American judge back home to know what the Gestapo was all about, even he capitulated.[83]

If the charge of having waged aggressive war was the only way in which Americans could be convinced that their participation in the war and in the Trial was morally justifiable, then it was worth including. Moreover, the reasons against having it were not particularly convincing. M. Gros, the French representative to the conference, was its main opponent and he based his opposition entirely on the absence of a legal basis for the charge—the absence of any international instrument to rely on. That the Kellogg-Briand Pact was inadequate for that purpose was clear enough. However, Justice Jackson's reply that in this Trial the future was at stake also, and that one could not fix one's eyes solely on the past for justifications, was well taken.[84] There was, to be sure, a certain Machiavellian streak in his arguments. M. Gros suggested that interference in the domestic affairs of nations on humanitarian grounds had been undertaken throughout the last century, and was thus at least hallowed by tradition, which the charges of conspiracy to wage aggressive war and waging it were not. Non-intervention was a sacred principle to Americans, Justice Jackson replied, all the more so since they had no intention of letting foreign nations meddle with their own domestic racial policies. Therefore all the charges that affected Nazi crimes within Germany and prior to the war had to be tied to the international crime of waging aggressive war. A mere charge of brigandage, again somewhat more traditional, and so appealing to the Frenchman, would not be sufficiently remote from intervention in domestic affairs.[85] America in short could only be convinced of Nazi guilt if waging aggressive war was made the most serious crime, and America must be convinced if she was not to forget what the war had been all about and what had happened in Europe. If the memory faded, isolation was sure to reassert itself. When M. Gros reminded Justice Jackson that Secretary Lansing and James Brown Scott had rejected proposals for an international trial of Germany's leaders for crimes against peace in 1919 because they saw no basis in international law for such a trial, the latter replied that America had come a long way since then.[86] In fact, he clearly feared that this was not the case, and that America needed a good deal of nudging. That was his second reason for demanding a trial for conspiracy to wage and waging aggressive war. How much effect it actually had on American public opinion is, of course, impossible to guess. That it was a sufficient political justification for the charge was, however, generally accepted.

There was a third motive which animated Justice Jackson, a desire to do something for the future of the rule of law in international relations in general and the future conduct of war especially. He did not believe that, by outlawing aggressive war in the course of trying the Nazi leaders, future wars could be prevented, but he thought that aggressive war might become less likely, or at least controlled. It was his genuine belief that his "codification" of international legal condemnation of aggressive war at the Trial could achieve this. This was aiming at the remote future and, like most such moves, it failed. There was indeed no reason to believe that it could be more than a gesture, inasmuch as it was directed not just at the men being tried or those in Germany who had supported them. It was meant to affect all men in the present and the future, and no trial, not even a spectacular one such as the Nuremberg Trial, can achieve such enormous consequences by itself. There is no international criminal court yet, and nothing effective along these lines is even imaginable at present. The Trial could do something for Germany. To demand more was unreasonable, an extravagance of the legalistic imagination.

Even if law were as powerful a force in world affairs as Justice Jackson believed—even if it were able to modify, in the absence of other political institutions and interests, the course of future wars—it would, at the very least, be necessary to define aggressive war in order to know what acts are to be considered criminal. This is virtually impossible on purely theoretical grounds. General Nikoschenko's refusal to consent to a general definition, even for the purposes of the Charter under which the Nazis were to be tried, gives an indication of the ideological reasons which make an international agreement unlikely. Justice Jackson meant by aggressive war any resort to violence aimed at altering the international *status quo,* for any reason whatever. It is obvious that any state with a revolutionary mission could not regard this as criminal, or even as aggressive. If this conception of aggressive war as the supreme international crime does not appear to have much of an effective political future, it does have deep roots in American thought. Justice Jackson was by no means alone in thinking that it is the illegitimacy of war that makes all the difference. It is only another manifestation of an indifference to historical reasoning about the causes of wars, and of a preference for legalistic decisions about their rightness and wrongness.[87] Behind it lie also an exaggerated voluntarism and other remnants of liberalism, which see war as a conspiracy organized by a few evil men, and as such quite analogous to domestic crimes of violence. The vast majority of men in an organized civil society are interested in maintaining peace and order, which only a relatively small number of deviants try to disturb by engaging in criminal activities. There is of course a grain of truth in the theory. Most ordinary people, who suffer wars, do not want them. It does not, however, follow that the causes of every war can be attributed to the machinations of a few political criminals. Some indeed are like that; others are not. No simple formula can take care of the origins of all wars. In any case, it is impossible to judge every war in terms of criminal aggression and legitimate self-defense. These notions presuppose a legal system which defines both crime and the occasions and form that self-defense may take. Even self-defense is, within a legal system, not just mere self-help at the discretion of the individual who feels threatened, but something defined, qualified, and limited by law. In the absence of such legal definition the idea of self-defense as rendering war legitimate has only the effect of making the "defensive" belligerent feel that he is morally entitled to use any military means whatever to win his just cause. The psychological consequences of legalism may well be an intransigeance fed by self-righteousness.

All these shortcomings of the notions of criminal aggressive and legitimate defensive wars were not evident at Nuremberg. On the contrary, the Trial did much to reinforce this ideology. The reasons for this are easily discerned. They lay in the character of the Nazis and the European war. The organization of the Third Reich, the ideology of Nazism, and the determination of the Nazi leaders to fight a new war from the first, especially when contrasted with the reluctance with which the other European states entered the war, corroborated the American image of an aggressive war by supplying a perfect historical example thereof. At the Trial there really was enough personal responsibility for the war to make it possible to try men for aggression without doing any violence to history. It is to the Tokyo Trial that one must look to fully appreciate the difficulties which this entire way of thinking can create.

If the legal basis of the charge of waging aggressive war was not very solid, relying on such a general expression of sentiment as the Kellogg-Briand Pact, it was no more and no less ephemeral than that of all the other charges. It is only the future futility of this part of the "codification" of international law, and the fact that it was a charge that the defense was not allowed to discuss fully, that is objectionable. At Tokyo there were, however, problems which did not arise at Nuremberg. First of all, it is doubtful whether a trial as a legal drama could have had any great political effect in a non-European country so lacking in legalistic traditions. Secondly, the war in the East was one that could not be easily discussed in terms of proximate causality, which Nazism had made possible, indeed sensible, at Nuremberg. Lastly, the American prosecutor at Tokyo, Mr. Keenan, unlike Justice Jackson, chose to put his case in natural law terms. That their positions did not, on that account, differ much, is only another demonstration of the extent to which American-style natural law thinking has assimilated traditional American political values. The absolutist terminology of natural law, however, gave to the prosecution an air of national partiality that was fortunately lacking at Nuremberg. Nor would it have been as glaringly evident at Nuremberg, even if it had been used, because Germans (unlike the Japanese) at least share in the legalistic tradition of which natural law thinking forms so immense a part. Indeed, it may well be true that the very considerable revival of natural law among German jurists is part of the general return to legalism to which the Trial contributed so much. In Japan there was no cultural basis for any of this. It is not, however, true that the Tokyo Trials did any great harm. Rather, they achieved nothing whatever, as far as Japan was directly concerned. At worst they provided one of the influential members of the Tribunal, the Indian Justice Pal, with an opportunity to expose the weaknesses of America's political position in Asia. With or without a natural law justification, aggressive war, defined as any resort to violence aimed at altering the international *status quo,* could and did appear as nothing but an ideological defense of colonialism. This one example suffices to show what difficulties lurk behind the notion of outlawing aggressive war, with the American idea of aggressive war providing the legal definition of this crime. Nazism happened to fit the liberal demonology that lies beneath it. It is questionable whether other past wars or any future ones will provide such a perfect *mens rea* for purposes of criminal trials. The First World War did not; neither did the war in the Far East.

What could a trial teach the Japanese? What political traditions could it restore? None. The "situational ethics" of the Japanese are inherently unlegalistic. An acceptance of each situation as demanding specific ethical responses and a near-fatalism in matters of personal behavior have long acted against government by general rules and personal responsibility to such norms. Until the war personal conflicts were rarely resolved by a resort to courts; they were handled informally by local worthies, who made communal cohesion, rather than what is due to the individual claimant, the main object of conciliation.[88] To see the deep roots that legalism and trials have in Western culture one need think only of the part which legal imagery plays in literature, in metaphor, and in religious discourse of every kind. The court of love, the court of conscience, the trial of wits, the court of honor,

Judgment Day—how much these phrases tell us about ourselves! How many trial scenes appear in dramas and novels!
How central to our everyday speech and to our imagination
is the picture of a contest between diametrically opposed
wills, judged according to some general rule! Even fate as
we think of it behaves legalistically. The trial, the supreme
legalistic act, has served us with an image around which we
have structured a vast variety of experiences—ethical, religious, and aesthetic. Of all this there is no trace in Japan. The
result is that a trial could not and did not dramatize anything
for the Japanese. The general view was that it was a bit of
a bore, but that the conquerors were behaving as one would
expect conquerors to behave. They were responding to their
situation, and so were the defeated leaders now on trial.
There was no great sympathy for the latter, and no interest
in the legalistic gymnastics of the former. The defendants
themselves appear to have had much difficulty in understanding the Trial, refusing to accept the extremely competent
advice of their American counsel, preferring to follow their
own legally irrelevant patterns of thought.[89] Nevertheless, it
would be quite erroneous to say that the Tokyo Trial was an
outrage—it was merely a complete dud.

Mr. Joseph Keenan in the remarkable summary and defense of his work as chief prosecutor and of the Tokyo Trial
as a whole, written when it was all over, displays some feeling
for these difficulties. He nowhere defends the Trial in terms
of its contribution to Japanese politics directly. He never even
mentions Japan's immediate future. His entire case is based
on natural law, universal and thoroughly supra-local in its
perspectives, and on the future of international law in the
world as a whole. Metaphysics and the future of international
law were his preoccupations. Enough has already been said
about the improbability of international law and trials exer-
cising significant influence upon the future of international

relations. Even though it is the role of law to reduce conflicts, not all conflicts can be mitigated by law, and surely not by occasional utterances (however striking) about the outlawing of aggressive war or war crimes. It was the natural law justification of the Tokyo Trial, and especially of the charge of waging aggressive war, that was both novel and revealing. It was also important since natural law theory was not only presented by Mr. Keenan but played a part in the opinion of the President of the Tribunal, Justice Webb, and in the dissent of Justice Bernard. It also was an object of Justice Pal's general attack on the notion of aggressive war in his dissent.

As at Nuremberg no one was inclined to defend war crimes, though the personal responsibility of those being tried was a great issue. In any case one does not have to believe in natural law to recognize that such acts as the Rape of Nanking and wanton mistreatment of prisoners of war merit punishment. The defense, as at Nuremberg, relied on the general absence of positive legality for its main arguments. The three dissenting judges on the Tribunal, Justices Bernard of France, Pal of India, and Roeling of the Netherlands, however, centered their objections to the judgment on the novel charges of conspiracy to wage and the waging of aggressive war. It was therefore to these issues, even more than to the validity of the Trial as a whole, that Mr. Keenan eventually addressed himself. According to him, aggressive war can only be defined and recognized in terms of natural law philosophy. In that metaphysical order of values it is indeed the supreme crime, since it is not merely murder but wholesale murder. It follows that since not all killing is murder a defensive war fought "on the plane of right reason" is ethically perfectly justified. What makes a war aggressive, by natural law standards, is that it is a violent attempt to alter the political and geographic *status quo*. To be sure, natural law does not stand against evolution or historical accident. The dominant position of the Western powers in the modern world is due to their cultural superiority, and their rule, if not perfect, was justified. Thus any war to alter the balance of power in the Far East was aggressive, irrational, and against the law of nature. While this definition of aggressive war—violent attack on established international positions—is conventional, its derivation is not. Mr. Keenan drew it from what he called "the Christian-Judaic absolutes of good and evil," and from the classical natural law writers, especially Victoria and Suarez. This, he claimed, insured its universal validity.[90] However, that is far from self-evident. What on earth could the Christian-Judaic ethic mean to the Japanese? Even if we assume that Christians and Jews share an ethic, which is a debatable proposition, why should their values be binding on the Japanese, few of whom are Christians, and none of whom are Jews? How can one even suppose them to know of these values? To them such a law of nature could, at best, be an alien moral tradition—at worst, the nationalistic ideology of the victors. Mr. Keenan, lastly, was already living in the age of atomic war. His version of the natural law doctrine of the just war, however, came from another era. When judged by the standards of so weighty an authority on the meaning of natural law as Pope John XXIII, Mr. Keenan's views were obsolete. "It is hardly possible to imagine that in the atomic era war could be used as an instrument of justice," the Encyclical *Pacem in Terris* declares. This shows how shaky a foundation natural law was for the purposes Mr. Keenan had in mind at Tokyo.

The partiality of natural law, and its ideological limitations, were enhanced at this Trial by the fact that American defense counsel did not accept it. Indeed, Mr. Keenan seems to have directed his remarks less at the Japanese than at their American counsel and their "judicial heresy." To him the

Trial "served as a cockpit for a death struggle between two completely irreconcilable and opposed types of legal thinking"—positivism and natural law.[91] Since, by admission, the quarrel between natural law and positivism involved differently minded American lawyers, the propriety of making the trial of Japan's wartime leaders the occasion for a showdown between them may well be questioned. In any case, if this was the ultimate significance of the Tokyo Trial, as Mr. Keenan believes, it was a struggle between two rival legal ideologies. As such, whatever judgment was passed on the accused, it was a political trial in the most simple sense—a contest between rival ideologies. Whatever claims to universal legal validity legalism in its natural law form may make, it was clear here that it represented only the preferences of one group among those who conducted the Trial. As in any political trial, one must, therefore, ask, "What was its political purpose?" In Mr. Keenan's eyes it seemed to be not the immediate results of staging a fair trial, nor Japan's future, but only the elimination of the "positivist" ideological enemy and the results of this victory in the remote future of mankind. At best he looked for no more than the moral vindication of America's pursuit of the war in terms of the justice of its cause as defined by natural law—a convenient identification of American national interests with the law of nature. One may well doubt whether this was likely to endear the latter, as an ideology, to the losers, or, indeed, to give the Trial much stature in their eyes, in the eyes of other Asians, or of Westerners who did not accept either natural law or Mr. Keenan's views on the "just war."

A third circumstance served to render the natural law a less convincing basis for the charges of aggressive war than Mr. Keenan thought it to be. Many observers have noted that natural law is capable of too many interpretations in any concrete situation to provide an objective and impersonal basis for international criminal trials.[92] At Tokyo there was a telling illustration of this point. Justice Bernard based his dissent on natural law too, but in his view it rendered the charge of waging aggressive war illegitimate. In short, the very charge which Mr. Keenan's natural law supported, Justice Bernard's natural law rejected. For Mr. Keenan natural law meant that the fairness of the Trial and the fate of those tried were matters of little importance compared to "the grander and wider aim of the trial, (i.e.) to advance the cause of peace and right notions of international law." [93] Such is the bent of the "grand" ideological consciousness. Justice Bernard's natural law, on the contrary, was the sum of the principles of legality and judicial fairness. The justice done to the men on trial was therefore his main concern. He found that the Tribunal had a right to judge them on the basis of universally recognized rules, transcending both municipal and positive international law. What gives these rules their validity is that they can be known by all and so are binding on all. Moreover, they are what makes the judicial process itself possible—the idea of justice. Speaking as a European he saw only the crimes against humanity as self-evident political crimes demanding punishment. The destruction of an entire population was something everyone knew to be wrong, and as such something that one could try and punish under natural law in the absence of positive legislation. He did not think that this was true of waging aggressive war. For him natural law imposed the strictest standards of procedural fairness, which meant proving the direct personal guilt of a crime of commission, not mere omission, on the part of every one of the defendants. Since the best international lawyers neither before nor since the war were sure of what aggressive war was, or whether it was a crime, one could not expect the Japanese leaders to have known more about it. The law of criminal conspiracy did not appeal to Justice Bernard either,

both because he did not think there had been a conspiracy
and because it evaded the necessity of proving individual
guilt for specific criminal acts in each case. The whole notion
of aggressive war was too vague, in his eyes, to make it possible to prove individuals responsible for it, and natural law
therefore forbade raising the charge or condemning anyone
for it.[94] A greater distance from Mr. Keenan's version of
the law of nature can hardly be imagined. Justice Bernard's
notion was designed to prevent the Tokyo Trial from becoming a political trial of the classical sort; Mr. Keenan's aimed
at nothing else.

Justice Bernard's dissent, though based on natural law, did
not differ substantially from the dissent of those who did not
invoke the law of nature. Justice Roeling also objected to the
American theory that aggressive war was the supreme international crime, the crime which must be punished in order
to maintain the international legal order. On the contrary,
he noted that, until international society finds means for
effecting peaceful changes, war cannot be outlawed except on
paper.[95] In these opinions he was vigorously supported by
Justice Pal, whose long and minutely reasoned dissent con-
tains, to this day, the most serious and profound discussion
of all the issues involved in these Trials. Natural law, he observed, was a Western notion, meaningless to the men being
tried and to their fellow citizens. In any case, it cannot serve
as the enforceable law of the world community because there
*is* no world community. To enforce "the common good" internationally is impossible, because no one, certainly not one
set of nations, can be the custodian of that good.[96] To attempt
to do so in a trial for waging aggressive war is merely to up-
hold the international *status quo*. It is a point Mr. Keenan
had conceded. The trouble with such a procedure lies in the
fact that only nations which benefit from the *status quo* can
think of peace in such static terms. Nations which strive for

political freedom or national self-determination cannot think of such peace as legitimate or of such aggression as criminal. The American idea of aggressive war as a crime allows the dominant Western powers "to repent of their violence and permanently profit by it" at one and the same time.[97] Only when war ceases to be the sole available means for bringing about social and political change can individuals be held criminally responsible for having broken the peace.[98] Whatever the future may be, law for the present cannot cope with war. One may well ask at this point whether international criminal law can fulfill in any degree the great function of criminal law—the deterrence of potential criminals. Surely two isolated trials like those at Nuremberg and Tokyo cannot achieve that. Precisely because law is a conservative force, a legalistic approach to war and peace is bound to yield a static conception of peace which has nothing to offer a world without a common interest in peace, which includes members that have more to gain by war than to lose by it.

This is a radical conclusion, and Justice Pal did not go so far. He separated the Far Eastern War from that in Europe and limited his remarks to the special conditions of the former, which he saw as part of a general revolt against colonialism. No doubt many Asians, especially those who (unlike the Filipinos) had had no direct dealings with the Japanese invaders, shared his views. This was a predictable event, and one bound to reduce the Tokyo Trial's value very considerably. In any case, as one might expect, he dwelt at length, and with some effect, upon racism as a policy designed to promote aggressive war. His point is well taken, when one remembers the result of the exclusion of Japanese and Chinese immigrants by the United States.[99] Justice Pal did not fail to recall that the Japanese had tried to get some international legislation against racial discrimination through the League of Nations, but that Lord Robert Cecil had moved

against discussing it because it involved matters domestic to
the British Empire.[100] There was, of course, more than
racism involved in Japanese-American relations and in Jap-
anese-Chinese conflicts. What does appear clear, though, is
that the events which led up to the war were long in the
making and involved such complex clashes of interest and
traditions that to think of the war as the product of a simple
conspiracy is absurd. That there was brutality during the
war Justice Pal conceded readily, but that there was a conspiracy either to start a war or to wage it, especially criminally, he denied. It was the character of international life itself
which led to all these events. After a perusal of Justices Roeling's and Pal's reviews of the course of history in the Far
East it is difficult to find conspiratorial forces at work. Why
should one assume that these events had but one determining
cause—a Japanese conspiracy? Conspiracy, however, is what
a trial for the crime of waging aggressive war must presuppose, else there is no *mens rea*.[101] The historic causes of the
war simply defy legal judgment.

At times Justice Pal appeared to imply that no war could
be regarded as just a matter of aggression and defense, and
that conspiracies to wage war were figments of an unhis-
torical imagination. However, he made two distinctions
which attenuated his somewhat rigid historical determinism.
His remarks were directed at the Japanese-American war,
not at the whole Second World War, and he made a sharp
distinction between Nazi Germany and Japan. Japanese government, if no model of liberalism, was also not a totalitarian
system, he felt. It was a traditionalist order in which public
opinion remained an operative force.[102] In short, the implication is that some governments are, and others are not,
closed conspiratorial groups, and a war waged by the former
may indeed be tried on charges of premeditated aggression.
To these considerations one may add another. While there
is no world order, there is a European one. The Nazis were

tried by their fellow Europeans for having disrupted an order of which all were a part and to which all at least paid lip service. Indeed, what made Nazism in one respect a far more serious event for Europe than the subsequent emergence of Soviet communism is that the former arose within the very heart of so-called Western civilization. It was an intra-European affair, subject to European standards of judgment. It is not meaningless to speak of a European order, and of violations of that order, whereas the phrase "world community" is cultural and political nonsense. There was the possibility of bringing Germany back to a Europe in which there was much that was as ancient as it was worth maintaining. There were elements of a *status quo* which legalism could defend. One could try the Nazi leaders as destroyers of a society of which they were members without injuring the facts of history and with some benefit to the future of Europe. It was certainly not, as the French representative on the Tribunal suggested, merely a convenience to separate the Nazis from the Germans. He claimed that the roots of the war lay in the eternal barbarity of the Germans and in centuries of false ideas prevalent among them.[103] He did not really think the Nazis were individually responsible for their behavior; it was all a matter of the remotest antiquity which simply made the Germans what they were—made even Hitler, conceivably, no more than a standard German politician.[104] It is not a convincing argument. The structures of Nazi government and ideology were quite novel and so were the results they produced in Europe. The *Führerprinzip* and the autonomy of Hitler's entourage from all restraint (other than his own) made it perfectly possible to fix responsibility. Where power is exercised so exclusively, responsibility is not hard to fix, both for the causes of war and for crimes against humanity.

If the causes of war never were properly discussed at Nuremberg, the dissenters at Tokyo at least gave an ample airing to the whole issue. In that respect the latter Trial was superior. Unfortunately this airing only showed that the charge of waging aggressive war was without much merit. When it came to trying the Japanese leaders for crimes against humanity another difficulty arose. They were charged not with direct acts of commission, but with failure to prevent atrocities. Justice Pal showed no inclination to mercy where war crimes had in fact been committed. He agreed that those who had performed such acts should be punished. In this he was again at one with Justice Bernard, who also felt that, though failure to prevent atrocities was not a crime, crimes against humanity were the supreme international crime. What these dissenting opinions, unlike the actual judgment, reveal are the great difficulties inherent in the Trials. Of these, two are especially troublesome. Apart from the relatively unique case of the Nuremberg Trials, is it generally possible to blame one set of statesmen for having caused a war directly, without refusing to consider so many relevant considerations as to falsify history? Secondly, if we say, as Justice Pal did, that there can be no proximate causality on which responsibility can be based for the waging of war, how can one ascribe responsibility for crimes against humanity, whether these are conventional war crimes or new crimes? Do these, also, not have their origins in the remote past—in a thousand years of national history, for instance? If war as a premeditated, unilateral act is rare indeed, why should one think of genocide as always a punishable policy? Is there a difference? No one likes to ask such questions, and no one can really answer them.

### JUSTICE AND THE REMOTE PAST

Why is it that so many observers should agree that aggressive war is not an international crime and that individuals may not be held responsible for it, while they regard crimes against humanity as crimes which must be punished? The answer does not lie in the different causes of war and of mass exterminations. It is not possible to believe that wars are inevitable social processes, natural and beyond individual control, while genocide, for instance, is an avoidable, unnatural policy for which individuals are fully responsible. The difference must be found simply in the history of our differing attitudes to war and to other forms of organized political violence. It is not a matter of logic at all, but of habitual social sentiments which have grown up among us and which determine our judgment.

War has for most of history been regarded as a normal part of social life. It is not regarded as an ignoble activity. Even those who object to aggressive wars admire the qualities of the soldiers engaged in them, if not the ends to which their valor is put. Given the impossibility of distinguishing between aggressive and defensive wars there only remains war, hallowed by tradition, for ages regarded as a natural part of social life. A mere legal pronouncement that some wars are criminal is not likely to alter the general view that war, as such, is not a crime, or the belief that any war in which one's nation-state is involved must be supported. Our view of crimes against humanity is different. It is not that they are rare, but that they do not enjoy the traditional approbation which war evokes. What made so many people feel that the extermination policies and other crimes of the Nazis were unprecedented, indeed unique, was that Europeans had lately come to think of this sort of thing as simply impossible in their midst. That is why "How could it happen?" is a question asked over and over again. Consequently one also feels that by punishing such acts one might make them, if not impossible, at least less likely in Europe. It is thus not really a matter of the difference between the causes of war and the causes of organized atrocities, but of the common responses to them. War is acceptable, mass exterminations are not. That is why one is prepared to punish crimes against humanity and to hope that they will again be universally abominated.

The feeling that crimes against humanity had become unthinkable tends to lead one to regard them as sudden and unnecessary interruptions of a civilized order. This makes them look more like individual crimes within organized society, which also appear to be aberrations from normal conduct. It also affects thinking about their causes, making them appear somehow less rooted in the historical past than the war itself. There really is no particularly good reason for this belief. It enables us to blame the cause of the exterminations directly on the individuals who performed them, and thus makes it easy to hold them criminally responsible. The fact, however, is that the crimes against humanity were an organized corporate enterprise expressing a policy deeply rooted in a national ideology, just as were the military policy, establishment, and operations. One is not dealing here with a handful of deviants, but with a social movement, and this makes the relationship between the causes of and responsibility for these acts exceptionally problematic. As far as the Major War Criminals at Nuremberg were concerned, one can speak intelligibly of personal responsibility and hence of punishment. Where power is so great the personal impact of the agent is also great. Here the test *sine qua non*, or, "But for x, y would not have occurred," can be applied to show that certain individuals were not the indirect or remote cause of the policies but that they, in fact, framed and implemented them. There is also plenty of evidence of *mens rea*, in view of the secrecy with which extermination policies were carried out and the frequent denials of their existence. Lastly, given the Major War Criminals' positions of power and competence in the Third Reich, the other conditions required to show that their acts were intended and freely and purposefully pursued were present too.[105] The same, however, cannot be said with equal force of their subordinates. Only the *sine qua non* test applies to them, and in a vague way, in that someone had to do the actual killing and that these men did the fantastic things which their fellow Germans and other Europeans did not do. Since they were, however, replaceable minor cogs in a bureaucratic machine, the *sine qua non* test of causality has but little force in assessing their responsibility. Of *mens rea* there is also little enough. It is hard to impute conscious criminality to these lesser figures, since all the acts that were subsequently regarded as reprehensible were praised and rewarded by all the authorities and approved by the rest of society at the time of their commission.

To be sure, those who did not choose to participate in these actions were not forced to do so against their will, nor were they punished, as a common soldier would have been if he had failed to obey his draft call. No man could claim that he acted out of fear. However, in the absence of any moral leadership or guidance from the "respectable" sections of society, it is, perhaps, unreasonable to expect average persons to do anything but "go along" with a political movement as all-pervasive and well-established as Nazism was in Germany. To expose the full extent of the bestiality of their behavior as part of the effort to discredit Nazism in general was, of course, necessary. However, to dispose of these men by trials in which crime and responsibility and punishment for crime became the main issues was not the best means available to the Occupation to this or any other politically useful end. Awakening the Germans to their past as a means of influencing their future political conduct was what then mattered most. A way to review the past without structuring history to fit the pattern of repeated trials could have been found. What had to be done about those who were actively engaged in such organizations as the concentration camps and who occupied dominating positions there was to purge them with varying degrees of completeness, as was done in Japan. This would have been merely a selective continuation of the war, which was, after all, fought in order to destroy the Nazis. A simple administrative hearing to determine the relevant facts—that is, what was the accused's position in a criminal organization and what did he do there—would have sufficed to determine policy in these cases. Indeed, it has since become clear that a failure to distinguish between the purposes of purges and of punishment did much to confuse and invalidate American occupation policies in Germany.[106] The object of purging was to get certain select groups and individuals permanently or temporarily out of political circulation in Germany. It is not that these trials set "bad" legal precedents, or precedents of any kind at all, but that purges would have achieved the chief political ends more effectively. This was not a policy that required legalistic thinking or values. It was rather an essential continuation of the war and a part of any plan for the reconstruction of German civil society.

These considerations of the nature of responsibility for war and for crimes against humanity do not, however, bring one closer to one of the problems presented by the trials—that of historic causality. This issue emerged both at Nuremberg and at Tokyo because the crime-of-waging-aggressive-war charge inevitably produced discussions of the causes of war, a discussion that would probably never have arisen if crimes against humanity had been the central charge. The result was the confrontation of two entirely different and incompatible notions of causality, the historical and the legal. What is really involved is not the difference between the historic origins of the war and of the atrocities, but between the meaning of causality as it is used in historical discourse and in the course of the judicial process, especially in criminal cases. And this issue is of sufficient interest to deserve a digression.

There is a certain kind of historical narrative that is largely biographical. Here the notion of causality is not different from that of common sense or of the law. To say that Booth caused Lincoln's death is a statement that any historian could make, and one that would not differ from a lawyer's view of causality for purposes of fixing responsibility. There is the *sine qua non* test: but for Booth, Lincoln would not have been shot. A historian might ask and a lawyer would have to ask whether there was a *mens rea* to complete the review of the factual, causal analysis of an act the criminality of which is about to be assessed. Many authors on legal and historical causality fail to recognize, however, that when history concerns itself, not with individual agents, but with impersonal "factors" or large-scale social events, which cover with one word innumerable individuals and individual acts, causality has very different meanings. It is, of course, true that in using causality historians do more than just explain the sequence of events. They also try to weigh the degree of importance, of influence, that various actions and events had upon subsequent known events. However, it is false to think that when they speak of the Black Death causing prices to rise all over Europe, causing the Germans to massacre the Jews, causing the weavers to strike in Flanders, or causing considerable friction between landowners and laborers in England, they mean by "causing" the same sort of thing as when they say, "Booth caused Lincoln's death." In the first case no individuals and no individually identifiable acts are involved. It is quite a different level of abstraction, in which personality and physical identity are not involved at all. One is dealing here with clusters of circumstances, not with people. To say that such purely conceptual entities cause something to occur means really that a vast number of unknowable incidents can be retrospectively seen in the form of a picture of general conditions which differs from the picture that we have of the previous period. Here cause is simply a way of saying that social change—itself a highly abstract notion—occurred. Again it is a matter of clusters of inter-related events, actions, and persons whose general direction we trace without really knowing exactly who caused what to occur. We are talking of general patterns of social be-havior during a considerable period of time. There is neither proximate nor remote causality here, but only shifting ab-stractions, metaphors, or composites which we fabricate in order to reduce the past to communicable form. These wholes cause nothing. They themselves are caused by the creative imagination of historians.

What gives historical thought its deterministic character is that it deals so largely with these impersonal entities. It is this, too, which separates it from legal and common-sense views of causality, which are primarily concerned to estab-lish the exact character of individual acts and the specific circumstances under which they took place. Both historians and lawyers look to the past to discover just what did hap-pen—which, since it did happen, *had* to happen. However, in order to fix responsibility we want to know both the exact impact that an individual's actions could and did have, given the conditions under which he acted, and his state of mind at that time. To use a paradigmatic case: for purposes of legal judgment it matters whether a man throws down a plate and causes it to break, or whether he distracts his wife, who then drops a plate. Causality, considered in this way, has ob-viously no relation to the sort of causality implied when his-torians speak of the causes of the Reformation, of the French Revolution, or of the Industrial Revolution. To say that any person or identifiable group of persons was the cause of any of these is clearly impossible. No individual can cause all that, in the sense that he can be said to cause Lincoln's death or cause a plate to break. He can be held responsible for those of his actions which we subsequently recognize as part of the general situation called the French Revolution, for instance, but he cannot be said to have caused it.

That the chain of causality is pursued into the more distant past by historians than by moralists and lawyers is not what makes the difference between their ways of thinking about causes. Historians do not feel compelled to go back to Adam every time, either. The cut-off point is settled in a relatively casual way by professionally shared ideas about relevance and traditional chronological divisions, by the special interests of the historian, and by his judgment of the duration of the situation which he wishes to describe and explain. In law the purposes of punishment, the ends of praising and blaming, determine the cut-off point. Those who wish to replace legal punishment by cure and rehabilitation will clearly wish to go far back into the psychological past of a criminal. Those who are interested in simply ridding society of dangerous deviants as quickly and efficiently as possible will be apt to stop very early. For them the "but for," *sine qua non* test will be all that needs to be proved. Those lawyers whose eyes are fixed on deterrence and on maintaining the principle of legality in criminal cases will want, in addition, proof of *mens rea,* amplified by a variety of conditional considerations which ensure that the agent causing the prohibited result did so in a truly voluntary, direct, and premeditated way. In all these cases the purpose of causal inquiry, the fixing of responsibility, and subsequent punishment will determine the scope and remoteness of the causes considered. If there is no general rule which can determine the cut-off point for the historian's search for causes, neither are lawyers at one about the proximity or remoteness of the causes that they must examine in order to fix criminal responsibility. What is clear, however, is that the criteria of the historian and those of the lawyers are entirely different and not interchangeable. To hold an individual legally responsible for causing a war or a revolution involves a cut-off point no historian could or would use; to bring the historian's sense of causality to bear on legal cases would doom lawyers to eternal indecision.

War is obviously a highly abstract term. A syllable is here being used to cover a multitude of actions on the part of an enormous number of people. This is true of all those occasions when organized groups of men engage in the protracted military combat which we call war. As such, the causes and courses of wars fall into that part of historical discourse in which causality is merely another term for social change. However, there are different kinds of war, and in some the circumstances are such that identifiable individuals make decisions and perform acts which are the causes of war in a relatively direct way. When an absolute monarch enters a war with an army of mercenaries—when war, as it once was, is "the sport of kings"—he can be said to be a cause of that war in a sense that is quite different from the causes which bring a corporate government of pluralistic societies depending on conscripted armies and complex industrial and technological organizations to engage in war. To say that Louis XIV caused the War of the Austrian Succession is a statement of a biographical sort which does no violence to social history. That is so because of the character of that war. To be sure, this is still not the Booth-Lincoln situation. There was more to armies and wars, even then, than just Louis XIV. It is a matter of degree. If, however, one says—as many have—that imperialism caused the First World War, one is not dealing with causality in that sense at all. This is due to the extreme abstractness of notions such as "imperialism" and "World War." They also fit the *kind* of war that is being discussed. It was a war in which so many groups of people engaged in such a variety of actions that any possible terms one uses to explain its origins and course are bound to be general, remote, and composite. That is why there is so little agreement about the causes of that war, though all agree that none of the participants wanted the actual war they got. In the case of the Second World War, the structure of Nazi government and ideology renders it far more plausible to speak of the Nazi leadership as the cause of the war. The years of conflict that preceded the Japanese-American war and the structure of Japanese government make an analogous explanation of that war less satisfactory. In neither case does historical causality really approximate causality as it is used in criminal cases, biography, or daily life, where a limited situation involving individual agents and acts exists. This is as true of the organizations that carried out Nazi extermination policies as of its military establishment and international policies. One can say that as individuals the Nazi leaders caused and were responsible for specific acts that contributed to the outbreak and conduct of the war, and for extermination projects. One could not say that as individuals or as a group they caused Nazism, of which the war and the atrocities were a part; for when we use the term Nazism we speak as historians, not as lawyers.

The reasons, then, for distinguishing crimes against humanity from crimes against peace are not a matter of causes but of consequences. It is, however, worth remembering that any conceivable large-scale twentieth-century war is a crime against humanity. Indeed, how different was what happened on Flanders fields and in the bombed cities of Europe from what happened at Buchenwald? The nature of contemporary war has eliminated all the conditions that once made it possible to distinguish the two. Not only is the distinction between the civilian and the soldier gone, but all that once made war comparable to personal combat, with its virtues of valor, loyalty, and honor, is gone. That only leaves the slaughter. What once was the appropriate reaction only to wanton mass murder must now, of necessity, be one's view of war, too. That is the ultimate reason why the distinction between aggressive and defensive war is worse than futile.

### TRYING THE REMOTE FUTURE

In the two great Trials at Nuremberg and Tokyo the past was being judged. The only suggestion that the past behavior of the men being tried, or their treatment by the Tribunal, was unimportant came from Mr. Keenan, who wrote that the immediate purpose of proving the case against the defendants was "ephemeral" when "placed in juxtaposition with the long-range aim of aiding in the creation of a jural situation," the construction of international criminal law. What mattered was not the trial itself but its impact "upon the history of human relations as they existed on the international scene." [107] What he meant was that the Tokyo Trial was to be seen as a victory for natural law over positivism. Since Mr. Keenan's very American brand of natural law included a faith in historical progress, it was a pretty modern political ideology that justified the present in terms of the remote future. As such, however, it was a very mild variant of the theory of historical responsibility. As a whole, Nuremberg and Tokyo were trials at which past acts were tried, and the justification for them must be that of any criminal trial—their effect on the immediate future and on those closest to the men on trial. There is, however, a theory of punishment that has nothing to do with the past at all. This is "preventive punishment," which punishes a man, not for something he is alleged to have done in the past, but for what he might do in the distant future. As such, it is of course not punishment at all, but "an hostile act," as Hobbes said long ago.[108] It does not really create any intellectual problems, once one sees that the word "punishment" is being misused to cover acts of simple elimination. The ideological justifications vary from preserving the Aryan race from the Jews to eliminating counterrevolutionary elements. Whether this is rational prevention based on a sound guess about those who might eventually prove troublesome, or just the inner dynamic of permanent revolution which must continually create new enemies, does not really matter much either. From the point of view of legalistic and liberal values it hardly matters whether terror is a policy used to achieve conscious ends, or the paranoid compulsion of autocratic regimes.[109] From the point of view of law, all that can be said is that legalistic values are absent here.

It is only when the legal process is used as an instrument to implement a policy of terror that a legal problem can be said to arise at all. Even in the case of the Moscow Trials of the late 1930's, there would be little to say if they had not found their "glossators among the metaphysicians."[110] On their face these trials were political trials of the most commonplace, obvious sort. The accused were charged with very specific crimes, such as espionage and treason, which are recognized as capital offenses almost everywhere.[111] The evidence was clearly fabricated, the prosecutor bullied the defendants, and the judges were obviously not interested in due process. The means used to obtain confessions remain clouded by discussion, but whether ideological as well as physical instruments were employed does not here matter. What is certain is that both the type of crimes charged and the confessions were essential to the purpose of the trials, which aimed not only at the physical elimination of the accused, but also at the utter destruction of their personal reputations. To this end it was clearly necessary that they not only confess, but confess to crimes which were universally abhorred. Treason and espionage, especially on behalf of Germany,

were acts that could find no sympathy, even among the
ideologically most indifferent Russians. As examples of political trials the Moscow trials offer nothing new, nothing unfamiliar to the history of such prosecutions. To the history
of Marxist ideology they add merely a footnote to the chapter
devoted to the transformation of dialectical materialism into
a conspiratorial view of history, corresponding to the experiences and needs of the Russian revolutionaries and of the
Soviet regime.[112]

All this was not clear to those metaphysical glossators who
wanted to justify the Moscow trials philosophically. Of these
Maurice Merleau-Ponty was the most notable, both because
of his eminence as professor of philosophy at the Sorbonne
and because he was not a member of the Communist Party.
To him Vishinsky's behavior seemed "bizarre." It was "bizarre" because Vishinsky tried to prove the accused simply
guilty of past crimes—a thoroughly bourgeois notion. What
the trials really were was a "drama of historical responsibility," of "subjective innocence and objective treason." To revolutionaries true justice has nothing to do with past actions.
It holds people responsible for the unintended, as yet unreal-
ized, future consequences of their acts.[113] History no longer
refers to the past at all; it means the future seen in terms of
the predictable course and final end of revolution. One could,
of course, simply say of revolution, as of war, *"Silent enim
leges inter arma,"* for that is what it comes to. It would also
be true. But it would not justify a trial and the attribution
of personal responsibility for some sort of crime. No dialec-
tician would stop with so old-fashioned and obvious a truth.
Hence the theory of historical responsibility—responsibility,
in Jean Paul Sartre's words, for "involuntary consequences"—
is necessary. Whatever the motives of the accused and the
actual character of their acts at the time of commission, if

these acts had an effect harmful to the progress of revolution they were responsible and indeed guilty on the basis of revolutionary justice. Here error was crime. The point is, of course, that even the erroneous character of the "criminal" action remains to be revealed in the future and is a matter of conjecture at the time of the trial, since the revolution is still far from complete. In short, neither the accused nor their judges really know what will and what will not contribute to the future success of the enterprise to which both are equally devoted. To secure the position of those who eliminate the traitor because he erred in his predictions, it is evidently necessary to believe that the judges have an exact knowledge of the remote future, as well as of what its achievement demands. For judgments of historical responsibility there must be one authoritative view of the entire course of the future, and the future is not only a matter of what must happen but also something that imposes obligations on the present. It is both the source of all knowledge of social fact and of all social values. As in all total ideologies, there is a slight confusion between "is," or rather "will be," and "ought." The confusion would hardly matter if it did not serve as an excuse for the killing of so many people. According to the glossators, offering political alternatives to Stalin was regarded as a crime because only Stalin's unchallenged power could lead the Russians to victory against the Germans.[114] It was a comforting belief for troubled Marxists. The subsequent revelations made by Stalin's heirs about his political competence should suffice to show what must be the fate of all ideas of historical necessity. That does not mean that, even if history as the study of the remote future should turn up with an accurate guess, it could be used as a standard for attributing criminal responsibility in the present. A man's historical reputation may be assessed in that night when the owls of Minerva fly, long after the results of his actions are known. Only an ideologized metaphysician could see the remote future as a substitute for rules of law.

To be the present executioner of the dictates of the remote future demands something more, even on the ideological level, than just the belief in total prescience. This was shown, even if indirectly, at the Moscow trials by those who felt authorized to assess historical responsibility. Such terms as "the very logic of things," the necessary "course of events," the "logic of the struggle" imply that a potential future result is not only inherent in every action but that an act may be judged in these terms, because failure to foresee the future is a sign of more than just a want of intelligence on the part of the agent—it reveals a conscious desire to produce some social evil.[115] Some element of *mens rea* was necessary to any sort of trial or act of condemnation. To offer a bare assertion of "revolutionary necessity" is a hard-boiled pose more likely to appeal to a philosopher in Paris than to a politician in Moscow bent upon a successful policy of terror and propaganda. As a result, the trial added to the general belief in objectively "right" and "wrong" political decisions the assumption that the results of decisions also correspond to the conscious ambitions of those who make them. A "wrong" decision implies a desire to harm "the cause," partly because the right course is so obvious and so authoritatively set forth by the Party, and partly because the world is full of conspirators who even reach the highest places in the Party. There need be no mistakes, and, if there are any, there is an obvious explanation for them: conspiracy to undermine the revolutionary cause. Any political trial in its search for *mens rea,* where often none exists, will present the past in conspiratorial terms. The Moscow trials, however, were only one manifestation among many others of a general obsession with conspiracy. As was noted, the trial as a whole did not revolve

about any question of historical responsibility, but was limited to simple criminal charges and patterns of argument.
The interplay between the "subjective" and "objective"
meaning of various acts was only used occasionally to confuse the accused. In the postwar trials of Rajk and Slansky
even the occasional use of this sophistry was abandoned, as
the charges of conspiracy and espionage became more comprehensive and more implausible as well. What gives the
real sense of conspiracy to these trials, and to the politics of
which they are a part, is the reduction of history to a radical
either-or.[116] Either one is for us or against us, and those
against us are a vast and ubiquitous conspiracy. Without the
possibility, indeed necessity, of such either-or judgments,
there would be no way of recognizing the latent tendencies
of acts which might appear on the surface as mere differences
of opinion. In fact, the total wrongness of differences of opinion, as such, depends on the belief that one side must be on
the criminal side of the either-or equation. This is the vision
and reality of politics as perpetual total war, of which political trials are but one small battle among many fought to
eliminate the enemy.

The either-or, for-us-or-against-us mentality does more, in
spite of Merleau-Ponty, to explain political trials under totalitarian regimes than any theory of historical responsibility.
In Nazi Germany the Catholic Boy Scout organization was
dissolved on the basis of a decree outlawing communist activities. Since anything that threatened German unity was held
to aid communism, it followed that a divisive group, competing with the Hitler Jugend, was in effect a communist organization.[117] In other words, "objectively" Catholics are communists, even if "subjectively" this might not be quite the
case. If legalistic methods of condemnation are used in either-
or persecuting politics, the "subjective" and "objective" mirrors
to reflect *mens rea* are bound to be used. However, this pre-

sents only a minor sidelight on totalitarian politics, since trials are not frequent or important instruments of terror. Obviously, for policies of mass extermination (whether of Jews or kulaks) trials are not convenient. The occasional staging of trials to dramatize the evil of the enemy and the watchfulness and power of the regime is thus not particularly important in the general course of terrorism or extermination. It is only among those lawyers totally blinded by their professional habits and formalistic ideology that the very existence of trials demonstrates the existence of legal systems in operation and provides an occasion for legal analysis. That is what comes of putting brackets around the political circumstances in which trials take place. Neither do the trials at Moscow offer anything of philosophical interest. The real duel is not between rival ideologies, any more than between different types of legal systems. It is rather a duel between the fanaticized and the skeptical consciousness in politics. At least one voice "from the other shore" has lately testified to that. It is the "Infallible Institution" acting on behalf of the "sectarian spirit," not the existence of a doctrine at all, that is the real evil, according to Laszek Kolakowski. It is not just doctrine, which by itself might allow individuals to make their own judgments as to the value of their acts, but the blind submission to one's superiors, and that on a speculation about the future into the bargain, that is the real menace. Under such conditions it becomes impossible to speak of any rules; for if necessity is the rule, and necessity is only known to those above, there can be no rules. Necessity does not know them, and those who enforce necessity do not want them. In the end it is not a question of good or bad ideologies, but of skepticism or submission.[118] For law and legalistic values this is an important consideration only in that it points to the deeper issues of politics. What happened at Moscow was not a "perversion" of law. There were no laws to be perverted, because the political conditions which make it possible to arbitrate conflicts and to limit arbitrary power by judicial action were absent; this was not a matter of types of law at all, but of terroristic politics.

It is, in fact, not impossible to have a considerable adherence to legalistic values and to have due process of law far more extensive than that displayed in Moscow in the 1930's, and still have a flourishing system of political repression in which only the most extreme forms of personal insecurity, those created by perpetual, full-scale terror, are abolished. This is, of course, a great deal. From a liberal point of view it is not enough. As a conservatizing, stabilizing force, law is obviously incompatible with the ends that terror is meant to achieve. As long as these ends remain primary, even without terror, and with an increased respect paid to the idea of legality, it is unlikely that even the security of expectations which law can give will be fully realized. It is not the revolutionary pretensions of the regime which render it incompatible with law, however. Vishinsky himself, long ago, rehabilitated the ideological respectability of law as a stable, organizing force.[119] It is the propensity of legalistic thought to encourage people to think of their claims, to assert their due, which is remote from such a regime. It is the individualistic, not the conservatizing, possibilities of law that render it incompatible with repressive politics. It is the point where law and liberalism meet that is unreachable. There can be a very considerable degree of legalism before that point is reached, however, as we have seen in the case of Nazi Germany.

The great contribution which a study of totalitarian politics can make to legal theory is to show the impossibility of thinking of law as something just "there"—a given entity filled with varying values, but still a solid system to be dissected integrally and in isolation. This procedure becomes impossible once one sees that certain ideologies and regimes are radically incom-

patible with any sort of stable legal rules. It also shows how
relatively limited are the political ends that law can serve. This
becomes very evident when one considers Nazi Germany, for
Nazism was an actively anti-legalistic ideology.[120] It was not
just that the policy of eliminating all opposition and all non-
Aryans was too sweeping for legalistic politics. Hitler simply
detested judicial procedures and ways of thought. This was
quite in keeping with his belief that simple solutions to all
problems were available and possible, if only carried through
with undeviating consistency. His radical followers understood this perfectly well from the very first, though his many
conservative adherents did not wish, or were not able, to grasp
it. It should be understood that the latter were no more liberal
and often no less brutal than the former. One of them, for
example, was Frank, the governor general of Poland. What
he objected to was not Nazi policy, of which he fully approved,
but its being carried out in a formally nonlegal manner.
He wanted rules for extermination, stable procedures for
condemning, and he wanted the judiciary left free to come
to decisions on the basis of these rules. In other words, guilt,
to be sure, guilt of crimes against Nazi law, was to be established by Nazi courts before punishment. It meant also a desire
to maintain that "Dual State" in which only racial and political
offenders were dealt with by direct police action, while other
offenders were treated according to ordinary criminal law,
and private law remained intact as long as only relationships
between Aryan citizens were involved.[121] This, however, was
not Hitler's idea of a Third Reich. Both the decisions arising
from "healthy folk instinct" and his own frequent interference with cases that he felt had been wrongly—invariably, not
harshly enough—decided were part of the same impatience
with, and outright dislike for, law as an idea, as an institution,
and as a way of dealing with deviants and disputes. All that
mattered was his own embodiment of the folk instinct, which

was inherently and intentionally indefinable and incapable of being contained by, or expressed in, rules. Whatever there was to Nazi ideology, apart from war and anti-Semitism, was thus a set of passions hostile to law. It was, of course, very much to the advantage of the more conservative Nazis not to see this fully, as long as they could avoid it. When they did see it, it did not, for them, mean that Nazism as a whole should be rejected. They only wanted it to remain at a halfway stage of its development, which would allow the partial maintenance of Germany's traditional legal system, and the prestige and autonomy of its legal caste. That this was an unlikely possibility is evident. That it should have been entertained is, however, a matter of great importance, for it reveals that legalism as an ideology is compatible with political attitudes and institutions which are not even remotely liberal, or even civilized.[122] To be sure, legalism was not compatible with radical Nazism, which essentially meant Hitler himself, but it could claim the adherence of men who did not cringe at crimes against humanity. As an ideology, legalism is capable of being combined with the politics of repression, though not in its most extreme form. This is a thought which should be sobering to those who believe that law and legalism are all that is needed for a decent political system and for the protection of freedom. Neither the autonomy of a judiciary (if its members are fanatics) nor the prevalence of rules (if they aim at repression) is any help to liberalism. They may fulfill the formal and ideological demands of legalism, they may create stability, but they produce neither freedom nor decency. For that, the spirit of humane skepticism must prevail.

## DOMESTIC POLITICAL TRIALS

If the value of political trials depends on the politics they promote, it follows that the political trials of totalitarian regimes are outrageous not because they are political, but because they promote reprehensible politics. The Nuremberg Trial of the Major War Criminals was justified only by the political values which it achieved. What of political trials that take place neither in totalitarian regimes nor in a situation (such as that in Europe in 1945) where no law and order prevail? In other words, what of political trials in stable constitutional systems where legalistic values and institutions predominate? What, in short, of political trials in the U.S.A.? The basic issue remains the same: is there a justification for coercive elimination of political enemies—for selective domestic war? It is not the courts' involvement in such a policy that is the primary issue. In the United States that is inevitable, in any case. All political issues in America sooner or later become legal cases. The question of political persecution in America is bound to be discussed in terms of its compatibility with the provisions and spirit of the Constitution. The way one answers that question, however, is going to depend on one's estimate of the danger presented by politically obnoxious and anticonstitutional groups, the degree of horror they inspire, and the extent to which one fears that the persecution of a few may end in restricting the freedom of all. As in most cases, one's political preferences will determine one's interpretation of the Constitution. The argument here is based on the belief that within constitutional systems the less persecution, the fewer political trials, the better. Not that these can never be justified, but the justifications offered for those that have taken place are inadequate and do not compensate for the loss of liberal values. It is, however, not argued here that either persecution or political trials have been so extensive as to inspire any fear and trembling or even to impair the constitutional order decisively. There is no cause for gloom and doom.

Before one can even begin to discuss political trials in the U.S.A., it must be noted that in the period since the Second

World War there has been no truly classical political trial in a federal court. Not only are the Bill of Rights and the other protections offered by the Constitution in force, but the extremely restrictive definition of treason, inspired by the Founding Fathers' distaste for political trials, has been interpreted so as to make successful prosecution for treason virtually impossible at present.[123] This in itself excludes the most usual form of political trials. Another curiosity is the extraordinary tenacity of legalism, even in extrajudicial persecutive politics. Looked at from afar it is astonishing, considering its aims, to observe the degree to which the Committee on Un-American Activities observes all the rituals of legalism. No less striking is the fact that nothing short of a *de facto* trial would do in the Oppenheimer case. This does not improve the policies here involved, but it does much to justify de Tocqueville's view that the "habits that freedom has formed" are more enduring than "the love of freedom itself." [124] That this renders even persecutive politics less virulent is also not to be forgotten, any more than that it does *not* make them more respectable.

There have been only three cases that could be, even partially, regarded as political trials. The second Hiss trial was one, but not because Hiss was falsely convicted. He very likely was guilty as charged. It was the atmosphere under which he was tried and the fact that the whole incident was meant to indict the New Deal and to promote the political fortunes of its opponents which made it a *cause célèbre,* and in effect a political trial. However, that does not mean that it was a political trial in the classical sense, with all the indifference to the actual deeds of the accused which that involves. The second political trial was that of the Rosenbergs. Again it was not a classical case. Espionage comes so close to an ordinary crime as to hardly qualify as a subject for a political trial. The difference here was that at the time the actual crime of

espionage took place the United States was allied with the
power on behalf of which the crime was committed. At the
time of the trial, however, the Cold War was in full bloom,
and the trial and sentence more than reflected this condition.
It was not that there was no evidence to prove that the Rosenbergs had committed espionage, but to accuse them of having
committed it on behalf of an enemy power, and to punish
them accordingly, involved a resort to the attribution of historical responsibility, which is the staple ideological support of
contemporary political trials. Yet surely that is what Judge
Kaufmann did when he accused the Rosenbergs of having, by
their acts, contributed to the death of their fellow Americans
in Korea. The assumption is that during the Second World
War they were able, not only to foresee the Korean War, but to
voluntarily and purposefully contribute to communist success
in it.[125] This is a judgment of "objective" historical responsibility, by which past acts are judged in terms of consequences
that were anything but evident at the time when the criminal
action took place. Only thus could espionage on behalf of a
state not at war with us be punished as wartime espionage. The
trial as a whole at least did turn upon past criminal acts. As
such, we may call this a semipolitical trial.

The most future-directed judgments were those given in
the *Dennis* cases by Judge Hand and by some of the justices
on the Supreme Court. As in all trials involving the communist
party of the U.S., the question is not one of outlawing a
political group by administrative fiat, or of using the courts
as just another instrument of persecution. The communist
party cases are none of them simple political trials of that sort.
They are, however, the only ones worth discussing, because
they are the only ones in which the problem of the elimination
of political enemies is the central issue. Moreover, the *Dennis*
case is the most significant of the various cases involving the

communist party because here the crucial question was fully faced: is it possible to proscribe politically dangerous organizations under the Constitution and to punish individuals for having committed political crimes? It was a matter which concerned the constitutional limits on persecutive politics in their application to specific individuals, not a simple criminal trial. Yet even in this context some of the issues that appear in so many contemporary political trials do emerge. Both historical responsibility and the vision of conspiracy turn up. The reason for this lies in the nature of the object of persecution, the communist party of the U.S. While the true enemy is world communism, the law can reach only the local manifestation of this movement, consisting of a small, unsuccessful, universally despised group, which has, so far, done nothing of any consequence. It is one of the paradoxes of politics that large communist parties, such as those of Italy and France, which really are dangerous, are beyond judicial prosecution, with a leadership secure in its parliamentary immunity and a voting bloc of followers so large as to be untouchable in a constitutional system, of which they have become a recognized, if immobilizing, part. It is only the subversive party which is, as yet, minute and unsuccessful that can be legally prosecuted without danger and difficulty. It must, however, in the nature of the case, be prosecuted less for what it has done than for what it might eventually do. This means seeing it as a conspiracy now, and trying it for acts that lie in the future—for historical responsibility. The First Amendment, moreover, creates an additional obstacle, since the conspiratorial activity of the communist party is a matter of talking, and speech is meant to be unhindered. Both the conspiratorial present and the dangerous acts of the future must therefore be built largely on the implications of words spoken in the present. The crime, in short, is verbal, and to outlaw certain types of speech in America is not easy. The judicial process is not designed for such proceedings and the judges neither like them nor perform brilliantly in them.

The notion of historical responsibility entered into the trial of the leaders of the American communist party when Judge Learned Hand held the Smith Act constitutional as applied to them.[126] He held that their activities were a sufficient danger to the Republic to warrant the withdrawal of the protection of the First Amendment from their subversive utterances. For proof of danger he did not turn, however, to the American domestic scene, but abroad. He looked at the Cold War, at the Berlin Crisis, at the fate of Eastern Europe. Rejecting "clear and present" as too constrictive a formula for estimating the danger presented by communism, he replaced it by a calculation of "probability." The assumption was that "the gravity of an evil" is an entity apart from its remoteness in time, something that almost compensates for it, that can be added to or subtracted from "probability." Moreover, he forgot that the probability of any historical prediction depends entirely upon its distance in time. The more distant the future that is contemplated, the smaller the probability that any guess made about it will be accurate. To be sure, Judge Hand did not resort to the crudest form of historical responsibility and hold Dennis *et al.* guilty of what they had not yet done. He was weighing the right of Congress to protect the nation against subversion, against the protection offered by the First Amendment to subversives, and he decided that Congress' powers here were not constitutionally limited to dangers obvious and immediate, but extended to those which were merely probable and distant. The fact remains that, for him, the criminality of the communists depended on the obnoxiousness of their doctrines and their future danger, not their past acts. Now it is hard to see whom the First Amendment protects if not the obnoxious. It is hard to see how the American communists could be regarded as criminally responsible for acts that were still no more than probable. The reason that the "clear and present" danger test had to go was that the American communist party is no such danger, while Soviet Russia is. The trouble is that putting every American communist in jail would not affect the danger from abroad one iota. Yet, in order to legitimize the Smith Act, Judge Hand pretended that it did, or at least might do so, and to such an extent as to outweigh the First Amendment. He did not even offer a clue as to the dangerous acts Dennis *et al.* might perform some day. He only referred to what Soviet power had already achieved and could do in the future. It might have been better to pretend that Dennis *et al.* presented a "clear and present danger," a notion no less convincing than the belief that the danger from Soviet Russia would be mitigated by their conviction. At least it would have kept the doctrine of historic responsibility out of American constitutional law.

What was on Judge Hand's mind was more frankly stated by Justice Frankfurter when Dennis *et al.* eventually came before the Supreme Court.[127] Rejecting the "clear and present danger" test as a "dogma," he called for a balancing of interests. As it happens, that is just what Justice Brandeis had said the "clear and present danger" test meant. It was to allow a balancing of free speech against the danger presented by organizations that spoke in order to violently overthrow constitutional government.[128] Justice Frankfurter was hardly fair in calling such an idea a dogma. However, what he wanted was a very different sort of balancing act, one in which the Court refrained from examining the danger altogether. It was the First Amendment as against Congress' right to decide what was dangerous that was to be weighed, not the danger itself. Since Justice Frankfurter considered Congress to all intents and purposes omnipotent in deciding what was good and bad for America, his balancing act had predictable results.

Not that he thought Congress wise. Far from it. He evidently thought the Smith Act futile, dangerous, and illiberal, but Congress' right to folly was the main object of his solicitude, and the First Amendment was not to stand in its way. If, as this view implies, the function of the Court is not to restrain Congress, but only to legitimize its acts by providing rationalizations which allow them to be fitted into the Constitution, there is no reason to suppose that any persecutive measure should ever be regarded as unconstitutional. Where national defense is the professed aim of statutes, the Court, in Justice Frankfurter's view, can only acquiesce.[129] Since we have lived, and can expect to live, in a state of semiwar for many years, this means that the war we wage abroad can, with reasoning such as Judge Hand supplied, be imported into the domestic scene. A persecutive law does not aim at punishing; it is "an hostile act," an individualized act of war in which guilt and responsibility matter little, since prevention by elimination is, as in war, the end. Such a state of affairs is hardly what any court desires, but as long as the subversive has done nothing but talk, the danger created by talk must be proved in court, and the judiciary, in accepting Congress' estimate of danger, will have to participate in this war.

What Justice Frankfurter's self-restraint implies is of some importance to an understanding of political trials in general. His criticisms of the Smith Act were bound to remain a mere exercise in self-expression, because he did not believe that the Court should pit its judgment against that of Congress. They did, however, point to the real trouble, to the persecutive spirit that inspired the law and that threatened the fabric of a liberal society. Given the passions and pressures in the midst of which the Court found itself, it was, perhaps, only reasonable to prefer accommodation to the temper of the times to a futile battle which might lead to even more direct limitations on judicial autonomy than the generalized pressure of an aroused public. To say, however, that this position is not a political one, or that it is an expression of perfect judicial independence, or, even worse, no decision on the merits of the law at all, is just absurd. When the Court leaves Congress free to act, it in effect gives its stamp of approval to those actions, *obiter dicta* notwithstanding. In acquiescing to Congress one may preserve the fiction of a nonpolitical Court by making its decisions uncontroversial. It is a political calculation that any judge faced with a political trial must make. It would have been a sensible and honorable one if Justice Frankfurter had been a member of another court, in a judicial system which knew no judicial review. As it happened, he was not.

It was left to Justice Jackson to face the other essential problem: that the Court was being asked to participate in the perversion of law. This is what Judge Hand had failed to see and Justice Frankfurter had tried to evade. The judicial process, Justice Jackson observed, is not designed to deal with radical political movements. It deals with individual offenders against law, not with the elimination of political groups. To attempt such tasks is to injure the judicial process, because the principle of legality cannot survive them. It is not just the futility of trying to cope judicially with mass movements, but the effect of such efforts on legality that concerned him. No doubt, he had had plenty of occasion to think about the principle of legality since his Nuremberg days. The remembrance of that trial seems to have influenced him in another way as well, for he went on to trot out his old *pièce de résistance,* the law of criminal conspiracy. Its virtue on this occasion was not that it would "get them." It was the only way out of having to assess imponderables, and of indulging in prophecy; for the judicial process, Justice Jackson insisted, is not to deal in prophecies. Prophecy of the future cannot replace assessment of past acts, all the more so since prophecy reflects only the personal preferences of the judicial prophets. The law of criminal conspiracy, at least, had a solid basis in Anglo-American law. He was not unaware of its disadvantages, its dragnet purpose, but he thought a watchful and independent judiciary could prevent its possible abuse. What it would allow the court to do, he thought, would be to avoid weighing the First Amendment against potentially dangerous subversive speech.[180] Moreover, the communist party was a conspiracy in fact. This was what separated it from all other radical groups of the past, which had been small and sporadic in their activities, and whose dangerousness was easily estimated without resort to prophecy; for only their immediate effects had to be considered, and these were familiar and followed predictable patterns. There was no need for speculation there. As part of a world-wide movement, communism in the U.S. was not a group of this sort. Its actions and future were imponderable. By treating communists as part of a criminal conspiracy, one was doing justice to the facts, and avoiding any alteration in the basic structure of judicial action. There was conspiracy of an unpredictable sort; there was the law of criminal conspiracy to cope with it. At least the whole problem of freedom of speech would not even be touched.

It is, of course, true that in ideology and in its internal organization the American communist party is conspiratorial, and it is not irrational to allow the government to protect itself against conspirators. The history of the law of conspiracy, however, is such as to inspire only misgivings. It hardly seems an improvement to avoid basing individual responsibility on prophecy by not proving it at all. It is too harsh to accuse Justice Jackson of having advocated that the government should be free to punish expressions of opinions when and how it chose.[131] His intention was, probably, to leave freedom of expression entirely intact by treating communism not as a matter of speech at all, but as a form of criminal conspiracy.[132] This would have isolated communism as a political problem, without affecting the position of the First Amendment in the constitutional scheme of things. His view of conspiracy was very general and untechnical, as at Nuremberg, and for precisely the same reasons. His legal soundness has, therefore, been much criticized. His political ends alone, however, are relevant here. Nevertheless, one cannot help being glad that the Court has firmly set its face against any use of the law of criminal conspiracy.[133] His real service was not in his obstinate devotion to the law of criminal conspiracy, but in being the only one of the justices who made perfectly clear what political trials in the contemporary world mean. They mean committing the judiciary to the politics of the remote future and of persecution. All the judges who realize this want to avoid it. Some can see no way out of it, except to hold all persecutive statutes unconstitutional. Others choose passivity. Justice Jackson looked for a substitute. In the end he, like Justice Frankfurter, concurred in the result which makes the First Amendment a dead letter as far as native communists are concerned. Ultimately Justice Frankfurter's remarks about the Smith Act are the most relevant. Beyond its constitutionality there lies the damage to a free society done by the very idea of such legislation. It is not just that the integrity of the judicial process is impaired. That is merely incidental to the politics of persecution, though perhaps this ought to be, as Justice Jackson felt, the first concern of the judiciary.

If the mobilization of the judiciary were a necessary muting of law in time of war one would not complain, especially if this war, like those of the past, had a foreseeable end. However, the Cold War is not like that, nor does it require the abandonment of the principle of legality. This abandonment is a necessity conjured up by an abandonment of pragmatic liberalism and a paranoia created by an interminable, frustrating, and exhausting conflict. To fight it out as a domestic crusade may be alleviating, but in the end it is only distracting.

It is not likely to wear down the legal institutions of the United States, or its legalistic temper. It is the spirit of the law that suffers. As in all political trials, it is not the trial itself that is important, but the political values involved. The question is always, "What politics?"

The political trial, the trial of elimination, can only be a destructive device in countries where liberal constitutional politics prevail. It is the enlistment of the judiciary in the ranks of a persecuting order, not their political uses as such, that is damaging. Nothing can be gained by abandoning the principle of legality in criminal cases, for here the strictest legalism, in its conservative function, supports and reinforces constitutional government and personal freedom. In a totalitarian system political trials are no better and no worse than the politics of such an order in general. There they are neither significant nor exceptionally shocking, in view of what terror does without benefit of legalistic apparatus. Where there is no established law and order, in a political vacuum, political trials may be both unavoidable and constructive. They represent, under these conditions, an obviously lower level of legalism than domestic trials (even political ones) within a constitutional system. That does not mean that they cannot embody and promote some legalistic values. It is entirely a matter of degree. Above all, it is not a question of trials being political institutions, but of the political values they serve. Legalistic values and institutions are, in fact, compatible with quite a range of other political ideologies—with liberalism and with repressive politics too, as long as the latter is not too extreme and radical. Law can perform its conservatizing and stabilizing work under many conditions, though not under all. That is, however, also why liberalism cannot rest satisfied with the mere preservation of due process of law. Legalism is not really threatened in the United States, and it is a great deal that American communists receive an open and fair trial instead of being carted off to concentration camps. Most men might be grateful for less. It is certainly more than many can expect. Yet it is no consolation for those who demand more because they see the questioning mind and tolerance as positive virtues, indeed as that very transcendence of mere animal reactions which we call civilization.

# Conclusion

Discussions of social theory do come to an end, but they are rarely, if ever, conclusive. There are no last words on this subject, and one ought not to expect them. To be sure, there are always those who demand "positive" ideas and prescriptions for belief and action. This, however, expresses only the inner needs of those who find the doubting spirit and the tentative mode intolerable. There is little comfort for them in this book and in its closing pages. To persons of a more skeptical turn of mind, honest criticism is not a form of destructiveness. On the contrary, it is the natural form of intellectual discourse, seen as a shared enterprise of argument and counterargument. This has, at any rate, been the spirit throughout the writing of this book. It cannot, therefore, end on a categorical note or with a rhetorical flourish. Nor is it possible to summarize all the preceding arguments in a neat capsule. So this must necessarily be an inconclusive end.

In treating legal theory as a part of political theory in general this book is far from novel. It represents, rather, a return to an older way of dealing with the subject which was abandoned only in the nineteenth century. To a very large degree the isolation of legal theory was merely a part of that specialization which is now a permanent feature of our intellectual life.

There are, therefore, many aspects of general jurisprudence which must necessarily remain the professional concern of lawyers as such. However, the restrictive scope of modern legal theory and its attendant formalism were also expressions of political preferences of various kinds. As these have been challenged here, so has the isolation of legal philosophy which they involved. The relationship of law to morality and to politics is not among those topics that can be discussed as part of any specifically "legal" science. The main argument here has, thus, been that a theory which concerns itself solely with the issue of validation—with only one question, "Is this law or is this not law?"—is excessively artificial and does only scant justice to the social actualities with which it purports to deal.

The reasons for this unduly narrow scope of modern legal theory are, as we saw, numerous and diverse. To some degree they can be found in traditional legalism, but other ideological preferences have also contributed. Whatever its causes, the separation of legal and political thinking, especially on the issues discussed in this book, ought to be ended. Our political thinking from antiquity onward has been permeated with legalistic notions and terms, just as legal theory, openly or not, is conditioned at every point by ideological commitments. As an alternative to this divorcing of inseparable forms of thought, it has been suggested here that it might be helpful to speak not only about law and non-law, but of degrees of legalism. It might also be useful to deal with at least some legal phenomena not as matters locked in the statute book and courthouse, but as events occurring in a vast variety of political contexts, each of which gives any such situation its full character. Taken alone, these remarks would, indeed, sound vague, but the preceding pages have made at least an attempt to show what is implied here, especially when one reviews a specific set of events, such as political trials.

If there are proposals as well as criticisms here, neither are meant to be dogmatic. Nor does one flatter oneself that all this is particularly original. But then, political theory should not strive for novelty. Its function is, at its best, evocative. This is is no small task. To give a lucid account of half-conscious, general, and often amorphous shared reactions to common social experiences is not a modest project. One hardly expects to succeed, but it is, for all that, worth trying. This is especially true when, as in the present case, one has chosen to be polemical. It was done not only out of a concern for the technical improvement of political theory as a mental discipline, but also for ideological reasons. What may well be called the liberalism of permanent minorities has quite openly informed these pages all along. To say this, is not an effort to excuse oneself for a lapse from academic good form. It is rather a simple facing-up to the perennial character of political thought. It is a purposive activity at any conceivable level of sophistication or simplicity. There appear to be only two ways of coping with that. Either one recognizes one's moral impulses and their bearing upon one's conceptions, or one does not. In neither case do they disappear. One ought indeed to ask: "Why should they?" And so, properly enough, this very doubting book ends with a question.

NOTES

INDEX

# NOTES

1. J. A. G. Griffith, "The Law of Property," in Morris Ginsberg, ed., *Law and Opinion in England in the 20th Century* (London, 1959), pp. 117–119.

2. S. A. de Smith, *Lawyers and the Constitution* (London, 1960), p. 5.

3. Griffith, "Law of Property," p. 120.

4. Harold Laski, *Studies in Law and Politics* (London, 1932), pp. 163–180, 230.

5. F. M. Watkins, *The State as a Political Concept* (New York, 1934), pp. 51–56.

6. A. P. Blaustein and C. O. Porter, *The American Lawyer* (Chicago, 1954), pp. 36, 100.

7. A. M. Carr-Saunders and P. A. Wilson, *The Professions* (Oxford, 1933), pp. 52–54.

8. Roy Lewis and Angus Maude, *Professional People* (London, 1952), p. 208.

9. Alexis de Tocqueville, *Democracy in America,* ed. Phillips Bradley (New York, 1951), I, 275.

10. Max Weber, *Law in Economy and Society,* trans. Edward Shils, ed. Max Rheinstein (Cambridge, Mass., 1954), pp. 227–229, 298–300, 304–305, 307–309, 316–317, 320–321.

11. Willard Hurst, *The Growth of American Law* (Boston, 1950), pp. 345–352.

12. Blaustein and Porter, *The American Lawyer,* pp. 34, 123.

13. B. R. Twiss, *Lawyers and the Constitution* (Princeton, N.J., 1942), p. 113.

14. E. L. Brown, *Lawyers and the Promotion of Justice* (New York, 1938), pp. 71–74, and *Lawyers, Law Schools and the Public Service* (New York, 1948), pp. 20–29; John Dickinson, *Administrative Justice and the Supremacy of Law* (Cambridge, Mass., 1927), pp. 333–358; Hurst, *Growth of American Law,* pp. 260–276; H. D. Lasswell and M. S. McDougal, "Legal Education and Public Policy," *Yale Law Journal,* 52:203–295 (1943); Arthur Vanderbilt, *The Doctrine of the Separation of Powers* (University of Nebraska Press, 1953), p. 143. This is but a small sampling of the huge number of attacks on the case method. All its critics are at one in their belief that everything can be accomplished by changes in the curriculum. Max Radin was quite alone in deriding this belief in his article "Modern Legal Education" in the *Encyclopedia of the Social Sciences.* Jerome Frank, while he recognized the superficiality of the "legal science as a social science" ideal, also put his hope in changes in the curriculum, with psychoanalysis as an added instrument of professional reform: *Courts on Trial* (Princeton, N.J., 1949), pp. 190–221, 225–246. For an English lawyer's view of the barrenness

of English learned jurisprudence see R. M. Jackson, *The Machinery of Justice in England* (Cambridge, 1953), pp. 350–353.

15. Max Weber, *Law in Economy*, pp. 236–237, 304–305, *The Protestant Ethic and Capitalism*, trans. Talcott Parsons (London, 1948), pp. 14, 25–28, and *The Religion of China*, trans. and ed. H. H. Gerth (Glencoe, Ill., 1951), pp. 100–104, 147–152, 210–211, 226–249.

16. F. A. Hayek, *The Constitution of Liberty* (Chicago, 1960), pp. 133–249. For a very friendly criticism along the same lines as that offered here, see J. W. N. Watkins, "Philosophy," in Arthur Seldon, ed., *Agenda for a Free Society* (London, 1961), pp. 31–49. On the logical problems of treating law as a matter of general rules distinct from direct commands, see J. F. G. van Loon, "Rules and Commands," *Mind*, n.s., 67:514–521.

### Part I: Law and Morals

1. W. W. Buckland, *Some Reflections on Jurisprudence* (Cambridge, Eng., 1945), pp. 1–5, 42–47.

2. This is the object of all the contributors to A. G. Guest, ed., *Oxford Essays in Jurisprudence* (Oxford, 1961). On some occasions Professor H. L. A. Hart seemed to suggest that this was to be the only valid program for legal theory. See, e.g., "Definition and Theory in Jurisprudence," *Law Quarterly Review*, 70:37–60 (1954); H. L. A. Hart and L. J. Cohen, "Theory and Definition in Jurisprudence," *Proceedings of the Aristotelian Society*, Supplement, vol. 29, 1955.

3. B. E. King, "The Concept of a Lawyer's Jurisprudence," *Cambridge Law Journal*, 11:416–417 (1951–1953).

4. See Glanville Williams, "The Controversy Concerning the Word Law," in Peter Laslett, ed., *Philosophy, Politics and Society* (New York, 1956), pp. 134–156.

5. See Norberto Bobbio, "Considérations introductives sur le raisonnement des juristes," *Revue Internationale de Philosophie*, 8:67–83 (1954), and "Nature et fonction de la philosophie du droit," *Archives de Philosophie du Droit*, 7:1–11 (1962), for excellent critiques of these procedures.

6. M. R. Cohen, *Reason and Law* (Glencoe, Ill., 1950), p. 80.

7. George Sabine, "Political Science and the Juristic Point of View," *American Political Science Review*, 22:553–575 (1928), offers an excellent explanation of why there is no special juristic point of view from which history can be analyzed.

8. See Max Rheinstein, "What Should Be the Relation of Morals to Law?" *Journal of Public Law*, 1:287–300 (1952).

9. John Austin, "The Uses of the Study of Jurisprudence," in H. L. A. Hart, ed., *The Province of Jurisprudence* (New York, 1954), p. 371.

10. H. L. A. Hart, *Law, Liberty and Morality* (Stanford, 1963).

11. For lists of differential characteristics, see A. P. d'Entrèves, *Natural*

*Law* (London, 1951), pp. 80–94; Roscoe Pound, *Law and Morals* (Chapel Hill, 1924). See also the contributions of Del Vecchio, Delos, and Le Fur in "Droit, Morale, Moeurs," *Annuaire de l'Institut de Philosophie de Droit et de Sociologie Juridique* (Paris, 1936). For the difficulties encountered by the "pure theory" of law in separating law and morals, see Alan Gewirth, "The Quest for Specificity in Jurisprudence," *Ethics*, 69:155–181 (1959).

12. H. L. A. Hart, "Legal and Moral Obligation," in A. I. Melden, ed., *Essays in Moral Philosophy* (Seattle, 1958), pp. 82–107, and *The Concept of Law* (Oxford, 1961), pp. 163–176; Luigi Baglioni, "Value Judgments and the Law," *Philosophical Quarterly*, 1:423–432 (1950–1951).

13. A particularly good account of the Christian position is to be found in N. St. John Stevas, *Life, Death and the Law* (Bloomington, 1961), pp. 9–49. A Protestant theologian's clear statement on the same issues is offered by Joseph Fletcher, "An Ethical View," in "Sex Offenses," *Law and Contemporary Problems*, 25:244–257 (1960). There are also two exceptionally concise statements by official Roman Catholic sources, evoked by the Wolfenden Committee Report. One is a statement by the Archbishop of Westminster, the other the report of the British Roman Catholic Advisory Committee on Prostitution and Homosexual Offences and the Existing Law. Anglican views on the same subjects can be found in the report of the Church of England Moral Welfare Council. All these have been reprinted in part in R. C. Donnelly *et al.*, *Criminal Law* (Glencoe, Ill., 1962), pp. 140–143.

14. W. D. Lamont, *The Principles of Moral Judgment* (Oxford, 1946), pp. 78–95.

15. T. H. Green, *Lectures on the Principles of Political Obligation* (London, 1941), pp. 34–35, 194–196.

16. Jerome Hall, *Principles of Criminal Law* (Indianapolis, 1947), pp. 138–168, *et passim*. For a criticism of similar confusion by an English jurist, see the fine article of Richard Wollheim, "Crime, Sin and Mr. Justice Devlin," *Encounter*, 13:34–40 (1959).

17. Thus Bentham: "Legislation has the same centre with morals, but it has not the same circumference." *The Theory of Legislation*, ed. C. K. Ogden (London, 1931), p. 60.

18. H. L. A. Hart, "Legal Responsibility and Excuses," in Sidney Hook, ed., *Determinism and Freedom* (New York, 1958), pp. 81–104.

19. Heinz Eulau, "The Depersonalization of the Concept of Sovereignty," *Journal of Politics*, 4:3–19 (1942).

20. Hans Kelsen, *General Theory of Law and the State*, trans. A. Wedberg (Cambridge, Mass., 1949), pp. 115–117, 401.

21. A good example of such partiality run riot is S. I. Benn and R. S. Peters, *Social Principles and the Democratic State* (London, 1959), pp. 30–56, *et passim*.

22. J. O. Urmson, "Saints and Heroes," in Melden, *Essays*, pp. 198–216.

23. It is interesting to note that contemporary forms of romantic morality

have found their way into legal theory. "Authenticity" has become the great dividing line not only between convention and genuine morality, but also between law and morals. Law is said to belong to that inauthentic world of social norms which are always in tension with the true inner self of man. This is especially the view of Luis Ricacens-Siches (a disciple of Ortega y Gasset), *Latin American Legal Philosophy*, ed. J. L. Kunz (Cambridge, Mass., 1948), *passim*.

24. See, e.g., C. K. Allen, *Aspects of Justice* (London, 1958), pp. 60–61.

25. Leon Petrazycki, *Law and Morality*, trans. H. Babb (Cambridge, Mass., 1955), *passim*.

26. Bronislaw Malinowski, *Crime and Custom in Savage Society* (London, 1926), pp. 55–59, 63–68. For a discussion of Malinowski's views on law, see Isaac Shapera, "Malinowski's Theories of Law," in Raymond W. Firth, ed., *Man and Culture* (London, 1957), pp. 139–155.

27. Franz Alexander and Hugo Staub, *The Criminal, the Judge and the Public* (Glencoe, Ill., 1956), pp. 125–135, *et passim*.

28. Sabine, "Political Science and the Juristic Point of View," pp. 553–575.

29. P. H. Nowell-Smith, *Ethics* (London, 1954), pp. 236–239, 271–273; Anthony Quinton, "On Punishment," in Peter Laslett, ed., *Philosophy, Politics and Society* (New York, 1956), pp. 83–91; John Rawls, "Two Concepts of Rules," *Philosophical Review*, 64:3–32 (1955); R. A. Wasserstrom, *The Judicial Decision* (Stanford, Calif., 1961), pp. 118–171.

30. Maurice H. Mandelbaum, *The Phenomenology of Morals* (Glencoe, Ill., 1955).

31. See W. D. Lamont's review of Mandelbaum's *Phenomenology*, in *Philosophical Quarterly*, 8:84–85 (1958).

32. Mandelbaum, *Phenomenology*, p. 251.

33. W. D. Lamont, *Principles of Moral Judgment*, pp. 52–53.

34. *Dennis v. U.S.*, 341 U.S. 508.

35. For two such calls from very diverse sources, see, e.g., Michael Oakeshott, "The Concept of a Philosophical Jurisprudence," *Politics*, 3:203–222, 345–360 (1938); Philip Selznick, "The Sociology of Law," in R. K. Merton and Leonard Broom, eds., *Sociology Today* (New York, 1959), pp. 115–127, and "Natural Law and Sociology" in John Cogley, ed., *Natural Law and Modern Society* (Cleveland, 1963), pp. 154–193.

36. That the choice has traditionally been between too much or too little detail is well brought out in A. P. d'Entrèves, "The Case for Natural Law Re-Examined," *Natural Law Forum*, 1:5–52 (1956). For an example of a call for "natural right" with no specified content, but as a dire need nonetheless, see Leo Strauss, *Natural Right and History* (Chicago, 1953), pp. 1–80.

37. Most notably J. C. Murray, S.J., *We Hold These Truths* (New York, 1960).

38. This has been the burden of Kelsen's case against natural law; for

instance, *General Theory*, pp. 391–446, *What is Justice?* (Berkeley, Calif., 1957), pp. 137–173.

39. Among recent opponents of natural law who have made an excellent case by pointing to its diversity, the most exhaustive list is that of F. E. Oppenheim in "The Natural Law Thesis," *American Political Science Review*, 51:41–53 (1957). A list provided by a supporter offers at least seven varieties of natural law current in Germany at present: Freiherr von der Heydte, "Natural Law Tendencies in Contemporary German Jurisprudence," *Natural Law Forum*, 1:115–121 (1956). Another exhaustive account may be found in Paul Weiss, *Our Public Life* (Bloomington, Ill., 1959), p. 142.

40. For this functional approach see D'Entrèves, *Natural Law*, pp. 7–62, and in a more limited way, Franz Neumann, *The Democratic and the Authoritarian State* (Glencoe, Ill., 1957), pp. 69–95.

41. E.g., Jacques Maritain, *Man and the State* (Chicago: Phoenix Books, 1956), p. 85; Heinrich Rommen, *The Natural Law*, trans. T. R. Hanley, pp. 129–134. I cite these precisely because they make every effort to be fair to their opponents, whom, nevertheless, they cannot understand.

42. Kelsen, *What is Justice?* pp. 198–208. For a most effective reply, see F. E. Oppenheim, "Relativism, Absolutism and Democracy," *American Political Science Review*, 44:951–960 (1950).

43. G. W. Constable, "What Does Natural Law Jurisprudence Offer?" *Catholic University of America Law Review*, 4:1–21 (1953–1954). Brendan F. Brown, "Natural Law: Dynamic Basis of Law and Morals in the Twentieth Century," *Tulane Law Review*, 31:491–502 (1956–1957).

44. For a natural lawyer's rejection of such attacks, see Friedrich Kessler, "Theoretic Bases of Law," *University of Chicago Law Review*, 9:98–112 (1941–1942), and "Natural Law, Justice and Democracy," *Tulane Law Review*, 19:32–61 (1944–1945). See also, W. L. Morison, "Some Myths about Positivism," *Yale Law Journal*, 68:212–233 (1958–1959).

45. Rev. J. R. Connery, S.J., "Letter, September 25, 1958," reprinted in Donnelly *et al.*, *Criminal Law*, pp. 139–140.

46. Murray, *We Hold These Truths*, p. 52.

47. Gunter Lewy, "Resistance to Tyranny: Treason, Right or Duty," *Western Political Quarterly*, 13:581–596 (1960).

48. Neumann, *The Democratic and the Authoritarian State*, p. 159.

49. A. L. Goodhart, *The English Law and the Moral Law* (London, 1955), p. 145.

50. D'Entrèves, "The Case for Natural Law," p. 37; Maritain, *Man and the State*, pp. 85–86.

51. Erich Fromm, *The Sane Society* (New York, 1955), pp. 12, 72, 173, 276–278. For a review of various theories of "positive mental health," see Maria Jahoda, *Current Concepts of Positive Mental Health* (New York, 1958). The most interesting part of the discussion is the remoteness of this

ideology from the concerns of practicing physicians. The medical man begins with disease and its possible cure, the ideologue with health and its necessary promotion. It is a difficulty as old as Plato and Aristotle. It ought to remind us to stay away from medical analogies and to beware of those who employ them. See W. E. Barton, "Viewpoint of a Clinician," *ibid.*, pp. 111–119.

52. E.g., Malcolm Sharp, "Realism and Natural Law," *University of Chicago Law Review*, 24:648–660 (1956–1957). Selznick, "The Sociology of Law." For Frank's view see *infra*.

53. F. S. C. Northrop, *The Complexity of Legal and Ethical Experience* (Boston, 1959), pp. 32–33, 54–55, 73–76, *et passim*.

54. Weiss, *Our Public Life*, pp. 62, 80ff.

55. L. L. Fuller, "Reason and Fiat in Case Law," *Harvard Law Review*, 59:376–395 (1945–1946), and "Human Purpose and Natural Law," *Natural Law Forum*, 3:68–76 (1958).

56. Sir Frederick Pollock, "The History of the Law of Nature," *Essays in the Law* (London, 1922), pp. 31–79.

57. C. M. Kluckhohn, *Mirror for Man* (New York, 1957), pp. 9–40; Max Gluckman, *The Judicial Process among the Barotse of Northern Rhodesia* (Glencoe, Ill., 1955); Adamson E. Hoebel, *The Law of Primitive Man* (Cambridge, Mass., 1954). Professor Hoebel, at least, comes right out and expresses his hope that the study of primitive law will reveal the uniformity in man's legal aspirations and so help to establish world law.

58. For the difficulty in establishing the existence and character of separate public, private, criminal, and civil laws in primitive societies, see Radcliffe-Brown, "Primitive Law," in *Encyclopaedia of the Social Sciences*, and Shapera, "Malinowski's Theories of Law."

59. Thus Kelsen claims that "pure theory" fits any legal system from that of the Ashantis to that of the United States: *What is Justice?* pp. 235–238.

60. Gluckman, *The Judicial Process*, *passim*.

61. For a full account of these theories, see C. G. Haines, *The Revival of Natural Law Concepts* (Cambridge, Mass., 1930).

62. Sir Patrick Devlin, "The Enforcement of Morals," *Proceedings of the British Academy*, 1959. For the best criticism of Devlin's views see Hart, *Law, Liberty and Morality*.

63. Walter Berns, *Freedom, Virtue and the Fifth Amendment* (Baton Rouge, 1957). Mr. Berns regards Hobbes, and to a lesser degree Locke, as the founders of liberalism. Kant is never mentioned. Yet it was Kant who gave the most philosophic demonstration of the theory that government and law, in order to have any claim to morality, must be based on freedom and aim at the protection of individual autonomy. For a recent defense of freedom as an essential aspect of constitutionalism and as a basis for law, see C. J. Friedrich, *The Philosophy of Law in Historical Perspective* (Chicago, 1958).

64. For the debates among members of the National Law Institute and

other lawyers about the advisability of making homosexuality a crime, see Donnelly, *Criminal Law*, pp. 130–132.

65. M. S. McDougal, "Law as a Process of Decision," *Natural Law Forum*, 1:53–72 (1956).

66. Jerome Frank, *Law and the Modern Mind* (New York, 1949), pp. 3–12.

67. *Ibid.*, pp. 18–21, 75, 93–99, 141–143, 146–147, 186–189; Jerome Frank, *Courts on Trial* (Princeton, N.J., 1949), pp. 282–285, 378–391, 407–415.

68. Frank, *Law and the Modern Mind*, pp. 166, 243–260, *Courts on Trial*, pp. 247–253, 346–373, 422–423. By this time, not surprisingly, Frank discovered that natural law was what he had been after long ago—with less dogmatism than that of Aquinas, but still natural law. Brendan Brown, "Jerome Frank," *The Catholic Lawyer*, 5:133–142 (1959).

69. Frank, *Law and the Modern Mind*, p. 283.

70. R. W. M. Dias and G. B. J. Hughes, *Jurisprudence* (London, 1957), pp. 467–478.

71. H. L. A. Hart, "Review of Frank's *Law and the Modern Mind*," in *Mind*, n.s., 60:268–270 (1950).

72. Edgar Bodenheim, "Positivism, Realism and Legal Method," *Virginia Law Review*, 44:365–378 (1958).

73. Julius Cohen, "Towards Realism in Legisprudence," *Yale Law Journal*, 59:886–897 (1949–1950), shows up this traditionalist element in realism and ties it to the case method of teaching law, which seems to maim the intellectual powers of American lawyers.

74. Frank, *Law and the Modern Mind*, pp. 111, 136, 263. For a further critique of Frank see especially G. L. Field, "Law as an Objective Political Concept," *American Political Science Review*, 43:227–249 (1949).

75. Thurmond Arnold, *The Symbols of Government* (New Haven, 1935), pp. 21, 46, 128, 196–198, 233–236, 271.

76. Fred Rodell, *Woe Unto You, Lawyers*, pp. 121, 16, 14, 17; Frank, *Courts on Trial*, pp. 321–324.

77. M. R. Cohen, "Law and Scientific Method," in his *Law and Social Order* (New York, 1933), pp. 184–197.

78. Thorstein Veblen, *The Theory of the Leisure Class* (New York: Mentor Books, 1953), p. 156.

79. E. N. Garlan, *Legal Realism and Justice* (New York, 1941), p. 81.

80. Jerome Frank, *If Men Were Angels* (New York, 1942), pp. 33–35, 54–65, 66–101, *Courts on Trial*, pp. 14–36, 62–79, 165–185, 321–324, and *Law and the Modern Mind*, pp. viii–xvi.

81. Felix Cohen, "Judicial Ethics," *Ohio State Law Journal*, 12:3–13 (1951), and Irdell Jenkins, "The Role of Ethical Values in Legal Decisions," *ibid.*, pp. 36–52.

82. M. R. Cohen, *Reason and Nature* (Glencoe, Ill., 1953), pp. 408–409.

83. Brendan F. Brown, "A Scholastic Critique of Case Law," *Ohio State Law Journal*, 12:14-22 (1951).

84. D'Entrèves, "The Case for Natural Law," pp. 5-52; R. S. Hartman, "Value Analysis and Legal Decisions," *Ohio State Law Journal*, 12:23-35 (1951).

85. Murray, *We Hold These Truths*, p. 91.

86. For a detailed account of how desperately judges try to avoid these decisions and many other valuable points about "morals" cases in the courts, see M. Shapiro, "Morals and the Courts: the Reluctant Crusaders," *Minnesota Law Review*, 45:897-961 (1961). All the cases referred to obliquely above are there discussed in detail. See also, Edmond Cahn, *The Moral Decision* (Bloomington, 1956), pp. 300-331.

87. Julius Cohen, R. A. H. Robson, and Alan Bates, *Parental Authority* (New Brunswick, N.J., 1958), pp. 1-22, 189-204.

88. *Ibid.*, pp. 98-99. See also, the debate between the authors and Edmond Cahn, in *Journal of Legal Education*, 11:513-516 (1958-1959), reprinted in Donnelly *et al.*, *Criminal Law*, pp. 130-132.

89. See H. L. A. Hart, "Immorality and Treason," *The Listener*, July 30, 1959, pp. 162-163; Stevas, *Life, Death, and the Law*, pp. 35-36, 40.

90. Hart, *The Concept of Law*, pp. 9, 30, 34, 40, 55-56, 58, 62, 99, 136-141, 234, 238-239.

91. H. L. A. Hart, "Positivism and the Separation of Law and Morals," *Harvard Law Review*, 71:593-629 (1958); L. L. Fuller, "Positivism and Fidelity to Law—a Reply to Professor Hart," *ibid.*, pp. 630-672.

### PART II: LAW AND POLITICS

1. H. L. A. Hart, *The Concept of Law* (Oxford, 1961), p. 7; Cicero, *De Inventione*, II, 160.

2. Hermann Kantorowicz, *The Definition of Law* (Cambridge, 1958), p. 49; George Sabine, "Justice and Equality," *Ethics*, 67:1-11 (1956-1957).

3. Chaim Perelman, *La Justice* (Bruxelles, 1945), pp. 15-21, 40-42, 59, *et passim*.

4. Michael Young, *The Rise of the Meritocracy* (London, 1958), and "Pressures at Eighteen Plus," *The Listener*, June 2, 1960, pp. 967-969.

5. Hans Kelsen, *What is Justice?* (Berkeley, Calif., 1957), pp. 350-375.

6. J. H. Hexter, *Reappraisals in History* (Northwestern University Press, 1961), pp. 185-214.

7. The above remarks constitute the core of contemporary American "realism"; e.g., George Kennan, *American Diplomacy* (New York: Mentor Books, 1952), pp. 88-89, *et passim;* H. J. Morgenthau, *Dilemmas of Politics* (Chicago, 1958), *Politics Among Nations* (New York, 1960), and *Scientific Man vs. Power Politics* (Chicago, 1946); K. W. Thompson, *Political Realism* (Princeton, N.J., 1960).

I have cited these because they have made legalism and its morality the butt of their criticism. In defense of Wilson, see Raymond Aron, "The Quest for a Philosophy of Foreign Affairs," in Stanley H. Hoffmann, *Contemporary Theories of International Relations* (Englewood Cliffs, N.J., 1960), pp. 79–91.

8. Carl Schmitt, "The Concept of the Political," in William Ebenstein, *Modern Political Thought* (New York, 1960), pp. 360–362.

9. Hans Kelsen, *Principles of International Law* (New York, 1952), p. viii.

10. Hans Kelsen, *Peace through Law* (Chapel Hill, 1944), pp. 13–14.

11. *Ibid.*, p. 16.

12. Walter Schiffer, *The Legal Community of Mankind* (New York, 1954), pp. 165–186. While I have relied on his critique of Oppenheim and Scelle, I think it exaggerates the optimism of the former. Oppenheim was not a model of realism in the years before 1914, but he did not expect law to triumph quickly. It also does not appear to me necessary to claim that the positivist school of international law is really another form of natural law. Not every moral theory or political ideology is a species of natural law, and to cover them all with one label does not serve to explain them. The same shortcoming is evident in Haegerstroem's critique of Kelsen: Axel Haegerstroem, *Inquiries into the Nature of Law and Morals,* trans. C. D. Broad (Stockholm, 1953), pp. 257–298.

13. Kelsen, *Peace,* p. 21. Oppenheim believed that Machiavellism was a thing of the past, that there would always be bad men, but that states had become moral: *The Future of International Law* (Oxford, 1921), pp. 54–55.

14. Hans Kelsen, *General Theory of Law and the State,* trans. A. Wedberg (Cambridge, Mass., 1949), p. 54.

15. Kelsen, *Principles,* pp. 313–314, 417–418.

16. Kelsen, *Peace,* p. 3.

17. Oppenheim, *Future of International Law,* p. 14.

18. *Ibid.*, pp. 21, 24, 46, 50; K. S. Carlston, *The Process of International Arbitration* (New York, 1946), pp. vii, 259–260, 264.

19. E.g., C. W. Jenks, *The Common Law of Mankind* (London, 1958), pp. 78–79.

20. Quincy Wright, *The Role of International Law* (New York, 1961), pp. 77–80.

21. Charles de Visscher, *Theory and Reality in Public International Law,* trans. P. E. Corbett (Princeton, 1957), pp. 91, 39–40, 167–168, 190–191, 332.

22. See the utterances of the past president of the A.B.A. and now its chief spokesman on world law, as reported in the *New York Times,* June 18, 1961.

23. Arthur Larson, *When Nations Disagree* (Louisiana State University Press, 1961), is the program for the A.B.A., and the above passages are essentially a summary of his proposals.

24. Kelsen, *Principles,* pp. 304–307, 380–386, *Peace,* pp. 23–34, *General*

NOTES TO PART II

*Theory*, pp. 146–150; J. L. Brierly, *The Law of Nations* (Oxford, 1955), pp. 68–69, 285–292.

25. Jenks, *The Common Law*, pp. 79–80.

26. Hart, *The Concept of Law*, pp. 208–231; Kelsen, *Principles*, pp. 401–447.

27. Schiffer, *The Legal Community*, pp. 260–268; Brierly, *Law of Nations*, pp. 55–56; Kelsen, *Principles*, pp. 100–102. That this illusion is absurd in an age when governments are so heterogeneous in ideology and structure has been eloquently explained by de Visscher, *Theory and Reality*, pp. 88–100.

28. P. E. Corbett, *Law in Diplomacy* (Princeton, 1959), p. 273.

29. De Visscher, *Theory and Reality*, p. 99.

30. For Savigny, see *On the Vocation of Our Age for Legislation and Jurisprudence*, trans. A. Hayward (London, 1831); Max Rheinstein, ed., *Max Weber on Law in Economy and Society*, pp. 198–223, *et passim*.

31. For the "stages of legal growth" theory see Roscoe Pound, *Interpretations of Legal History* (London, 1923), and "Legislation as a Social Function," *Proceedings of the American Sociological Association*, VIII (1912), 148. I have singled him out because his sociological theory of law proclaimed itself to be such a decisive break with legal formalism. In fact, it never really broke away from the main stream of legalism, except for occasional outbreaks of rhetoric. This itself serves to explain Pound's subsequent return to legal conservatism, especially after his condemnation of American realism and his subsequently growing antipathy for administrative law. A careful reading of the early polemics shows them to be considerably less radical than they seemed at the time of their writing, before the First World War.

32. Kelsen, *Peace*, pp. 19–23, *Principles*, pp. 15–17, 23, 36, 101–102, 105–108, 139; Hart, *The Concept of Law*, p. 226; Wright, *Role of International Law*, pp. 32, 80.

33. V. A. Roeling, *International Law in an Expanding World* (Amsterdam, 1960), pp. ix–x.

34. Jenks, *The Common Law*, pp. 136–139; Larson, *When Nations Disagree*, pp. 225–229.

35. Brierly, *Law of Nations*, p. 73.

36. E.g., Jenks, *The Common Law*, pp. 408–442.

37. Corbett, *Law in Diplomacy*, p. 273.

38. See George Schwarzenberger, *A Manual of International Law* (London, 1960), I, 315–358.

39. I. L. Claude, *Swords into Plowshares* (New York, 1959), pp. 219–249.

40. The most notable among the latter is Dr. V. A. Roeling (see his *International Law*). Less radical, though similarly inclined, is Jenks, *The Common Law*.

41. This belief allows the more optimistic of the world law enthusiasts to think that the Soviets may yet be talked into submitting to the jurisdiction

of the Permanent Court of International Justice: e.g., Jenks, *The Common Law*, pp. 106, 115–116, 119–120, 129, 134–135, 142, 148–153, 163, 169–170, offers a qualified optimism based entirely on the principles of *domestic* Soviet law; Larson, *When Nations Disagree*, pp. 98–99, 182–185; Wright, *Role of International Law*, pp. 79–80. In contrast, see Julius Stone, *Quest for Survival* (Cambridge, Mass., 1961), pp. 12–13, 31–32. I am much indebted to this and to all the others works of Mr. Stone, so much so that I wish to acknowledge it generally rather than in dispersed notes.

42. E.g., Kelsen, *Prinicples*, pp. 444–447. In this, as in most instances, Kelsen remains the best representative of orthodox international law theory. Even those who do not share his adamant opposition to the law of nature follow him on all other matters. His influence is perhaps best seen in what is the most sensible and most commonly used introductory text on the subject, Brierly's *Law of Nations*.

43. See especially A. V. Lundstedt, *Superstition or Rationality in Action for Peace?* (London, 1925), and "The Responsibility of Legal Science for the Fate of Nations," *New York University Law Quarterly Review*, 10:326–340 (1932–1933); Karl Olivecrona, *Law as Fact* (Copenhagen and London, 1939), pp. 193–210; Haegerstroem, *Inquiries*, pp. 278–289. Although Haegerstroem is the acknowledged founder of this school, his views on international law are, as he explained, drawn from Lundstedt's critique.

44. One example among many of such reasoning is Malcolm McDermott, "Law and the Liberal Mind," *Tennessee Law Review*, 21:178–187 (1950).

45. In the following paragraph, and indeed thoughout this entire chapter, I am much indebted to Otto Kirchheimer, *Political Justice* (Princeton, 1961). If I do not cite this book page by page it is only to avoid an excess of notes, and because my debt to it is too general.

46. Z. K. Brzezinski, *The Permanent Purge* (Cambridge, 1956), pp. 72–76.

47. C. J. Child, "Germany 1939–1945," in Arnold and V. M. Toynbee, eds., *Hitler's Europe* (Oxford, 1954), pp. 26–30.

48. See "Treason," in *Encyclopedia of Social Sciences*, for the fate of the Statute of Treason of 1352 in the hands of the judiciary. See also Bryce Lyon, *A Constitutional and Legal History of Medieval England* (New York, 1960), pp. 632–633, and Willard Hurst, "Treason in the United States," *Harvard Law Review*, 58:226–272, 395–441, 806–846 (1944–1945).

49. Henry L. Mason, *The Purge of Dutch Quislings* (The Hague, 1952), pp. 58–84).

50. Henry Weihofen, "Retribution is Obsolete," in C. J. Friedrich, ed., "Responsibility," *Nomos*, 3:116–127 (1960). This article is especially significant because it specifically deals with the crimes committed during the occupation of Europe in the Second World War. It errs on one very significant point—the prospects of re-education. Mr. Weihofen is full of praise for the Dutch attempts to re-educate collaborators. It appears, however, that these efforts were not successful, because citizenship is not a matter which can

be taught. It is a matter of lifelong experiences and behavior. Mason, *The Purge*, pp. 140–157.

51. E.g., Robert Jackson, "Nürnberg in Retrospect," *The Canadian Bar Review*, 27:761–781 (1949), and "Trial of the Trials," *Common Cause*, 3:284–294 (1949–1950); Lord Justice Lawrence, "The Nuremberg Trials," *International Affairs*, 23:151–159 (1947); Justice Birckett, "International Legal Theories Evolved at Nuremberg," *ibid.*, pp. 317–325; Max Rheinstein, in August von Knierim, *The Nuremberg Trials*, trans. E. D. Schmitt (Chicago, 1954), pp. x–xi.

52. A perfect account of this state of mind is Simone de Beauvoir, *L'Existentialisme et la Sagesse des Nations* (Paris, 1948), pp. 125–165.

53. "Aide-Memoire from the United Kingdom, April 23, 1945," reprinted in *International Conference on Military Trials, London, 1945,* Department of State Publication No. 3080, pp. 18–20 (hereafter referred to as *Conference*).

54. This argument was used also at the Tokyo Trials: J. B. Keenan and B. F. Brown, *Crimes against International Law* (London, 1960), p. 45, and J. A. Appleman, *International Crimes and Military Tribunals* (Indianapolis, 1954), pp. 247–250.

55. Of those who saw danger ahead the following are most representative: Montgomery Belgion, *Victors' Justice* (Hinsdale, Illinois, 1949) and Lord Hankey, *Politics, Trials and Errors* (Chicago, 1950). For an over-optimistic view of the trials as a "good" precedent see Quincy Wright, "The Law of the Nuremberg Trial," *American Journal of International Law*, 41:38–72 (1947).

56. E.g., R. K. Woetzel, *The Nuremberg Trials in International Law* (London, 1960), pp. 46, 120.

57. *International Tribunal for the Far East. Dissenting Judgment of Justice R. B. Pal* (Calcutta, 1953), pp. 620–621.

58. *Conference*, pp. 379–381.

59. H. F. A. Donnedieu de Vabres, *Le Procès de Nuremberg* (Paris, 1947), pp. 239–246.

60. For similar conclusions reached on more legalistic grounds, see G. A. Finch, "The Nuremberg Trial and International Law," *American Journal of International Law*, 41:20–37 (1947).

61. See W. E. Benton and Georg Grimm, eds., *Nuremberg: German Views of the War Trials* (Dallas, 1955). All the articles, whatever view they take of the Trial, dwell on the principle of legality. As one contributor put it (K. S. Bader, p. 157), the Trial reminded German lawyers of the duties of defense counsel—precisely because it was a political trial conducted with a degree of fairness that was infinitely greater than any of those they had seen in the recent past.

62. *Conference*, pp. 335, 437. The argument was taken up again at Tokyo, as were all the other legalistic justifications derived from analogy to municipal law. Keenan and Brown, *Crimes*, p. 45.

63. Woetzel, *Nuremberg Trials*, pp. 165–166; Keenan and Brown, *Crimes*, pp. 5–6, 73–77. For Justice Pal's vigorous refutations, which have been repeated here, see *Dissenting Judgment*, pp. 54–62.

64. Jackson, "Nürnberg in Retrospect," p. 778; Keenan and Brown, *Crimes*, p. 50.

65. E.g., Quincy Wright, "Legal Positivism and the Nuremberg Judgment," *American Journal of International Law*, 42:405–414 (1948); Keenan and Brown, *Crimes*, pp. 11, 56, 160; Pal, *Dissenting Judgment*, pp. 60–64.

66. Julius Stone, *Aggression and World Order* (Berkeley and Los Angeles, 1958), pp. 15–19, 145–148.

67. Mason, *The Purge*, pp. 61–64, 123–131.

68. Jackson, "Trial of the Trials," p. 292. As Justice Jackson noted, "He took pride in his accomplishment."

69. *Conference*, p. 48.

70. *Ibid.*, p. 438.

71. H. J. Spiro, *Government by Constitution* (New York, 1959), pp. 211–236, 282–286.

72. Benton and Grimm, *Nuremberg*, pp. 77–79, 85, 127–135, 175–176, 203; Knierim, *The Nuremberg Trials*, pp. 263–175. Knierim was concerned with the subsequent American trials held at Nuremberg, of which he disapproved entirely. Nevertheless, even this imperturbable mind boggled at the evidence that emerged in the course of the *Einsatzgruppen* case.

73. J. D. Montgomery, *Forced to Be Free* (Chicago, 1957), pp. 59–67, 127.

74. Bernhard Duesing, *Die Abschaffung der Todesstrafe in der Bundesrepublik Deutschland* (Offenbach/Main, 1952), pp. 224–232, 276–310.

75. Sybille Bedford, *The Faces of Justice* (London, 1961), pp. 83–153.

76. Stone, *Aggression*, pp. 139–144.

77. *Ibid.*, pp. 11–13, 15–25.

78. E.g., *Conference*, pp. 84, 273–274, 302, 304–306. In fact, almost the entire conference to set up the Charter was devoted to wrangling over the charge of crimes against peace and the law of conspiracy. In the end Justice Jackson simply wore down his French and Russian colleagues.

79. E.g., *ibid.*, pp. v–xii. This opinion was shared by the American chief prosecutor at Tokyo: Keenan and Brown, *Crimes*, pp. 160–161.

80. *Conference*, pp. 333, 362–364.

81. *Ibid.*, pp. 112–113, 299–300, 362–364.

82. *Ibid.*, p. 383.

83. Donnedieu de Vabres, *Le Procès*, pp. 101–103; *Conference*, p. 241.

84. *Conference*, pp. 299–300.

85. *Ibid.*, pp. 329–335, 360–362, 381–382, 385–386.

86. *Ibid.*, pp. 295–300.

87. For an extensive discussion along the same lines see R. W. Tucker, *The Just War* (Baltimore, 1960). During the period between the wars, A. V. Lundstedt in Sweden followed similar reasons in his indictment not

only of the Versailles Treaty but of international law in general (Lundstedt, *Superstition or Rationality in Action for Peace?*). His disciple, Heinz Lunau, took up the attack after the war. Their main point here is well taken, that international law tends to treat nations as if they were analogous to individuals, and pretends that international law is analogous to municipal law. It is doubtful whether this is really as great a cause of international conflict as they suppose. Reacting against the grandiose claims of international law, these authors have made that harmless and insignificant institution their pet villain. As for the Nuremberg Trial, it tried individuals for personal acts— not a nation or a state. To that extent their critique does not apply to it at all. See Heinz Lunau, *The Germans on Trial* (New York, 1948), pp. 115–151.

88. For discussion of Japanese reactions to the Tokyo Trial and for Japan's non-legalistic tradition, see Kazuo Kawai, *Japan's American Interlude* (Chicago, 1960), pp. 4–8, 22–24; Takeyoshi Kawashima, "Law," in "Postwar Democratization in Japan," *International Social Science Journal*, 13:21–34 (1961); Edwin O. Reischauer, *The United States and Japan* (Cambridge, Mass., 1954), pp. 244–245. I am also much indebted to my friend, Mr. Tatsuo Arima, formerly instructor of government at Harvard and a specialist in Japanese intellectual history, who explained many aspects of Japanese thinking to me.

89. Solis Horwitz, "The Tokyo Trial," *International Conciliation*, no. 465, pp. 525–526 (November 1950); R. J. C. Butow, *Tojo and the Coming of the War* (Princeton, 1961), pp. 470–540.

90. Keenan and Brown, *Crimes,* pp. vii, 60–64, 66, 72, 155.

91. *Ibid.,* pp. 158 and 13.

92. Woetzel, *Nuremberg Trials,* p. 169.

93. Keenan and Brown, *Crimes,* pp. 50, 157.

94. Typewritten transcript of Justice Bernard's dissent in the Treasure Room of the Harvard Law School Library, pp. 1–3, 7, 15–18, 20–23.

95. Typewritten transcript of Justice Roeling's dissent in the Treasure Room of the Harvard Law School Library, pp. 11, 19–20, 32, 35–44.

96. Pal, *Dissenting Judgment,* pp. 47–48, 68–70.

97. *Ibid.,* pp. 115, 135.

98. *Ibid.,* pp. 114–116.

99. Reischauer, *The United States and Japan,* pp. 16–17, 23.

100. Pal, *Dissenting Judgment,* pp. 315–320.

101. *Ibid.,* pp. 650, 408, 499, 554, 557–559; also Roeling's dissent, pp. 64–178.

102. Pal, *Dissenting Judgment,* pp. 671–672.

103. Donnedieu de Vabres, *Le Procès,* pp. 273–274.

104. This has been lately suggested by A. J. P. Taylor, *The Origins of the Second World War* (London, 1960). It might be recalled that this author also

shares the "eternal Germany" views of M. Donnedieu de Vabres. See his *The Course of German History* (New York, 1946).

105. In the following pages I have relied very heavily on H. L. A. Hart and A. M. Honoré, *Causation and the Law* (Oxford, 1959). Unhappily the authors do not deal very exhaustively with the problem of historical causality. The various legal cases and paradigmatic cases drawn from daily experience which they present all deal with situations occurring in a limited time span, and they involve few identifiable persons. When they do mention historical causality, they go astray in regarding something like the Black Death (their example) as equivalent to an individual agent for purposes of causal discussion (p. 59). I am, however, much indebted to this discussion, and especially to pp. 79–122 and 348–363.

106. Montgomery, *Forced to Be Free, passim.*

107. Keenan and Brown, *Crimes,* p. 155.

108. *Leviathan,* ed. Michael Oakeshott (Oxford, 1947), pp. 203–204.

109. See C. J. Friedrich, ed., *Totalitarianism* (Cambridge, Mass., 1954), pp. 60–84, for a debate on this issue between J. G. Gliksman and Hannah Arendt.

110. J. Donnedieu de Vabres, "Les Valeurs Philosophiques et le Droit Moderne," *Revue de Metaphysique et de Morale,* 53:55–80 (1948). This article is perhaps the most profound and intelligent analysis of political justice and its implications for legal philosophy, and I am deeply indebted to it, even where I do not fully agree with the author.

111. Nathan Leites and Elsa Bernaut, *Ritual of Liquidation* (Glencoe, Illinois, 1954), pp. 11–12.

112. *Ibid.,* pp. 204–220.

113. Maurice Merleau-Ponty, *Humanisme et Terreur* (Paris, 1947), pp. 27–75, *Les Aventures de la Dialectique* (Paris, 1955), pp. 81–99, 273–313, and *Signes* (Paris, 1960), pp. 329–330; Jean-Paul Sartre, "Merleau-Ponty Vivant," *Les Temps Modernes,* 1961, pp. 304–376.

114. E.g., Isaac Deutscher, *Stalin* (New York, 1949), pp. 372–385.

115. Leites and Bernaut, *Ritual,* pp. 113–142, 143–165, 166–175.

116. *Ibid.,* pp. 113–142, 350–381.

117. Ernst Fraenkel, *The Dual State* (New York, 1941), pp. 16–19.

118. Laszek Kolakowski, "Permanent and Transitory Aspects of Marxism," trans. G. Krzywicki, in Pawel Mayewski, ed., *The Broken Mirror* (New York, 1958), pp. 158–159, and "Responsibility and History," *Eastern Europe,* vol. 6, no. 6, pp. 12–15 (1957), vol. 7, no. 2, pp. 17–21, no. 3, pp. 24–28, no. 5, pp. 12–16 (1957).

119. H. W. Babb and J. N. Hazard, eds., *Soviet Legal Philosophy* (Cambridge, Mass., 1951), pp. 303–341; Barrington Moore, Jr., *Political Power and Social Theory* (Cambridge, Mass., 1958), pp. 154–178. For a relatively optimistic view see H. J. Berman, *Justice in Russia* (Cambridge, Mass., 1950).

120. For law in Nazi Germany see Fraenkel, *Dual State, passim;* Friedrich

Roetter, "The Impact of Nazi Law," *Wisconsin Law Review*, 1945:516–562; Martin Broszat, "Zur Perversion der Strafjustiz im Dritten Reich," *Vierteljahrshefte für Zeitgeschichte*, 6:390–445 (1958); Helmut Heiber, "Zur Justiz im Dritten Reich: Der Fall Elias," *ibid.*, 3:275–296 (1955); C. J. Child, "Germany 1939–1945," pp. 26–30, 128–153; *The Justices Case,* vol. III of *Trials of War Criminals before the Nuerenberg Military Tribunal* (1951), pp. 469–503.

121. Fraenkel, *Dual State, passim.*

122. See *Justices Case,* pp. 284–310, for the views of one such conservative Nazi, Schlegelberger.

123. Willard Hurst, "Treason."

124. *Democracy in America,* I, 250–251.

125. Giles Playfair and Derrick Sington, *The Offenders* (New York, 1957), pp. 235–238. Unlike other critics these authors do not suggest that the Rosenbergs were framed or not guilty of espionage. They question the punishment on the same grounds as those offered here. Indeed, they use the incident to illustrate their case against capital punishment and, indeed, all punishment in general, which does not follow necessarily from this case.

126. *Dennis v. U.S.,* 183 Fed. 2d 201 (1950).

127. *Dennis et al. v. U.S.,* 341 U.S. 494 (1951).

128. *Whitney v. California,* 274 U.S. 357, 378–379 (1926).

129. This continues to be the Court's position at present; see R. M. McCloskey, "Deeds without Doctrines," *American Political Science Review*, 56:71–89 (1962).

130. It is worth noting that without invoking the law of criminal conspiracy Justice Brandeis had also tried to evade assessing imponderables by holding the I.W.W. to be a conspiratorial organization aiming at serious crimes (274 U.S. 375, 379).

131. R. M. McCloskey, *Essays in Constitutional Law* (New York, 1957), pp. 280–281.

132. This, oddly enough, is the conclusion of Professor C. H. Prichett, who nevertheless criticizes Justice Jackson's opinion severely in his *Civil Liberties and the Vinson Court* (Chicago, 1954), pp. 66–79, 244.

133. *Scales v. U.S.,* 81 S. Ct., 1469, 1484–1485 (1961).

# INDEX OF NAMES

Made in the USA
Lexington, KY
16 September 2011